LECTURES ON MORAL SCIENCE.

LECTURES

ON

MORAL SCIENCE.

DELIVERED BEFORE THE

LOWELL INSTITUTE, BOSTON.

BY

MARK HOPKINS, D.D. LL.D.

PRESIDENT OF WILLIAMS COLLEGE; AUTHOR OF "LECTURES ON THE EVIDENCES OF CHRISTIANITY," ETC.

BOSTON:
GOULD AND LINCOLN,
59 WASHINGTON STREET.
NEW YORK: SHELDON AND COMPANY.
CINCINNATI: GEORGE S. BLANCHARD.
1863.

GEO. C. RAND & AVERY,
STEREOTYPERS AND PRINTERS.

TO

The Graduates of Williams College

SINCE 1830.

Permit me, my friends, a word of explanation with those of you who may read the following Lectures. It seems called for by the difference between them now, and when they were heard by the most of you.

In 1830 I was elected to the Professorship of Rhetoric and Moral Philosophy in this college, and during the first year prepared and delivered twelve Lectures on Moral Philosophy. Of these, omitting the introductory one, the first paragraph was the following: "If the human constitution was made by a wise and good being, it must have been made for certain ends; and in those ends, whatever they may be, and nowhere else, can its perfection and happiness be found. To discover these ends and the means of attaining them, is the object of Moral Philosophy." Then followed such an examination of the constitution of man as I was able to make. This shows that the present lectures are but the carrying out of my original thought; but that those lectures should have been delivered for more than twenty-five years without essential alteration is what requires explanation, if not apology.

The explanation is, chiefly, from the pressure of other duties. During the remaining years of my professorship, my leisure was occupied with lectures on Rhetoric and Natural Theology, in connection with extra duties imposed by the declining health of Dr. Griffin. Subsequently, and till 1855, those of you then here will remember our studies together in Anatomy, and Mental Philosophy, and Moral Philosophy, and Natural Theology, and Butler's Analogy, and Vincent. Add to these, preaching; the administrative labor incident to my position; the publication of between forty and fifty pamphlets, and of a volume on the Evidences of Christianity, and it may not seem strange that when the years came round, as they seemed to, with increasing rapidity, I was only able to give the lectures as they were. Always feeling that my first duty was in the class-room, my strength simply sufficed for the demands of the passing day. In 1855 the Rhetoric of the class passed into other hands, but so much of work still remained that a revision of the Lectures was not undertaken till 1858. In the winter of 1861, the course, with the exception of the last lecture, for which there was not time, was delivered before the Lowell Institute.

When the Lectures were first written, the text-book here, and generally in our colleges, was Paley. Not agreeing with him, and failing to carry out fully the doctrine of ends, I adopted that of an ultimate right, as taught by Kant and Coleridge, making that the end. If, therefore, any of you still hold that view, — as doubtless many do, — it is not for me to say that you have not good authority for it, or to complain if you object to that now taken.

But whatever may be said of this central point, the Lectures have been much changed in other respects, and, as I hope, improved. Such as they are, with thankfulness that I am permitted to address so many of you, and with many pleasant recollections of our former discussions on this subject, they are now committed to your candid and indulgent consideration.

Your sincere Friend,

MARK HOPKINS.

WILLIAMS COLLEGE, OCTOBER 1, 1862.

PREFACE.

PHILOSOPHY investigates causes, unities, and ends. Of these it is the last two that are chiefly considered in the following lectures. "Happy," it has been said, "is he who knows the causes of things." But in a world where there are so many apparent discrepancies both natural and moral, he must be more happy who knows the arrangement of things into systems, and sees how all these systems go to make up one greater system and to promote a common end. An investigation of causes respects the past; of unities and ends, the present and the future. Of these the latter are more intimate to us, and he who can trace the principle of unity by which nature is harmonized with herself, and man with nature, and man with himself, and the individual with society, and man with God, — who can see in all these a complex unity and can apprehend their end, — will have an element of satisfaction far greater than he who should know the causes of all things without being able to unravel their perplexities.

From the place assigned to Moral Philosophy in the classification adopted in these lectures, an incidental consideration of the above harmonies seemed to be required. Hence it is hoped that the book may contain suggestions that will be valuable to some who may not agree with its doctrines on the particular subject of morals. It is particularly hoped that it may do something towards introducing more of unity into the courses of study, or some of them, in our higher seminaries. If the works of God, regarded as an expression of his thought, are built up after a certain method, it deserves to be considered whether that thought will not be best reached by following in their study the order that has been followed in their construction, and which is involved in that method. Something of this I have long aimed to do in my instructions, and with very perceptible advantage. With suitable text-books and a right arrangement of studies, much more might doubtless be done.

In treating of any natural system, as each part implies all the others, wherever we begin, and whatever method we follow, we are compelled to use terms whose full meaning can be reached only in the progress of the investigation. This is particularly true when, as in the present instance, instead of beginning with definitions, we seek for them. For this it is hoped that due allowance may be made.

It will be seen that important, and even cardinal points, are often but briefly touched in these discussions. I can only say that the work is, of necessity, suggestive rather than exhaustive, and that if these points are so treated as to show their place in the system, the outline may be readily filled up.

For remarks upon the present condition of the science, and for the general course of thought pursued, the reader is referred to the opening lecture, and to the summary at the close.

English literature is rich in ethical speculation. Several valuable treatises have recently been published in this country; but the ground of classification, and the general aspects and connections of the subject, as presented in the following lectures, are so far different from others, that it is hoped something may be gained to the science by their publication. To the authors of the treatises above referred to, and also to the friends who have aided me by their suggestions, I desire to express my indebtedness.

I will only add, that the work is written in the interest of truth, and not controversially.

CONTENTS.

LECTURE I.

LECTURE II.

LECTURE III.

LECTURE IV.

LECTURE V.

LECTURE VI.

LECTURE VII.

LECTURE VIII.

LECTURE IX.

LECTURE X.

LECTURE XI.

LECTURE XII.

LECTURES ON MORAL SCIENCE.

LECTURE I.

MORAL SCIENCE AND ASTRONOMY.—REASONS FOR THE SLOWER PROGRESS OF THE FORMER.—PROGRESS MUST BE SLOW.—TWO CLASSES OF SCIENCES.—USE OF STUDYING THE SCIENCE.

AMONG the sciences which earliest drew the attention of man were those of Astronomy and Morals. Of these, one respects the sources of that light which is from without, the other of that which is within. Of the one, the objects and phenomena are not only without us, but are separated from us by inconceivable distances; of the other, the phenomena are not only within us, but belong to that part of our nature which is special to us, and whose circle lies nearest to its central point.

Connected with each are practical judgments common to all. Both the heavens and the moral nature of man yielded him guidance before there was a thought of the science of either. The unscientific man rejoices in the light that comes from Arcturus no less than if he could analyze its beams, and is guided by the polar star no less surely than if he could measure its magnitude and distance. The day and the night, the changing moons and the revolving seasons, are alike to all. In the same way men agree in their practical judgments on the great subjects of morals. By their original nature there is within them a guiding light by which the learned and unlearned alike may walk. But in either case, when science began its work, and asked for causes, and reasons, and classifications, there were conjectures and diversities of opinion without end. Of the apparent movement of the heavens, and of a virtuous or heroic act, men judged alike; of the cause of that movement, or of the nature of virtue itself, they did not judge alike. Practically, men could agree in both; but in everything pertaining to the science of either, nothing could be more discrepant than their opinions, or, for ages, more discouraging and apparently hopeless than the attempt to establish any one doctrine that should be generally accepted.

If, now, the inquiry had been made in the early period of these sciences which of them would soonest reach perfection, the unhesitating answer would doubtless have been, — that of which the phenomena are within us, which are immediately testified to by our consciousness, and are always subject to our notice. Whether man would *ever* be able to perfect a science of the heavens, might well have been doubted; but that he should do this sooner than perfect the science of that which pertained to his own most intimate being, and which stood in the closest relation to his highest interests, could not have been believed. But so it has been. After ages of observation and conjecture, during which the phenomena seemed in hopeless confusion; after exhausting the efforts of some of the best minds in every age, the central truth of astronomy at length dawned, and the chaos of conjecture became the order of science. From a science of observation, astronomy has now become one of deduction, and if not altogether complete, is more nearly so than any other.

The success thus achieved in the field of astronomy was a great stimulus and encouragement to effort in other departments. From the vastness of its distances, the magnitude of its objects, the complexity of its phenomena, and from its inconceivable forces and velocities, there was connected with success here an excitement and sublimity which greatly heightened the purely scientific pleasure, and which inspired a confidence of future triumphs in whatever should be attempted. Nor was this confidence without a basis. In the advance of every form of physical science then known, no period of the world can be compared with that since the time of Kepler and of Newton. Meantime, forms of science then unknown, as chemistry and geology, have sprung into giant proportions; while the application of science to the arts, employing every substance, and harnessing every force in nature for the service of man, is revolutionizing not only society, but the face of nature herself.

In mental and moral science there has, too, been greater activity than ever before; but we are not, perhaps, in a position as yet to say how much there has been of progress. There are still discordant voices, and different schools, and those that say "Lo, here," and "Lo, there;" and perhaps the variety of systems proposed, especially in morals, was never greater.

Thus situated, it is an encouragement to think of the seas of doubt through which astronomy has waded. We remember that the perplexities of its votaries were once as great as ours can be now, and hope for a similar deliverance. The end of investigation is attained when we either comprehend all that is brought before us, or can draw the line which shall fix the natural limits set by God to our knowledge; and we are not of that desponding, or rather indolent class, who distrust the powers of the human mind to do, in all cases, one or the other of these.

So far as our present subject is concerned, it may aid us in doing this if we inquire for a little how it has happened that physical science, and especially astronomy, has so far outstripped moral science. What are the causes of a result so impossible to have been anticipated?

And first, we may mention a difficulty much insisted on by Chalmers, as pertaining to the observation of all mental phenomena. This arises from the fact that the mind is both the observer and the thing observed, and that some of its states at least (they say all) are of such a character as to preclude examination at the moment they exist. Thus, when a man is thoroughly angry his whole thought is directed to the object of his anger, and nothing can be conceived more incompatible with the state of an angry man than that he should be engaged in taking psychological observations on himself. The moment he turns his attention from the object of his anger to himself for the purpose of observing it, the anger is gone. It cannot, therefore, be studied directly, as we study the objects of our senses, but only as it is remembered.

This holds in all cases of violent emotion and should have its just weight, but not in the ordinary states of thought and feeling. If the view of Chalmers and of Brown before him were adopted in its strictness, no man would ever know his own present state, but only the states he had been in, and so could never deal with his present, but only with his past self. The moment his attention should be so far called to himself as to inquire whether he was angry, his anger must cease; and the prophet of old who thought he was angry, and said he did well to be, was mistaken. In thinking, we know not only the object of our thought, but ourselves as thinking. The consciousness is so far complex as to embrace both. So in the feelings. There is no more difficulty in supposing such a complexity of the consciousness as to embrace both an act and a feeling caused by an act, than there is in supposing that the same consciousness can embrace the remembrance of an act and the feeling caused by that remembrance.

There is doubtless at this point a real difficulty, but we think it less formidable than it is made by Chalmers and others.

To a successful investigation the first requisite is a clear apprehension of the subject to be investigated as distinguished from everything with which it may be confounded, or to which it is related. This discrimination in regard to morals has often failed to be made. This is the second reason.

Language accommodates itself, after a time, to the exigencies of thought; and when clear discriminations are generally or persistently made, there will be terms to express them. In the Latin language, the word for conscience and for consciousness was the same; it is so still in the French, Italian, and Spanish, and this was formerly true of the English. But if the moral consciousness were not now partitioned off, and its phenomena grouped by a word of its own, we may easily see how difficult it would be to disentangle those phenomena from the mass of other things covered by the same word; and while the language remained in that state it was scarcely possible that much progress should be made in the science. But as thought was concentrated and analysis progressed, that which was consciousness par eminence, the moral consciousness, appropriated the term conscience; and yet no one can now read even the scientific writers on the subject and not perceive that they still use the term with a wide diversity of signification.

It was this state of the language, or more properly of the public mind represented by it, that rendered possible in the Scotch universities such a state of things as is complained of by Chalmers. He says: "In the hands of some of our most celebrated professors, it" (*i. e.* moral philosophy) "has been made to usurp the whole domain of humanity, insomuch that every emotion which the heart can feel, and every deed which the hand can perform, have, in every one aspect, whether relating to moral character or not, come under the cognizance of moral philosophy." He calls the science as there treated "a strange concretion," "a vast and varied miscellany," which he wished "to marshal aright into proper and distinct groups."

How this subject has been regarded in England we may learn from an introductory lecture to a course on Moral Philosophy delivered in London by Sidney Smith. "Moral philosophy," he says, "properly speaking, is contrasted to natural philosophy; comprehending everything spiritual, as that comprehends everything corporeal, and constituting the most difficult and the most sublime of those two divisions under which all human knowledge must be arranged." "In this sense," he proceeds, "Moral Philosophy is used by Berkley, by Hartley, by Hutcheson, by Adam Smith, by Howe, by Reid, and by Stewart. In this sense it is taught in the Scotch universities, where alone it *is* taught in this island; and in this sense it comprehends all the intellectual, active and moral faculties of man; the laws by which they are governed; the limits by which they are controlled, and the means by which they may be improved." In accordance with this, we find in his course, lectures on external perception, on taste, and on wit and humor, while in his whole twenty-seven lectures he did not treat of the conscience, or of right and wrong, at all.

Such a blending of departments, all covered by one name, in a single professorship, could not be favorable to accurate analysis. There were reasons for it. Mental and moral science are nearly related; but all knowledge is related to all other knowledge at some points, and it would be scarcely more incongruous to assign geography to the astronomer because the earth is one of the planets, than to group external perception and the knowledge of duty under the same science because they both belong to the mind.

A third cause of the slower progress of moral science is its greater complexity.

All science supposes uniformity in the phenomena, and so, in their cause or law, which is what science seeks. If there be no cause acting uniformly, and tending to entire uniformity of results, there is no basis for science. But with such a cause, the complexity will be in proportion to the number of disturbing forces that may come in between it and the phenomena as seen by us. In astronomy these disturbing causes are comparatively few. Gravitation towards the sun only, would cause the planets to move in a perfect ellipse. But none of them do thus move, and it is obvious that disturbing forces might be multiplied so as to render a science of the stars, or at least any other than a hypothetical one, impossible. Here lies the obstacle to a science of the winds. There is doubtless uniformity of causation, but the phenomena, as known to us, are so modified that we cannot trace each one back to its cause, or predict the future. So of human conduct. Men are themselves unlike, and in endless variety. Motives are complex. The effects of education, of social position, of political institutions and of climate, are to be estimated; and even though all the actions of men might be referred to one principle, it would be impossible to trace them to it, or to predict with certainty the course of any one individual under its guidance.

When we look, then, at this greater complexity, and remember that the study of processes within us, mental and moral, is connected with no such pleasure as observation by the senses, and can have no such aid from others, we find a reason of no little weight for the slower progress of this science.

A fourth reason is to be found in the fact, which we should not have anticipated, that the nearer we come to that in our being which is most intimate and central, which is our very self, the more difficult observation and analysis become.

As early, certainly, as the time of Cicero, the mind was compared to the eye, because that sees other things but not itself. The power of making itself an object to itself belongs to the mind of man as he is distinguished from the brutes; it is the last power that is developed, and in most men is scarcely developed at all. But where this power is developed it begins with those phenomena which are most outward and least essential. Hence, not only in matter, but in mind, completed science will probably travel from that which is more remote, or more outward, to that which is nearer, or more inward.

It is now generally conceded that there are two kinds of knowledge, or cognitions, — one which we gain of, and from, the external world through the senses; and the other that which springs from the mind itself after its powers have been waked into consciousness. It is not supposed that there are innate ideas, but that the mind has fixed capacities by which, in connection with the exercise of consciousness, it necessarily and universally forms certain ideas and affirms certain truths. These ideas and truths, if such there are, must be more intimate to us than any other part of our mental furniture; but it is precisely respecting these, and the field which they claim, that the most subtle and difficult of all the problems in philosophy have arisen. That we have ideas through the senses no one has ever doubted, and they are readily classified and their characteristics given; but nothing could more strikingly illustrate my present point than the fact that the very existence of any such truths and ideas as those just mentioned has been doubted, and still is. The reception or rejection of these cognitions as elements of philosophy has been the dividing line between its different schools from Plato down. Probably the preponderance in numbers has been against them, and even now they are rejected by such men as Comte and Mill.

As we should anticipate from the fact just stated, the advocates of these cognitions have failed to give their characteristics, and thus to bring them out into distinct consciousness. Before Leibnitz, no one had ever mentioned their two great characteristics, — *necessity* and *universality*, — and it was not till the time of Kant that these were at all signalized and properly applied. Meantime, there was no uniform and accepted designation either for the cognitions, or the faculty in which they originated. The faculty was called "intuition," and the "dry light of the mind," and "common sense," and "the reason," and by Hamilton it is called "the regulative faculty," while the names for the cognitions themselves were still more numerous.

But remarkable as all this is, it is still more so that no one has even claimed to explore all the recesses and sound the depths of this faculty. Some ideas, as those of existence, identity, and space, are recognized by all of this general school as given by it, but no one has claimed to make an accurate and full statement of these native, necessary, and universal cognitions. They have lain, and still lie, like a nebula in the depths of the heavens, which no instrument has as yet been able fully to resolve.

Among and concerning these it has been that the great battle with skepticism — that is, philosophical skepticism — has been fought. Hume denied their validity. Their legitimacy and place was not recognized in formal logic, then the test of truth, and the mass of philosophers were in the unfortunate position of holding to principles clearly involving consequences which they could not accept. Skepticism had thus an apparent triumph. Meantime, Reid began groping about in this region, and found the means, as he and others thought, of bridging the chasm of inconsistency dug by the skeptics; but so great was the want of precise terms, and so subtle the elements he dealt with, that even the acute Brown not only did not comprehend him, but imputed to him opinions the very reverse of those he held. In such a state of terms and ideas, men are like Indians fighting in a thicket. It is not easy to find and dislodge your adversary; and when you do, he can easily gain another place of concealment, and deny that he has been dislodged at all. If a clear exposition of these truths of reason, or native cognitions, or first truths, or maxims of common sense, or fundamental laws of belief, or whatever we may choose to call them, could have been made before the time of Hume, he would probably never have been heard of as a philosophical skeptic. The mind of Hume had in perfection the acuteness of the skeptic, which enabled him to see defects, and so to destroy, but had not the comprehensiveness needed for construction.

But to take a plainer case. What can be more intimate to a man, or more perfectly known, than that of which he is conscious? If a man cannot know what he is conscious of, it would seem that he cannot know anything; and yet the whole question, between Reid and Hamilton on the one side, and the great mass of philosophers on the other, respects simply the fact whether there is or is not given in an act of consciousness, both a subject and an object that are not, in the last analysis, identical. What consciousness testifies to must be accepted. This all allow. Not to do it would be suicidal even to the skeptic; for he would have no ground for affirming that he doubted. The only question is, what it is that consciousness gives. If we say that it does thus give both the subject and the object, that simple affirmation sweeps away in a moment the whole basis of the ideal and skeptical philosophy. It becomes as the spear of Ithuriel, and its simple touch will change what seemed whole continents of solid speculation into mere banks of German fog. If we say that the subject and object are not both given, we are then left to find as we may a solid basis for our belief in the existence of an external world. But however we may decide it, the fact that the great philosophical dispute of the day would be settled at once by a precise statement of what is given in the consciousness of every man, shows clearly that our investigations become more difficult as we approach the centre of our being. It shows, too, how far apart, on subjects like these, men may be in their statements, whose belief is really the same; for the consciousness is really the same in all, and is accepted by all.

What has now been said relates indeed to the intellect; but the moral nature is not less central, and presents, to say the least, equal difficulties on this ground.

In connection with the above, it may be well to notice a peculiarity of all advances and discoveries made in this direction, as they are related to the mass of men who are not philosophers. It is, that the more profound and difficult the discoveries are, the more they will seem, when clearly announced, to be a matter of course, and no discoveries at all. Though few men are able to state what is really contained and implied in their own consciousness, yet, when it is stated by another, there can be in it nothing strange to them; they recognize it and say, "Yes," "Certainly," and it seems to them they could have made the same statement. The continent is discovered, the egg is set on end, and nothing could have been easier.

A fourth reason, which has been implied already, and which has operated both as cause and effect, has been the want of definite terms. Science requires that terms should be used uniformly in the same sense, and that they should convey the same impression to all who use them. This can be done perfectly only in mathematics, may be approximated in dealing with objects of sense, but is most difficult in all that pertains to mental and moral science. In these the terms are borrowed from material objects, and so can be applied only figuratively; and then in applying them there is a difficulty that does not belong to physics. When I point a child to a particular star and say, "That is Jupiter," I am sure that we both see the same object; and when speaking of it thereafter, we cannot fail of understanding each other. But when I speak to him of "the reason," as distinguished from "the understanding," or of "first truths of reason," as distinguished from "empirical knowledge," or of conscience, I speak to him of what is in my own mind, and he must respond respecting what is in his mind. But differing as we do in age, constitution, and education, we can never be sure that our impressions are alike. "What," said a master to his man who had refused to do his bidding on the ground of conscience, — "what do you mean by conscience?" "It is," said he, "something in here that says, I won't." In the opinion of Paley, if conscience be anything original and native to the mind, it cannot be distinguished from prejudices and habits. Some think it simply the power of moral discrimination; others add an emotive element to reward and punish, and others still an impulsive power. Some regard it as the voice of God, and nearly or quite infallible; others as simply a form of judgment, like any other, and equally liable to error. Here the same *word* is used; and so it is, only with a difference of meaning somewhat wider, when we speak of a sign of a tavern, and of a sign of the zodiac; and till there is agreement in the meaning of the term, no progress can be made in discussion.

How, then, shall we be freed from this difficulty? Who shall have the right to say what the term conscience shall include? No one. But as thought is concentrated, as it will be, more and more upon man himself, the facts of his moral nature will come into more distinct consciousness, and the discriminations thus made will demand the narrowing down of old terms, or the invention of new ones, and these will gradually become definite and generally accepted. When terms are thus gained, they will react upon thought, as instruments invented react upon the inventive power; for language is not only a product, but an instrument of thought.

This process is going on, slowly but satisfactorily, in moral, and particularly in mental science. In the latter, the old classification of the faculties was into those of the understanding and the will. This sufficed till further examination showed that all the facts could not be ranged under these. We not only think and will, we also feel; and accordingly, after long discussion and some aid from abroad, the threefold division of the faculties into those of Thought, of Feeling, and of Action, is almost universally accepted. Under each of these a distinct science, or, if you please, department, is formed, in which a similar process must go on. In that of thought, or, as he terms it, of cognition, Sir William Hamilton has introduced new terms and classifications, some of which will doubtless be adopted. The same will be done in the other departments, till the whole shall assume all the definiteness and completeness of which the science, from its nature, is capable.

This difficulty from a want of terms, and of uniformity in their usage, has been felt from the first, and will be appreciated the more as the subject is more studied. It is one concerning which it is easy to give precepts, but difficult to follow them. Of this difficulty no one has been more fully aware than Locke. He wrote largely upon it, and gave wise precepts; and yet used the word *idea* so loosely that on the great subject of the origin of knowledge it is still uncertain what he really believed. On the Continent he was so interpreted as to be made the father of materialism. Many of the English admitted of no such interpretation, and both parties sustained themselves by adequate quotations. On this subject I make no promises.

The next, and the last consideration I shall adduce to account for the slower progress of moral science, is the failure of men in practical virtue.

That there has been such failure no one will deny; and it has operated in various ways. When a science, as formerly that of war, is regarded as at the basis of the great business of life, it will be studied. Attention will be concentrated upon it, and it will be carried to the greatest possible perfection. But let the subject be one for which, while every one acknowledges its importance, few have any practical regard; let it be thought of as something which will do for the closet and the schools, but not for practical life; let there be a general impression that its maxims are repeated in a perfunctory way, as a cover to the real principles of action, and any earnest or general study of the science is impossible. Theories there may be. They are needed for conversation and the Reviews; but only as there is a real, heartfelt, practical interest in virtue, can there be a genuine struggle for the truth as vital. The general failure of men in practical virtue has created an atmosphere unfavorable to an earnest search after the truth in morals. The set of the current in society has been against it.

Again, under this head, in proportion as men are vicious, not only will they lack interest in the science, but they become disqualified for its pursuit.

This is in accordance with the laws of all the faculties. The faculties are strengthened by exercise; they can be strengthened in no other way; and they are exercised rightly only by doing just the work which God intended they should do. *The moral powers, as a whole, can be so exer-*

cised as to improve them only as duty is accepted and practically performed. Therefore we say that the man whose moral faculties have been dwarfed by disuse, or perverted by abuse, would not be well qualified to investigate the science of morals. The phenomena, it is to be remembered, are those of mind. While there is, therefore, in all a common basis for the science, yet both the seeing eye and the thing seen may be modified by custom and habits. If there be little moral culture, the moral phenomena will either be obscure, or will consist in a decided wickedness which is blinding and hardening, while, at the same time, the power of moral discrimination will be diminished. It may be said that it is the intellect that constructs science. But it must construct it out of the materials given, which will be different in a vicious mind; and it must also have clearness and power in the particular field in which it works. But no fact can be better established than that wickedness, in every form and degree, not only blunts the moral feelings, but weakens the power of moral discrimination. A perfect mental science would require, first, the normal action of the faculties to give the phenomena, and then an accurate observation of those phenomena. A perfect moral science would require the normal action of the moral powers, either in ourselves or another, and an accurate observation of the results; but by the prevalence of vice the facts are both distorted and obscured.

What has now been said of morals is equally applicable to taste. A man whose sense of beauty should be either uncultivated or perverted would be the less capable of apprehending and presenting perfectly the science of æsthetics. But there is in morals a special difficulty. A vicious man is strongly tempted either to deceive or to bribe his conscience, and can hardly be expected to judge fairly of any system that would either justify or condemn himself. In all moral and religious truth there is this difficulty. It is not that we have lost the power to judge, but that we will not use it. It is the old difficulty of the influence of the desires and affections and of our supposed interest on our judgment. We all know how passion and interest pervert the judgment, and what discordant opinions there are wherever men are under their influence.

If, therefore, there had been no incapacity from vice, and no wrong bias, or passion, or want of candor, we cannot but suppose that moral science would have been much more advanced than it now is.

In thus answering the natural inquiry respecting the relative progress of these sciences, I have desired also to do something in the way of caution and guidance for ourselves. What has been is now, and will continue to be. The same obstacles that have been encountered by others we shall encounter; and some of them are such that if we are forewarned we may be forearmed against them.

Against the first difficulty mentioned we can do nothing directly; but it is a satisfaction, and may be of some aid, to know the precise mode in which our observations are to be made. But we may gain definite views of the sphere and objects of the science; we may seek to simplify it; we may make independent search into the depths of our own consciousness; we may be careful in the use of words, conforming at least to our own definitions; and, above all, we may either enter upon, or become more earnest in, a course of practical virtue, and so both prevent the imbecility of vice, and disperse the blinding mists that always arise from a corrupt heart.

The difficulties just considered are such as to preclude the hope of any great and sudden advance in this science

— of any, at least, which shall be at once recognized and incorporated into the public mind. Even if completed in thought and expression by one man, — if it should have its Newton, — yet its full acceptance by the public mind and assimilation with it would necessarily be slow. In astronomy, the true system was opposed to the popular conceptions and forms of speech, and more than one generation was required for it to permeate the masses and thoroughly control the habits of thought. But in that the proofs were open to popular apprehension, and, for the most part, there were no desires and passions to obstruct conviction. But of all the changes in society, none are so slow as those which are conditioned upon changes in language and character. Even Christianity itself, with its wonderful evidence and its divine power, is far from having taken full possession of the public mind in any community, and simply because it had these obstacles to encounter. But, as we have seen, perfection in moral science, to say nothing of other obstacles, can be reached only through changes both in language and in character. If terms absolutely new would not be demanded, yet some, like the heathen words for God, would require to be expanded and ennobled, while others would require to have their elasticity and capacity reduced; and then, the delicacy of moral feeling and accuracy of perception to be attained only through virtuous habits, would be indispensable.

It follows from this that, in our cultivation of this field, we are not to be disappointed if we see no immediate or startling results. The changes to be anticipated are like those of geology in the formation of strata, — sometimes more and sometimes less rapid, but always relatively slow.

But since the progress of the science is so slow, and its

completion has been so long delayed, it may be asked whether it is of any use. Are there not, it may be inquired, in our nature practical principles, which do and will control the course of human affairs with something like the certainty of instinct, and quite independent of scientific speculation? Within the memory of many this question has been put respecting various branches of physical science. It would not be put now. But respecting metaphysical and moral science there are those who put it with sincerity and earnestness.

On this point, and as they are related to practical arts, there are two classes of sciences. In the one the science is wholly at the basis of the art, and is requisite to its results in any degree. The art of photography could not have been without chemistry, nor surgery without anatomy, nor the art of protecting buildings from lightning without the science of electricity. In such cases, and they are numerous, the science is first, and the practical results follow. The processes start from the sciences. In these cases no one questions the utility of science. In the other class the practical results are first and the sciences follow. The sciences start from the processes, which they simply recapitulate. Here science consists in the statement of the properties, the relations in space, and the successions in time of those things which our will cannot reach, or, if it can, cannot improve. Science may predict the place of a star; but the color of its light or the rapidity of its motion it cannot affect. God gives light and the eye, and we see; but we see no better after knowing the structure of the eye and the science of optics than before. Here the result is first, as perfect as it can be made, and the science is just a statement of the process by which the result was reached. It is in this class that the science of the mind belongs. Like the eye, its faculties are given, and act by their own law without reference to science, which can merely trace back and state such results as are common to all minds. It is solely with reference to these sciences that the question arises.

To this question, What is the use? there are two replies. The first is, that, even in the sense of the word as used by the objector, these sciences *are* of use. The processes may be perfect; we may not be able to affect the results, and yet the sciences may be of use indirectly. We cannot change the number or movements of Jupiter's satellites; but by means of their eclipses we can calculate the longitude. Entomology will not enable us to change the structure or habits of an insect; but it may suggest a mode of saving our trees. The laws of the winds are not subject to our control; but by a knowledge of them we may shorten our voyage.

Again, this class of sciences becomes greatly useful when the structures and processes of nature become deranged. When the eyes become flattened by age, science can remedy the defect, and when

> "A drop serene hath quenched their orb,
> Or dim suffusion veiled,"

it is by science alone that it can be removed. And so it is in most cases of displacement and derangement in the physical system. The science of anatomy, which is almost wholly at the basis of the art of surgery, would be of no practical use if nothing ever went wrong in the body.

A second reply to the objection urged is, that while we do not repudiate the conception of utility involved in what has just been said, we yet do not need it for the vindication of these sciences. We are capable of an interest in science for its own sake, which shows that we have an affinity with higher natures, and that the whole domain of the universe will finally be ours. The pleasure felt by the great discoverers of scientific truths is among the purest and most unselfish that can belong to man. It gives them a thought of God which they utter to the race, and it becomes a fountain of joy to millions. So it has been in astronomy. Every time the thought of God, as uttered by Newton, has been apprehended for the first time by any mind, there has been a commencement anew of the revolutions of the heavens, and the morning stars have sung together. And so would it be if the mighty forces and bright order that are without and afar could be seen to be, as they are, but a type and reflection of the forces and order within. Then would the great thought of God, not merely of a physical order in one department, but in all departments; and not of a physical order merely, but of one which should correspond in his one universe to a spiritual and moral order still more glorious, stand fully revealed, and should be a light and a joy forever.

I have only to add, that our opinions of the laws and processes of our being may be so held as to affect those processes scarcely at all, and hence that the practical results of man's opinions on these points are often less beneficent and less mischievous than would naturally be supposed. In our minds, no less than in external nature, the forces are what they are, irrespective of any opinion of ours, and will act, and no theory has any direct tendency to eradicate or diminish them. In the man who believes in disinterested benevolence, the desires and passions and selfish forces may still have the ascendency, while he who holds to the selfish theory may be often moved by the natural impulses of benevolence and sympathy. So it is that the selfish theory of morals, so long inculcated, has not wholly corrupted society; so it is that men are often better and worse than their theories; so it is that God holds in check the evils that would naturally flow from the errors of men.

LECTURE II.

THREE QUESTIONS.—THE CONSIDERATION OF ENDS.—AN END ATTAINED IN THREE WAYS.—ENDS SUBORDINATE, ULTIMATE, AND SUPREME.—AN END INVOLVES A GOOD.—THE NATURE OF GOOD AS FROM ACTIVITY.—THE GREATEST GOOD.

THE difficulties mentioned in the last lecture as obstructing the progress of moral science would also render it less desirable as a subject for a course of popular lectures. But with those difficulties it has two decided advantages.

The first is, that it appeals directly to the consciousness of the hearer. No learning is needed; no science, no apparatus, no information from distant countries. "It is nigh thee, even in thy heart." Some familiarity with terms may be required; but there is that in every man which may, and ought to make him a competent judge of all questions pertaining to this science. Let a lecturer but state the facts simply and truly, thus interpreting every man's consciousness to himself, and he may hope to carry his audience with him. Thus to state the facts will be my endeavor.

The second advantage is, that the questions involved are among the deepest and most vital that belong to our nature.

We proceed, then, to our subject, and begin with facts. That men regard some actions with approbation, and others with disapprobation, is a fact, just as it is a fact that they regard some portions of matter as hard, and others as soft. Of those actions which they approve, they say that they ought to be done; of those which they disapprove, they say that they ought not to be done.

In these facts we have our subject. Moral philosophy respects the character and conduct of men only as there are acts which they ought, or ought not to do. Wherever the word *ought*, indicating duty, can go, there is its domain; and the point beyond which that cannot go fixes its limit. Whoever can answer, in all cases, these three questions, 1st. *What ought to be done?* 2d. *Why ought it to be done?* and, 3d. *How ought it to be done?* has mastered the science of morals.

In answering these questions we may seek aid in various directions. I propose to inquire, at present, what aid we may derive from a consideration of ends as they stand related to all rational and moral action.

In acting morally, man also acts rationally; but it is the characteristic of rational action that it involves the conception of an end. Except in the apprehension of an end, there is nothing that a rational being can do, or that a moral being ought to do.

This relation of an end to all rational action may be seen if we observe what occurs in the production, study, and use of works produced by design.

In these the designer first conceives of the end, and then of the thing designed with reference to that. It is, therefore, the end in view that controls the structure.

In studying a work produced by design, we may first gain a conception of the structure, and pass from that to the end; but our interest in the study of the structure is from its apprehended relation to an end; and we are never satisfied with a knowledge of structure without that of the end.

The perfection of a work of design must consist in its

adaptation to attain its proposed end; and all use of it except for this end must be either inappropriate or wrong. Hence, a conception of the end must control not only the structure, but the use.

If the relation between the structure and the end be at once perceived, there will be no need of rules. If not, rules may be needed. These must grow out of the relation of the structure to its end, and will always express some mode in which the structure must be used to attain the end.

What is true of rules is true also of laws. These have often been confounded, but are essentially different. A law is imperative; a rule is not. A law has sanctions; a rule has not. A law tells us what to do; a rule, how to do it. A command to put forth continuous action directly, and without the use of means, as to love God, would be a law, but not a rule, and no rule could be given by which we could do it. But though there are laws which cannot become rules, yet rules may become laws when the observance of them is commanded, and enforced by a penalty. While, therefore, a rule prescribes a course of action that would lead to an end, a law may prescribe one that is itself an end. But even then, as a rule derives its value from its relation to an end, so must a law derive its value from what it is regarded as an end.

Again, regarding man as a moral being, if no end valuable in itself be supposed, it will be found impossible to conceive of him as under obligation to act in any particular way. For the very conception of obligation that of an end is a condition.

We see, therefore, that in all rational action the central conception is that of an end. In works of design it controls the structure in the mind of the designer; it is essential to a right understanding of the structure by him who would study it; it is in its relation to this that the structure has its perfection and appropriate use; and from this that the value of all rules and laws for, and in its use arises. Of whatever can be comprehended and used, even of man himself, all this may be affirmed.

Let us, then, apply these principles to man.

As man was made by a wise and good being, he must have been made for some end, and the conception of this end must have controlled the formation and adjustment of every part of his complex structure.

From the study of this structure we may gain some knowledge of its end. Aside from revelation, this is our only knowledge on this point. Nor is the amount of knowledge to be thus gained small. Of some parts of the body, as the hands, the feet, the eyes, the teeth, the end is revealed at once in the structure. It is this knowledge of structure as related to use that gives comprehension. Only in the light of it can we have complacency in the structure when right, or the power to correct it when wrong. In the same way the faculties of the mind, in their relation to each other, reveal their end, and thus the law of their use. An intelligent being whose end should not be revealed *in* itself would be an absurdity. If the end were not revealed *to* itself, it would be lost. It is the possibility and measure of such knowledge that determines the possibility and measure of any philosophy of man.

The perfection of man, viewed merely as a product of divine power, must consist in his adaptation and capacity to attain the end for which he was made.

That, and that only, is the right use of the faculties of man, — of all his susceptibilities and powers of agency, — by which they attain the end for which they were made.

If man could see the end for which he was made as God sees it, and dispose himself perfectly for its attainment, he would be in harmony with God; his faculties would work in harmony with each other, and he would do all that he ought to do.

Laws and rules for the conduct of man, whether confessedly human, or claiming to be divine, are valid only as they are based on a true perception of the relation between the human constitution and its proper end. If a course of conduct, prescribed by what claims to be law, could be shown to be opposed to the attainment of the end for which man was made, it would not be right to pursue it. The will of God is revealed in the end, and he cannot contradict himself.

In the following discussions the word *end*, as applied to man, will be of frequent use, and, to avoid ambiguity, it may be well to say that the idea it involves is complex. As intelligent and responsible, the end of man is to choose something; as an agent, it is to do something; as capable of enjoyment, it is to enjoy something; and as a creature made by God, his end is to *be* that which will enable him to do and to enjoy all that God intended he should. He is to be something, to choose and do something, and to enjoy something; and his whole end will be, to be what God intended he should be, to choose and do what He intended he should choose and do, and to enjoy what He intended he should enjoy. He who should fail in any of these would fail of attaining his whole end; and if the word should at any time seem to refer particularly to one of these elements, it will not be to the intentional exclusion of the others.

An end may be attained in three ways. And, —

1st. It may be attained by instinct. Here the agent

has no knowledge or rational comprehension of the end, but is guided by a blind impulse.

2d. An end may be attained by obeying a rule implicitly. Here there may, or there may not be a conception of the specific end, but the connection between the means and the end is never seen. In this way children are governed. Here the principle is not instinct, but faith. They follow the rule, that is, they do as they would if they understood the connection between the means and the end, and so receive the same benefit. To a finite being faith is a necessary principle of action, and becomes practical wisdom when there is a rational ground of confidence in the word of another because it is his word, or of implicit obedience to his commands.

3d. An end may be attained understandingly and rationally. The structure may be known, now regarded simply as a means; the end may be known; and there may also be a clear perception of the mode in which the structure must be used to attain the end. In this mode of action man would not act from law, but from a knowledge of the reasons of the law. He would be wholly a philosopher. Viewing the end as God views it; voluntarily choosing this end; applying all his powers as they were intended for its attainment, he would do all that he ought to do, would have the approbation of God, the approbation of his own conscience, and the sanction of reason.

But if, in thus attaining the end for which he was made, man would, as has just been said, do all that he ought to do, then have we answered, in a general way, one of the questions mentioned above. Would he thus do all that he ought to do? If we say yes, then *Moral Philosophy will be the science which teaches man the end for which he was made, why he should attain that end, and how to attain it.*

To the above definition it may be objected, that it includes theology and religion. It does so only so far as to justify a consideration of our duties towards God, and that is found in all treatises on morals. Moral philosophy differs from theology in taking for granted the being and attributes of God; and religion differs from morality because it includes all our duties towards men as commanded by God; and also because it implies an order of faculties, and a class of duties, as those of worship, of which mere morality could know nothing. Still, the science of duty, of obligation, must be one. No satisfactory account of the moral nature of man and of its full sphere can be given on any other supposition. We may, if we choose, divide our duties into those towards God, and those towards man; but moral science must go wherever the word *ought* can be applied.

But if not faulty on this ground, the definition has an advantage in regard to Christianity. We are able, in the light of it, to state precisely, which has not always been done, the relation between Christianity, as a remedial system, and moral philosophy. This is entirely different from that of natural religion. It is that of medicine to physiology. Physiology can know nothing of medicine except as it would restore the system to health; and moral philosophy, if we accept the above definition, can recognize as obligatory no precept peculiar to Christianity, except as it can be shown to be necessary, in our present state, to the attainment of the end for which man was made. Let this be shown of any such precept, and its obligation will not only be recognized, but it will be an evidence that the religion is from God; and a demonstrated capacity in the religion to bring man fully to his end would be a demonstration of its truth. From the constitution of man moral philosophy would find his end. In the end it would find revealed the will of God, and in the relation between the constitution in its various parts and its end would find revealed the law of God, and those rules in accordance with which his faculties must act for the attainment of the end. Christianity, on the other hand, is wholly remedial. It supposes man to have broken law, and it harmonizes with moral philosophy and can be accepted by it only as it can attain for man his original end, — or, it may be, something better, though of that moral philosophy could know nothing.

Shall we, then, accept the above definitions? Let us do so, so far, at least, as to make further explorations in this direction. The definition speaks of an end; but ends are of different kinds, and these we shall need to consider.

An end may be subordinate, ultimate, or supreme.

A subordinate end is one chosen for the sake of some end beyond itself. Thus books are chosen for the sake of knowledge, and the implements of husbandry for the sake of a crop. A subordinate end, regarded by itself, is not necessarily a good. It may be the reverse.

An ultimate end is one that is chosen for its own sake, and without reference to anything beyond. It must be some form of good. The enjoyment there is in viewing a beautiful prospect is valuable for its own sake, and is the ultimate end in making the ascent whence the prospect may be seen.

An ultimate end, it is to be noticed, is always the result of action, and never the action itself. It never lies proximate to the volition, and so cannot be the immediate object in any act of volition, and is never commanded. The formula is — "do this and live." It is the thing to be done that is commanded, and that is to be willed; the living is the result, and the ultimate end. So it is in everything. Eat the peach, — and enjoy it; take the remedy, — and get well; ascend the mountain, turn your eyes upon the prospect, — and enjoy it. The ascent and the turning of the eyes are the immediate result of volition; the enjoyment is not willed, but comes of its own accord as a result of the constitution of the perceptive powers and the landscape in their relation to each other. It is here as in the machinery which man constructs. He may build a mill, supply it with wheat, set it in motion, and to all these volition is in immediate relation. But the ultimate end of the mill is the flour, and that is ground by the mill. To that the will, as an executive act, is not proximate. Hence, ultimate ends, those ultimate for man, have no exchangeable value. They cannot be bought and sold, and in this sense are worth nothing. As the brain has no sensibility itself, but is the condition and fountain of sensibility for all other parts, so these, having no exchangeable value, are the condition and ground of all such value. Hence, after having chosen an ultimate end, an act, not of volition, but of choice, we are always to understand what it is that lies proximate to that, and to attain that must be the object of all immediate volitions and efforts. And hence, again, in accordance with our present scheme of thought, virtue will consist in the choice of the right end, followed, of course, if the choice be thoroughgoing, by the willing of that state or mode of activity which is believed to be proximate to that. That state is always proximate to the will; no means are required, and so a failure to be virtuous admits of no excuse.

This relation of volition to an ultimate end has not generally been stated with sufficient distinctness, and the result has been a constant puzzle. It is generally said that all men seek happiness, and yet no man ever made it the direct object of volition. No man can. That God holds in his own power. It is his immediate gift through that constitution and relation of things which he has established. We will that which he has made the antecedent and condition of happiness, and he gives the happiness. We say "open sesame," and the gate opens of its own accord. This is what men mean when they say they will do their duty and leave the event with God.

But besides an ultimate, there is also a supreme or chief end. A supreme end is also ultimate; but is that to which, in any possible conflict of ultimate ends, all others must be subordinated. Ultimate ends often, and necessarily, conflict with each other. The pleasure from each sense is ultimate; but it may be necessary to choose between that of music through the ear and that of beauty through the eye. In such cases we may indulge our preference; but no end may be chosen as ultimate when it would conflict with that which is supreme.

Any ultimate end may be adopted as supreme; but the wisdom of man consists in choosing that intended by God, which can be but one, and in giving to each of those thus made secondary its proper place.

The choice of this supreme end is the highest act of a rational being, and involves the activity of all his rational and moral powers. It is the characteristic of a rational action that it involves the conception of an end, and of a moral action that it involves the preference of an end. And as we regard a moral being as virtuous or vicious according to the end chosen, so do we regard a rational being as wise or foolish on the same ground. Wisdom and folly chiefly respect the ends which men pursue, rather than the means by which they pursue them. Here, then, we find a point at which the rational and moral natures coalesce.

But to be more particular. What the supreme end of man, as fixed by God, must be, will be determined by what he is in himself, and as related to other beings. The conception and choice of such an end will therefore imply a knowledge, implicit or formal, of himself, and of those beings and relations through which alone the end can be realized. This is the highest of all knowledge. There is in it the *Γνῶθι σεαυτόν** of the ancients, and something more.

In the conception of an end there is also involved that of some good. This cannot come from the intellect alone. There must be the activity of the emotive nature, — of that through which we enjoy, as well as of that through which we apprehend. But the recognition of a good through the intellectual and emotive nature acting conjointly, does not make it an end, much less a supreme end. To become such it must be chosen. This involves the moral nature, since the character of every man is determined by the end he chooses. But, further, that a good should become a supreme end implies that the will shall at once put forth determinate acts for its attainment. Thus the conception of a supreme end involves that of the action of the intellectual, the emotional, the moral, and the executive powers, that is, of the whole personality,— of the man in his unity.

An end, as has been said, involves some form of good. We next inquire, then, what is a good?

A good must be either some form of enjoyment, satisfaction, blessedness; or that which is the occasion, cause, or ground of such enjoyment.

There are many objects without us so related to our organs and faculties that enjoyment is the result of their

* Know thyself.

reciprocal action. Thus light acts upon the eye, and is the condition of seeing. Here we have the eye, the light, and the product of their joint action, that is, seeing. A peach eaten acts upon the palate, and is the condition of a pleasant taste. Here we have the palate, the peach, and the result. Are, then, the light and the peach a good? As conditional for these results, they are *good*, but not *a* good. When we apply the term good, we mean either to indicate that which is good in itself, or we have reference to an end, so that the question may be asked, Good for what? and if that question can be answered by indicating any use of the thing for an end beyond itself, then it cannot be, so far forth, *a* good, nor can it be any part of a supreme good. But all outward objects, and all possessions, sometimes called *goods*, have a use beyond themselves. If they were never to contribute to comfort, enjoyment, or utility in any way, they would be good—for nothing. It would seem self-evident that light never seen, the sapid quality of the peach never tasted, would not be a good.

We seem, then, driven, in our search for a good, to living, sensitive, conscious beings, whose faculties are in action. If there were no consciousness in the universe, there would be no good. But if found here, good must be either in some state of the being that is back of the activity; or in the activity itself; or in the results of the activity.

Let us illustrate this. Health is commonly regarded as a good. Doubtless, there is a state of the materials composing the body that is conditional for health, and is back of their activity. But of that we know, and can know, nothing. As known by us, health is that state of the body in which each part accomplishes perfectly its end.

When the teeth masticate, and the stomach digests, and the liver secretes, and the blood circulates perfectly, and every other organ and portion of the body performs perfectly its part, there is health. This state, however, is itself a form of activity, since a cessation of activity would be death. As a result of this perfect performance of its office by each part there is power, and a state of conscious well-being, in which a person is said to enjoy himself. Here it must be conceded that the whole worth both of the state and of the activity, if we choose to distinguish them, is from their results. If there were from them no power and no enjoyment, they would be good for nothing. Here, what we have to do, and all we have to do, is to secure that form of activity which we call health. The results follow by the constitution of God. All that was said respecting an ultimate end as not lying approximate to volition applies perfectly here.

And so it is in mind. There may be a state of mind back of activity, and so back of consciousness, that is good as related to results; but without those results appearing in consciousness it cannot be *a* good. If conceivable at all in such a state, which I think it is not, mind could never be known as mind, and, never emerging from it, would not rise above the dignity of matter.

As there is, then, no good without consciousness, which involves activity, it would seem that the good must be found either in the activity itself, or in its results.

But activity in itself cannot be a good. If it had no results it would be good for nothing, and those results may be evil and wretchedness, as well as blessing.

We turn, then, in this search, to the results in consciousness, of activity. We are so constituted that any form of normal activity, physical or mental, produces satisfaction, enjoyment, blessedness, according to the faculties that act. Of these the conception is simple and undefinable except by synonymous terms. They are that in which we rest, in which we are so satisfied that, within a given sphere, we look for nothing beyond. From our activity as excited in taste, by odors, by music, in admiration of beauty, in love, there may be a satisfaction which shall be the measure of our capacity in that direction. This all concede to be a good. We say, then, that in the satisfaction attached by God to the normal activity of our powers, we find *a good*, an end that is wholly for its own sake. We say, too, that it is only in, and from such activity that we can have the notion of any satisfaction, enjoyment, blessedness, either for ourselves or others; and that that form and proportion of activity which would result in our perfect blessedness would be right.

Such a form of activity will be to the mind what health is to the body, and in the maintenance of that will be found the highest duty and the highest good of man,—his wisdom and his virtue. From it must result to others all the good he is capable of doing; and to himself all he is capable of enjoying. Here, as in health, what man has to do, is to maintain the activity, and God gives the result.

It will appear, from what has been said, that there may be as many forms of good as there are faculties or forms of activity; and these forms of good may differ not only in degree, but in kind. Has man a sensitive nature? There is, from the activity of that, and from each modification of that activity, as in the different senses, a sensitive good. It is multiform, but one. Has he an intellectual nature? There is from the activity of that an intellectual good. We may, indeed, conceive of the intellect simply as a capacity for knowing, and as acting without the slightest enjoyment, — as light without heat. But this is not its actual constitution. Call it what you please, derive it whence you will, there is enjoyment in the very process and activity of the mind in the driest mathematical demonstration. Has man, again, an æsthetic, a rational, a moral, a religious nature? There is, from the activity of each of these, a corresponding good. It is clear, then, that the whole good of man would arise from a combination in the highest possible degree of all these forms of good; also, that *the highest good would be from the activity of the highest powers in a right relation to their highest object.* Nor is this highest good any mere happening, as is sometimes said of happiness; nor is it the mere satisfying of any craving; it is that result in God's creatures that was intended by him, and is an image of his own rational and holy blessedness in the activity of those powers in which we are made in his image.

Of the conditions of good the above statement is the most general that can be made, and admits of no exception. It implies nothing in relation to the direction of the activity as designed to produce our own good, or that of others. If there are in man no faculties except for promoting the well-being of the agent himself, then the well-being of the agent will be found in the highest activity of those faculties. But if there are also faculties capable of working disinterestedly, and that were designed to promote the good of others, then, whatever good can come to the individual through those faculties, will come from their highest activity for the very end for which they were made. That man, as social, has such faculties, there can be no doubt; and it may be that it is only in the activity of these for the good of the whole that the end and highest good of the individual can be found.

In the view just given, we have the basis of a conception of the spiritual universe analogous to that given in astronomy of the physical universe, but far higher. In astronomy, no less than in mind, activity, movement, is at the basis of all order, and beauty, and beneficence. But there the motion is impressed from without; here it is from within; there it is unintelligent; here it comprehends itself; there it is necessitated; here it is free; there there is no consciousness and no emotion; here the movement is reflected in the consciousness, and every faculty sings. Think, then, of creatures, intelligent, moral, free, with susceptibilities high and keen, in numbers far outnumbering the starry hosts. See in each a central personality — a mysterious selfhood, with its attendant faculties revolving, like satellites, harmoniously about it. See these planetary intelligences in their myriad heavens, each moving in his own bright orbit, at once of duty and of freedom, mutually giving and receiving, and singing together that song which was typified when the morning stars sang together of old, — and you have a spectacle which He who sits upon the central throne may well look upon with complacency, and pronounce "very good."

That the account now given is correct, appears from this. If we suppose enjoyment, satisfaction, blessedness, to be wholly withdrawn from the universe, we should feel, whatever state or form of activity there might be, that its value was gone. It would be a vast machine producing nothing. But if we suppose the highest possible blessedness of God and of his universe secured, we are satisfied. It must surely be difficult to satisfy those who cannot find an adequate end and good in their own highest blessedness, and in the highest blessedness of God and his universe.

If the statements now made be correct, we are prepared to answer the second question mentioned above. The first was, What ought to be done? and the general answer was, To ascertain the end for which we were made, and to seek to accomplish that. The second question was, Why ought it to be done? and the answer is, Because of the intrinsic excellency and worth of that end. Man, and all moral beings, are capable, as such, of a high and holy blessedness which can be compared with nothing else, which is the fruit and crown of all virtuous and holy activity, which has no exchangeable value, but has, in itself, an infinite worth.

If it be still asked why a man ought to seek an end which has this intrinsic worth, the reply is that this idea of obligation or *oughtness* is a simple idea, and therefore that we can only state the occasion on which it arises. Of its presence in connection with our choice of this end we can give no account, except that such is our constitution. This, however, does not compel us to say that we ought to seek a thing simply because we ought. The sense of obligation or *oughtness* may or may not precede the choice, but could have no place if there were not a ground of action besides itself. It does not come up out of vacancy. A man ought to choose that which is congruous to his nature. It would seem that an act of choice must be from something in the thing chosen thus congruous. He ought to choose his own well-being rather than the contrary; but he ought to choose it not simply because he ought, but because it *is* well-being. If there were nothing valuable in itself, there would be nothing that ought to be either chosen or done.

For those who adopt the general line of thought we are now pursuing, this question concerning good is fundamental, because there is involved in it the rule for right action. According to this, any course of action which will secure the whole good for which man was made must be right.

But among those who believe that the rule has its basis in the highest good, there is a difference of opinion as to what that good is. On this subject I cannot enter at large, but will refer briefly to two different views. These make the good consist in that which is conditional for the results, and not in the results themselves.

The first is that of Jouffroy. His view is that good consists in universal order. "When," says he, "reason first perceives that, as there is a good for us, so is there for all creatures whatsoever, and that thus the particular good of each creature is but an element of universal order, of absolute good, then does the idea of good, so disengaged and elevated to the sphere of absolute being, appear to our reason as obligatory."* Here two questions may be asked. The first is, whether the reason does necessarily form this idea of universal order. Since *the* reason has been so much spoken of, nothing has been more common than to mistake the results of abstraction and generalization for its immediate and necessary ideas. That this is not one of those ideas, may be inferred from the fact that men are not agreed in what the order consists. Universal order may be either that form and extent of activity which would secure universal blessedness; or that perfect distribution of good and evil which would constitute moral order, but would involve punishment and suffering.

But if this idea of universal order be an idea of reason, it would not follow that the highest good was in that. It would be only conditional for blessedness. This it doubt-

* Introduction to Ethics.

less is; but if no blessedness were at any time or in any degree to result from it, it would be in vain. No position or movement of matter, no activity of mind, however controlled and subordinated, that should have no results beyond itself, would be a good.

These remarks are made on the supposition that the blessedness is not considered a part of the order. If it be, then there is simply a confusion of terms. Order would be made to include not only, according to its usual acceptation, the constitution and movements of the universe, but its results.

The other view is that of a very able and distinguished cotemporary. This has its basis in the perfection of the individual as a moral being, as the other has in that of the universe as a constituted whole. "The highest good," says Dr. Hickok, "the summum bonum, is worthiness of spiritual approbation." *

From so able a thinker I differ with regret. But what is that in which a man's worthiness of spiritual approbation consists? It is in his choice of an ultimate end. The character is according to that. Does, then, the highest good of man consist in his choosing as an ultimate end his own choice of an ultimate end? This cannot be, and yet would seem to follow from the definition.

Again, if this be the highest good, it consists of something which can enter into the consciousness but a small portion of the time, and then only by special effort. Man can make himself and his state the object of his own thoughts; but introspection was not intended to be the business of his life, nor the form of his activity in which he should be either most useful or most happy. He was made to apprehend God and his works, and his fellow-crea-

* Moral Science, p. 43.

tures, and to love and admire these, and not to look withiu, except to correct what may be wrong, and to admire there, as elsewhere, indications of the divine wisdom and goodness. How, then, can that be the highest good of man which, if he really had it, he would think of only as the man who has healthy lungs thinks of his breathing? No doubt worthiness is conditional, and in a moral being necessarily so, for blessedness. But the word, though it may be used absolutely, naturally carries with it an indication of something beyond itself. A worthiness of what? Of approbation? And why not of the blessedness there is in and through that worthiness and that approbation?

In this and similar cases the ultimate appeal must be to consciousness. To that I appeal, only wishing the statements to be so made that the consciousness may apprehend distinctly the elements with which it is dealing.

In speaking hitherto of activities and their results, language has been used in its ordinary sense, as applied to outward things. It will be observed, however, that in the region of mind and of consciousness the results are themselves activities. There is, therefore, a sense in which it may be said that the activity *is* the blessedness. The difference is, that what we call activities here are those which are inaugurated and controlled by the will, while what we call results are those emotions and feelings which follow from the other, by the appointment of God. We do not, therefore, in this connection, regard ends as anything outward, but identify ends and activities.

LECTURE III.

KINDS OF GOOD.—SUSCEPTIBILITIES AND POWERS.—GOOD AS HIGHER AND LOWER.—FORCES AND FACULTIES—THEIR SUBORDINATION.—THE LAW OF LIMITATION.—METHODS OF ADDITION AND OF DEVELOPMENT.—NATURAL AND CHRISTIAN LAW OF SELF-DENIAL.

In the last lecture two questions were answered. The first was, What ought man to do? and the second, Why ought he to do it? Man ought to attain the end for which he was made; and he ought to do it because of the intrinsic worth of that end. In answering these questions we considered the nature of an end as related to rational activity, and also the nature of good as necessarily included in an ultimate end.

We now proceed to answer the third question proposed, which is, How ought man to attain the end for which he was made? There is a sense in which this question may be resolved into the first; for, if we know, in the fullest sense, what to do, we also know how to do it. But convenience and the common use of language justify the division now made.

In answering the above question we shall naturally examine the different forms of activity of which man is capable, and their resulting forms of good, that we may thus find for each faculty the law and measure of its activity. But this may be done with more advantage if we first discriminate between different kinds of good; and if we also find a criterion by which we may distinguish that which is higher from that which is lower.

As has been said already, there are as many kinds of good as there are forms of normal activity; but these forms of activity may be divided into two great classes broadly distinguished.

Man has *powers*, and he has *susceptibilities*. By his powers he acts upon external nature; by his susceptibilities external nature acts upon him.

Once awakened, the powers act, not simply because they are acted upon, but of their own proper activity. The susceptibilities have no activity of their own except as they are acted upon. In the activity of the susceptibilities the movement is from without inward; in that of the powers it is from within outward. In the one we receive; in the other we give.

When the susceptibilities are acted upon by their appropriate stimuli, the result is *pleasure*. So far as this term is employed distinctively, this is the form of enjoyment indicated by it, and is that which is sought by those who are called "lovers of pleasure." It has an inlet through each of the senses. It is the product of warmth, and food, and of the various kinds of nervous stimulation. That the production of this is an object in nature, is obvious from the number and variety of those arrangements by which sensitive beings receive pleasure from the objects around them. In this respect the works of God call for our grateful study. Particularly is the human organism admirable for this in its complex and wonderful adjustment to external nature.

But in this enjoyment there is no necessary activity of any rational or moral power. The right relation being established, man is no further active than as he has the vitality and susceptibility which must be the condition of any pleasure.

Between this form of enjoyment and that from the activity of the powers the differences are radical. And, —

1st. The law of habit, mentioned by Butler, by which passive impressions become weaker as they are longer continued, applies only to the susceptibilities and the resulting pleasure. "It is," says Paley, "a law of the machine for which we know no remedy, that the organs by which we receive pleasure are blunted and benumbed by being frequently exercised in the same way. There is hardly any one who has not found the difference between a gratification when new and when familiar, nor any *pleasure* which does not become indifferent as it grows habitual." It is, on the other hand, the law of the powers that they gain strength by activity, become more masterly, and more and more capable of being the source of a high joy and blessedness.

Here, then, is a radical contrast between the good from the susceptibilities and from the powers. The one is like a vessel full and sparkling at first, but gradually wasting away and becoming vapid; the other is like a fountain whose waters well up the more freely the more they overflow.

A second difference is to be found in the rank of these two forms of good.

Pleasure is a good in itself, and so an ultimate end; but for the most part it is also a means to something beyond itself. This is especially true of legitimate pleasure. It seems to have been intended as an inducement to the performance of acts which are to have remote consequences of which the agents themselves are often either ignorant or regardless. The pleasure of the child, and of the man too, in eating, and in muscular movement, is the inducement to do that which is necessary for the upbuilding of the body, but for which they generally have no care. On the other hand, the good from the activity of the powers, as in loving and in worshipping, is an end in itself, and has no reference to anything beyond itself.

There is a third difference. We always feel ourselves at liberty to forego the enjoyment of pleasure, and respect ourselves when we do this for the sake of the good which comes from the activity of the powers, but never the reverse. These two are often, and to some extent naturally, opposed, and it is a part of the conflict of life to keep pleasure within its proper limits.

We have thus, from our susceptibilities, a good which we may call *pleasure*. From the activity of our powers, voluntary and moral, we have a good higher and different in kind, for which we need a distinctive name, but which we will here call *happiness*. This will differ with the powers, intellectual, æsthetic, moral, spiritual, which are in exercise. By these, taking cognizance practically, æsthetically, scientifically of the works of God, apprehending the character and wants of man, being brought into relation to the attributes and character of God, man is capable not only of the appropriate enjoyment from such cognitions, but also of putting forth in love all the activity of his nature for the good of the whole. What of good there may be from these can be known only by experience, but clearly it need be limited only by our capacity.

My own belief is that that part of our nature through which we have the highest good lies open to the direct action of the Spirit of God, as the susceptibilities do to that of the objects around us; that thus we may apprehend him directly; and that in his response to this, in love, man is capable of a good that is ineffable, and may be called "*fulness of joy*," or *blessedness*. The capacity for this I suppose as much belonged to man originally as his capacity for perceiving beauty.

The above distinctions are practical, and, from the tendency there is in men to seek pleasure in opposition to their higher good, are worthy of careful attention.

We now turn from this broad classification of good to inquire for the basis of one that is more exact. We speak of good as higher and lower, and we have an instinctive feeling that some forms of good are higher than others. Is there a criterion by which we may determine what is higher and what is lower?

In answering this question, I hope for indulgence if I enter upon a range somewhat wide. Moral science has usually been studied as isolated. My wish is to connect it with the laws of that physical system which not only supports man, but has its culmination in him. I wish to show that there runs through both one principle of gradation, and one law for the limitation of forces and activities, and so of the forms of good resulting from them. If this can be done, it will add to both physical and moral science the beauty of a higher unity than has commonly been noticed, and will show that there could have been but one author for both.

All good, and all arrangements conditional for good, are the result of some activity. They are in or from it. Arrangements conditional for good are the product of forces, good itself of faculties. A faculty is a force united to personality and subject to the control of the will. What we need to find, then, is a common law for the subordination and limitation of both forces and faculties.

This we find in their relation to each other as conditional and conditioned. The forces that are at work around us and the faculties within us, from the lowest to the highest, may be ranked as higher and lower as they are or are not a condition one for another. That which is a condition for another is always the lower.

In anything we may choose to examine, — a house, or a portion of matter, — we shall find some conceptions or properties that may be spared, and yet the thing continue to be that thing. But we may continue our analysis till we reach certain properties or conceptions which are indispensable, which underlie all others, and are conditional for that thing. So it is with solidity, or the occupation of space, in matter; so with the foundation of a house. These may be of no importance in themselves, but all-important as conditions for something above them.

It is this relation of the forces of the universe and of their products to each other, as conditional and conditioned, that gives to it its unity. If its forces were diverse, it would not be a universe, — that is, if they were so diverse as to be free from this relation. Any being or thing conditioned upon nothing in the present system, and the condition of nothing, would be so utterly out of relation as to be alien from every conception of unity.

In seeking, then, for the law of subordination and limitation of the forces of the universe, we must begin at the lowest, and to find that, we must continue to drop from our conceptions of the universe every force and product that can be spared till we reach that which being taken away the universe would be dissipated, would become utter chaos, and so, having no unity, would cease to be a universe. What is that force? Plainly it is the law of gravitation. By this, particles of matter that would otherwise be chaotic, are aggregated, and its masses move in harmony. This is a universal force. It is conditional for the activity of every other, and is the lowest of all. The product of this would be mere unsorted matter aggregated and moving in systems, and would be the lowest conception we could form of a physical universe. It would be the first approximation towards a good, — the first step conditional for all others; for that which we find last in thus going back must have been first in the order of nature, if not of time.

Gravitation being thus given, what, in going down, is the last force we should have been obliged to drop before reaching this? What, in going up, would be the next step to fit matter for any use to which we can suppose it might be put? It would be to bring matter, chiefly of the same kind, into solid masses by what we call the attraction of cohesion. For this gravitation is plainly conditional, since matter must be aggregated before it can cohere. This gives us the next higher force.

The next force needed, for we will now pass up, is chemical affinity. By this, particles of matter having different properties are united, and form compounds. In the present state of our knowledge it cannot, perhaps, be proved that cohesion is always conditional for chemical affinity. If not, these two forces must be ranked with those groups to be spoken of hereafter. The compounds, however, formed by this force are conditional for the action of that power which we call life. The power of life assimilates nothing which has not previously entered into combination by this affinity.

Through the action of the three forces now mentioned we may have the conception of a world, inorganic, destitute of life, and having its unity solely from the fact that its forces are thus conditional and conditioned.

But the inorganic world is conditional for that which

is organic, and is under the control of that principle or force called life. And here, again, we have three great forces with their products. These are the vegetable, the animal, and the rational life.

Of these, vegetable life is the lowest. Its products are as strictly conditional for animal life as chemical affinity is for vegetable life, for the animal is nourished by nothing that has not been previously elaborated by the vegetable. "The profit of the earth is for all; the king himself is served by the field."

Again, we have the animal and sensitive life, capable of enjoyment and suffering, and having the instincts necessary to its preservation. This, as man is now constituted, is conditional for his rational life. The rational life has its roots in that, and manifests itself only through the organization which that builds up.

We have, then, finally, and highest of all, this rational and moral life, by which man is made in the image of God. In man, as thus constituted, we first find a being who is capable of choosing his own end; or, rather, of choosing or rejecting the end indicated by his whole nature. This is moral freedom, and in this is the precise point of transition from all that is below to that which is highest. For everything below man the end is necessitated. Whatever choice there may be in the agency of animals of means for the attainment of their end, — and they have one somewhat wide, — they have none in respect to the end itself. This, for our purpose, and for all purposes, is the characteristic distinction, so long sought, between man and the brute. Man determines his own end; the end of the brute is necessitated. Up to man everything is driven to its end by a force working from without, or from behind; but for him the pillar of cloud and of fire puts itself in front, and he follows it or not, as he chooses.

In the above cases it will be seen that the process is one of the addition of new forces, with a constant limitation of the field within which the forces act. The sphere of gravitation is wider than that of cohesion. Cohesion rests upon it as upon a base. The sphere of cohesion is wider than that of chemical affinity; that of chemical affinity wider than that of life; that of vegetable life wider than that of animal life; and that of animal life wider than that of rational life. Hence, the plan of the creation may be compared to a pyramid, growing narrower by successive platforms. It is to be noticed, however, that while the field of each added and superior force is narrowed, yet nothing is dropped. Each lower force shoots through, and combines itself with all that is higher. Because he is rational, man is not the less subject to gravitation, and cohesion, and chemical affinity. He has also the organic life that belongs to the plant, and the sensitive and instinctive life that belongs to the animal. In him none of these are dropped; but the rational life is united with and superinduced upon all these, so that man is not only a microcosm, but is the natural head and ruler of the world. He partakes of all that is below him, and becomes man by the addition of something higher.

If now we pass to the physical system of man, we shall find that it is composed of various systems and groups of systems which are conditional and conditioned in the same way.

Here again there are three divisions. In the lowest group we have those systems which are for building and repairing; in the next higher, those which are for support and locomotion; and in the third those which are for sensation and direction; and each lower group is conditional for the higher.

In the several groups, also, the same general order holds. Among the builders or repairers the nutritive or digestive system is the lowest. This is conditional for the circulatory, this for the respiratory, and this again for the secretory and assimilative. In the systems for support and locomotion, the osseous system is conditional for the muscular; and that system of nerves which is for sensation is conditional for that which is for motion and direction.

Whether these subordinate systems can all be placed in a right line is not important. It is now conceded that in the classification of animals and of plants there are groups within which no precise order can yet be traced. But in all cases, — and here is the principle contended for, — *if the end accomplished by any system or group be conditional for any other end beyond itself, it will be lower than that end.* Thus, building and repairing are lower than support and movement; and these are lower than sensation and direction.

Nor does this law stop here. It applies to the mind. In this, too, according to the latest and best classification, there are three groups, and each lower is conditional for the higher. There is first the intellect, including what are sometimes called the cognitive faculties, — all our faculties of knowing. These are conditional for the emotive or pathematic nature, including all the feelings and emotions consequent upon knowledge. These again are conditional for what Sir William Hamilton calls our conative powers, those of desire and of will.

In each of these we have a group, which we need not now examine; but we shall find running through each the same principle of order and arrangement already noticed.

We have thus a beautiful gradation from those "foundations of the earth" laid by God, and "the corner-stone thereof," up to the point at which "the morning stars sang together, and all the sons of God shouted for joy."

But in attaining and preserving the unity and order of the universe, God's methods are two. Besides this of addition, there is another applicable only to organic beings, that of development. In all organic beings there is something central and enveloped, and the being reaches his perfection by being developed.

In some respects this is the reverse of the other method. In that, in making our analysis, and seeing what we can spare, we reach that which is lowest; but in this, by the same process, we reach that which is highest. If we ask what the last thing is in the universe that can be spared, and unity remain, it is gravitation, the lowest force; but if we ask what the last thing in man is that can be spared and he remain a man, it will be that in him by which he is highest. In the method of additions that which is most fundamental, which is first in the order of our conceptions, is lower than that which is later, and serves it. But in the method of development that which is the most fundamental and first is the highest, and all else is lower as it is less or more essential to this. Here the lower are a condition for the development of the higher, but still are conceived of as coming in later. Here, therefore, when anything is spoken of as a condition, it is not to be regarded as a condition of being, but of development. In both methods the principle of arrangement already stated will hold; that is, if the end accomplished be a condition for any other end beyond itself, then it will be lower than that end, and all the means and apparatus for producing it will be lower than those for producing the higher end.

In the range of conditioned forces and systems above spoken of we find no good till we come to the gratification there is in the lowest sensitive being from the assimilation of food, and in the performance of those functions which are at once the condition for life, and by which life manifests itself. From that point the rank of the good rises precisely as the systems do through their whole gradation till we reach the highest of all.

We thus find the law of subordination both of forces and their products, and of susceptibilities and faculties, and of the good resulting from their activity. This we needed here because there is involved in it, or results immediately from it, what I shall venture to call *the law of limitation.* By this I mean the law which fixes the proper limit of every form of activity, and so of every kind of good except the highest; and so will enable us to live in the best sense of that much-abused expression, "according to nature."

This is a point of great importance in morals. According to an ancient theory, that of Aristotle, virtue and good consist in proportion, or the golden mean. It is readily seen that many things, that most things which men use and enjoy, are good up to a certain point, but that, carried beyond that point, they become, if not in themselves, yet relatively, evil. The pleasures of the senses and of the appetites are good, but may be readily carried to excess. Where is the limit? Amusement is good, the pursuit of money is good. Where is the limit? There is a wide range of questions which arise at this point in respect to the use of things lawful. How far may we go in dress? in expense? in conformity to fashion, and the usages of those around us? To determine these questions we need some plain criterion. Besides, there are those who think all pleasure and good alike except in intensity and duration. Paley thought so. The sensualist makes an irruption upon us and says that his joys are as high as any others, — that is, in his opinion, and that, on such a subject, the opinion of one man is as good as that of another. It is a mere question of taste and feeling, and there is no standard. We are also asked by another class, as by Whewell, "How are we to measure happiness, and thus to proceed to ascertain by what acts it may be increased? If we can do this, then indeed we may extract rules and results from the maxim that we are to increase our own and others' happiness; but without this step," which he plainly supposes cannot be taken, we "can draw no consequences from the maxim."* For such cases and inquiries we need a law of subordination and of limitation, a test and measure both of activity and of good.

If man would enjoy his whole good, it is obvious that his life must be a unity as the universe is, so that all the forces that conspire to make it up may act in harmony. This would give all possible good. But the method of attaining this is clearly set before us in the method pursued by God in making the universe one. As the forces in man, that is, his faculties, bear the same relation to each other that the forces in nature do, we shall find their proper limit by finding the limit which God fixes in proportioning the conditional and conditioned forces of nature. His method of doing this is to give to each lower force precisely the relative strength that shall make it most perfect as a condition for the activity of those above it, and which are conditioned by it. It is to carry that which is an end in one sphere no further than will fit it to become a means for the one next above. Gravitation

* Vol. I., B. III.

is a necessary means and condition of cohesion; these two of chemical affinity; these three of organic life, and so on; but no lower end is pursued one jot beyond the point where it may become the means of a higher end. Each force is limited at the point where it may best subserve the force above it. If gravitation were stronger than it is it would prevent the ascent of the sap altogether, or would cause a dwarfed vegetation. Man could not lift his foot, or only as he now pulls it from a clay-bed. The bird could fly but a short distance, and with weary wing. If its force were less, we should be liable to be blown away, the equilibrium of all bodies would be less stable, and the earth would be constantly sending off meteoric stones to astonish the inhabitants and puzzle the philosophers of other planets. As it is, gravitation will be found to have precisely that force which is best for the stable equilibrium of bodies, for the ascent of sap to its proper height, and in animals for agility and firmness combined. If chemical affinities were stronger than they are, the power of life would be unable to disengage the materials with which to build up the plant and the body; if they were weaker, that power could not prevent vegetable and animal decomposition and corruption even before death. Thus shall we find it throughout the whole range of forces in nature and in man. Hence the law of limitation will be, that every activity may be put forth, and so every good be enjoyed, up to the point where it is most perfectly conditional for a higher good. Anything beyond that will be excess and evil. It is a peculiarity of the works of nature as distinguished from those of men that her ends are also means, but she never pursues such an end beyond the point at which it would cease to be a means.

Here, then, is our model and law. Have we a lower

sensitive and animal nature? Let that nature be cherished and expanded by all its innocent and legitimate enjoyments, for it is an end. But, — and here we find the limit,—let it be cherished only as subservient to the higher intellectual life, for it is also a means. Let the intellectual nature have its full growth; let it scale every height, and sound every depth, for it is an end; but let it do this only in subservience to the higher emotive, moral and spiritual nature, for this, too, is a means. Thus let each of these, while it fulfils its own ends, so fulfil them as to minister to the sphere above, until we come to that which is not a means, but is of itself an end, and an absolute good. Men may enjoy pleasure, may use intoxicating drinks and narcotics to any extent they please, provided it shall interfere with no higher good. They may indulge in expense, amusements, fashion, as they will, if there is nothing higher and better that they can do. Certainly if there is nothing better they can do, they had better do that. The law applies universally so long as there is a good that is conditional for one above it, — so long as there is an end that is also a means. But when we reach the highest and supreme good, as that is conditional for nothing beyond itself, there can then be no excess. That is infinite; it is the ocean without a bottom or a shore.

Up to this point this system has fully met the wants of that part of our nature whose activities have a natural limit which cannot be passed without degradation and loss on the whole. At this point it meets those indefinite yearnings which testify to the connection of man with the Infinite, and are the presage of his immortality.

We may now readily see how far Aristotle was right. His system had a basis, and not a narrow one. Much of our good is the result of proportion and limitation, and of finding the golden mean. He was right so far as he went, but he needed the law of limitation, and he did not see the ocean.

It will be observed that none but a good man can adopt the model above proposed, for no bad act can be at once an end and a means. Lying, cheating, stealing, are means only, and can never become ends; but every good act is not only an end in itself, but is also a means of confirming him who does it in habits of goodness; and thus he who adopts this model will find provision in it that his path shall be as that of the just, "shining more and more unto the perfect day."

The law of limitation, above given, implies the natural law of self-denial.

This requires us to reject no good cynically because it is a good. It respects every part of the human constitution as made by God, and gives free play to every activity within its own limits. It says, with an apostle, that "every creature of God is good, and nothing is to be refused if it be received with thanksgiving." Any supposable strength in the appetites will only give force to the character, provided the governing powers keep them wholly under control. No matter how strong and spirited the horses if they are trained to perfect subjection. So with the desires. The desire of knowledge and of power and of esteem cannot be too great if they do not conflict with the affections and the moral nature. As they are stronger, they will but afford a richer soil in which these can strike their roots, and thus furnish the sap for a more abundant fruitage. And so it is with every lower form of activity. The stronger it is, the better for those above it, if it does not conflict with them. The stronger and more healthy the body, if a man be not at all animalized through it, the better for every mental faculty, and for every high and healthful form of affection and emotion. The law requires the restriction or denial of every appetite, desire, propensity, passion, at the point where it would interfere with something higher, and only at that point. This is the natural and original law. But if moral disorder has come in and become habitual, if great interests are at stake in circumstances of temptation and struggle, it may be wise, and even a duty, to ignore and reject many pleasures that might otherwise be indulged in, as the soldier who hastens to defend his country may not stop to enjoy fine scenery by the way.

This gives us the difference between the natural law of self-denial and the Christian law. The first would be the law for a man in health, simply requiring that nothing should be done to injure that. But Christianity is wholly a remedial system. "They that are whole need not a physician, but they that are sick;" and the law of self-denial as a remedy, or as a condition for the working of other remedies, may be as different from its natural law as the regimen of a sick man should be from that of one who is well. It has been from a consciousness of disorder that difficulties and obscurity have arisen at this point. There has been a feeling that self-denial, as well as self-torture, was compensatory; and then, when the lower powers had gone to excess, it is not strange that there should be a tendency to their undue repression, and even eradication. This has given rise to asceticism, and penances, and to a vast brood of superstitious observances. But precisely what the natural law is in its place, that the Christian law is in its place. Under Christianity self-denial is not a remedy, but the condition for the working of remedies, and its law is that it shall be carried just so far as is necessary for the best working of those great remedies which God has provided for the moral disorders of this world. This may often make self-denial very severe, but only as it is salutary. It may require the cutting off of a right hand, or the plucking out of a right eye, but only on the condition that they "offend," that is, cause you to stumble in your course towards heaven.

In what has been said hitherto, the dependence of the higher upon the lower forces and powers has been prominent. So long as these powers remain within the limits of unconsciousness, the right proportion is always preserved; but when they come under the direction of a finite, and especially of a perverted will, that proportion is not preserved. The danger is that the dependence of the higher upon the lower will be ignored, that the lower will in consequence be neglected and deteriorate, and then that the higher itself, the fountain of its sap being dried, will dwindle and wither. So is it always when a short-sighted selfishness would snatch too soon and grasp too much; so always when men would reach their ends by circumventing or evading those laws by which God has appointed that they should be gained.

The law — and this is especially true in organic life — is, that that which is highest can increase only through the ministration of the parts that are lower, and hence that the perfection of the highest in its sphere can be reached only as the lower are made perfect in their sphere. In training a child, would any one secure the highest, the best balanced, and the longest continued action of the mind, he can do it only by so attending to the body as to secure the priceless but subordinate blessings of health and a sound physical constitution. Would you have healthy feeling? Cultivate the intellect, else feeling will be fanatical. So has God constituted every organic being that "if one member suffer all the members suffer with it." Yea, and so that upon "those members of the body which we think to be less honorable we should bestow more abundant honor;" since the perfection of the more honorable members that are ministered unto can be attained only through the perfection of the less honorable that minister. Our end may be the perfection of the higher; our method must be to secure it through the perfection of the lower.

This method is one of wide application. It teaches us, while we aim at the highest, to care for the lowest; while we aim at the mind, to care for the body; while we aim at a perfect government, to care for the people and to seek to educate and elevate them; while we aim at perfect social organizations, to give woman her true place, not as inferior, but as different. No element of reaction upon progress can be swifter or more fatal than that of degraded mothers. It teaches us to care for children, and servants, and slaves, and criminals. Nature herself seems to cry out to us to do this. All history shows how men have disregarded this method and law, and it shows, too, how the law has avenged itself by bringing down the high and the low together. This is indeed the one great lesson of history. It needs to be pondered, more especially by republics, where the barriers of form and of force are so feeble; but whatever the form of government may be, the law is as pervading and resistless as that of gravitation, and the result is only a question of time. That result no form of heathen civilization has been able to prevent. It can be but one so long as successful men and successful classes seek with a blind selfishness to elevate themselves at the expense of others, — so long as men refuse to adopt the models of method which God has set before them, and thus to bind society together in an organic and a perfect whole.

LECTURE IV.

RELATION OF INTELLECTUAL AND MORAL PHILOSOPHY. — SPONTANEOUS AND VOLUNTARY ACTIVITY. — FACULTIES INSTRUMENTAL AND ULTIMATE. — INSTINCT. — THE APPETITES. — NATURAL — ARTIFICIAL. — THE DESIRES. — CLASSIFICATION OF THEM. — DESIRE OF CONTINUED EXISTENCE.

The nature and limitations of good having been already discussed, we now proceed to consider those powers from the activity of which good results.

This brings us to that point both of union and of cleavage between mental and moral science, at which, as we have seen, no little confusion has arisen. Theoretically the line between them is, or may be made, distinct; but practically the treatment of the one will include, in some measure, that of the other. What man ought to do will depend on what he is, and the circumstances in which he is placed. Mental science, or psychology, will, therefore, be conditional for moral science, which will make use of the first, and is the higher of the two. The province of psychology will then be to show what the faculties are; that of moral philosophy to show how they are to be used for the attainment of their end. Both have to do with the faculties of the mind, but in different aspects; as both the botanist and the agriculturist have to do with wheat, and the astronomer and navigator with the heavenly bodies. The botanist classifies wheat; the agriculturist raises it, and cares for a knowledge of its class only as it will enable him to do that. The astronomer investigates the nature of the heavenly bodies and their relations to each other; the navigator regards them solely as the means by which his course may be guided. And so the moral philosopher does not care for the nature and classification of the mental faculties except as a knowledge of these will guide him to their right use and proper end. So far, however, as this knowledge will thus guide him, as to a great extent it will, he is bound to have it.

The moral philosopher is, therefore, not excluded from the domain of the psychologist. It is *his* domain. It is the soil into which his science strikes its roots; it is indispensable for him that certain portions of it, at least, should be rightly cultivated; and if the psychologist does not do his work in those portions as he thinks it ought to be done, he has a right to revise it, and do it for himself. It is not to be allowed that the mere psychologist may lay down such doctrines as he pleases respecting the moral nature, and thus virtually determine the character of the science. It will, moreover, always be necessary to consider the faculty itself in determining its use, and to make our classifications with reference to the objects of moral science.

In accordance with this we shall, —

I. Distinguish the two great forms of mental activity. These are, — 1st. The *Spontaneous*. 2d. The *Voluntary*. And, —

II. We shall class the mental faculties as they are related to ends. And, —

1st. Of the mental *activities*, as they are either, 1st, spontaneous; or, 2d, voluntary.

As the inorganic world underlies and is conditional for the vegetable world; as the vegetable is conditional for the animal world; as the automatic or organic life of the body is conditional for its animal life, so is there an automatic and involuntary life of the mind that is conditional for its voluntary and responsible movements.

All life is inscrutable, and to our view automatic. How it begins it is impossible for us to conceive, since it manifests itself only through organization, while there is no organization that is not its product. In vegetables its results are seen in organizations entirely destitute of sensation and of will; and in the animals and in man, the conditions being complied with, it works with the same independence. The circulation of the blood in man, digestion, secretion, assimilation, have organs appropriated to them which the will does not reach, and they go on by laws as independent of the will as the circulation of the sap in vegetables. Through these organs and processes there are built up and presented to us the organs of sensation and of voluntary motion, but we cannot say what they shall be. We cannot cause this power of life to build up such a structure as we should like; we cannot add one cubit to our stature, or make one hair white or black.

But precisely as we find the heart beating, and accept the limbs already built up, so do we find the mind thinking, and the faculties acting, and accept them as they are given. Those cravings which we call appetite are upon man from no contrivance of his. He knows and can know them only as he finds them acting. He finds a succession of thoughts bubbling up, like water from a fountain, of which he knows not the source, and the flow of which he can no more stop than he can the flow of a river. No man ever thought at first by willing to think. Adam did not. He was created a thinking being, and thought as naturally and as necessarily as he breathed. Nor can any man stop thinking by willing it. He *must* think. He may control the current of his thoughts, but think he must; and if his thoughts had flowed on forever, as they do in dreams, without the intervention of a personal power, he would have been a thinking thing. Man, also, feels desires springing up. These he may or may not gratify, but there they are, a part of his nature. The natural affections, too, put forth their tendrils like the vine, and quite as independently of any will of man.

With these faculties the self-conscious, rational, personal being, with powers of supervision and comprehension, is endowed; into this nature is put, or rather we may say is so incorporated with it that it becomes a part of himself. This nature is an epitome of all that is below him, and he was put into it not only that he might govern himself, but govern it, as we saw in the last lecture, after the model of that government which God exercises over nature itself. This is the garden into which man is put that he may dress it and keep it.

Am I, then, distinctly understood at this point? Is it seen that there are activities going on within, not only our bodies, but our minds, with which our wills have as little to do as with the springing up of the grass? These faculties and activities are one thing, and *we* are another. We are responsible for the activities only as we can control them directly or indirectly.

In this original and spontaneous nature there are characteristics common to all men, and also diversities apparently as great as in natural scenery. Some natures are richer and grander than others; they tower up like the great mountains. Some are more easy of control, and some more difficult.

We now proceed, as was proposed, to the consideration

and classification of our various faculties and powers as they are related to ends.

In this aspect the faculties or powers may be divided into two great classes: —

I. Those which are instrumental for the attainment of ends beyond themselves. This is the first class. Here we find, —

1st. Those which indicate ends. These are the Instincts, the Appetites, the Desires, and the Natural Affections. And, —

2d. The Intellect, in the light of which we pursue ends. These are the Instrumental Powers, and do not necessarily imply a moral nature. They require to be governed.

II. The second great class of powers are those in whose activity we find ends beyond which there are no others. These are our Moral Nature. By them we elect and sanction ends. They govern, or, at least, ought to govern. These are the powers that belong to man as a person. They are Reason, Moral Affections, and Free-will.

The Instrumental Powers are neither good nor bad in themselves, but as they are used. Generically we share them with the animals, but they are much modified by being taken into connection with a higher nature.

Let us, then, first consider those powers which indicate ends.

In the conception of an end the primary element is not intellectual. If there were no original, no rational apprehension of good involving desirableness, congruity, automatic tendency, impulse, appetency or craving, revealing some want to be satisfied, or capacity of enjoyment to be met, we could have no conception of an end. In our analysis in this direction this is the last thing that we reach, and so is conditional for all the rest. The intellect is implied. There must be consciousness. Every mental operation, whether perceptive or impulsive, must take place in the light of that. But consciousness being given, the impulse towards an end or the apprehension of it as having in it a good, is the primary element in our conception of an active, as distinguished from a contemplative being. Without such impulse or apprehension, the objects we now seek might be known as they are in themselves, but not as ends for us. There would be no motive for the voluntary exertion of the intellect even. As a part of our nature, these impulses are generically the same in all men, but reveal themselves in different proportions, and in them we find what have been called the active powers of man. By this it is not meant that the contemplative powers are not active, but that they do not, and these do, lead to action.

The powers which indicate ends are commonly, and, as it seems to me, correctly divided into the Instincts, the Appetites, the Desires, and the Affections. Of these there is no question respecting any except instinct, the existence of which in man has sometimes been doubted.

Instinct, which we shall first consider, is defined by Paley to be "a propensity prior to experience, and independent of instruction." It leads animals obviously destitute of either understanding or reason to perform the same acts as if possessed of those powers in the highest degree. In building her cells the bee proceeds on the principles of mechanics and of the abstruser mathematics. In incubation the hen seems to have a knowledge of the doctrine of different specific gravities, and turns her eggs over regularly because the yolk is slightly heavier than the white. Animals with migratory, and those with acquisitive instincts, proceed on an apparent knowledge of the movements of the heavenly bodies for months in the future.

In all animals of the same species instinct is mostly uniform, and, as we descend in the scale of creation, becomes, in the inverse ratio of understanding and reason, more uniform, more blind, and more perfect. A pure and unperverted instinct may always be trusted implicitly. A marvellous and a beautiful thing it is to see "the stork in the heaven knowing her appointed times; and the turtle, and the crane, and the swallow, observe the time of their coming." Surely, here "He leadeth the blind in a way that they know not." Here extremes meet — the perfection of reason and the perfection of ignorance.

But as the light of understanding and reason increases, the glimmerings of instinct seem lost. Accordingly, most writers on morals have not noticed this as one of the active powers, or, if they have, have spoken of it as confined almost wholly to animals. But if instinct is needed by rational creatures we shall be sure to find it, for God does not care less for them than for the ant and the bee. It would be in accordance with all we have hitherto seen of the order of the universe, and of the mode in which its unity is secured, if we should find this, like gravitation, passing up and blending itself with the activity of the very highest power of its own order. Or, if any should suppose that this, the lowest form of intelligent action, cannot blend with those intuitions of reason which it so much resembles, it is yet pleasing to see in its certain guidance the best analogon and symbol of perfect reason, just as gravitation, which is the lowest motive power, is the best symbol of love, which is the highest of all.

I suppose, however, that something of instinct does blend with the activity of our highest powers. For this, it is not necessary that we should be under the guidance of any specific instinct, for wherever there is a tendency in our nature that is automatic, there we find the instinctive element. Hence we may, and do, speak of rational instincts. In every created nature, however high, there must be tendencies and yearnings by which the true end of the being shall be revealed to itself, and in which the first movements towards that end shall originate. That a good of any kind should begin to be sought in any other way, is not conceivable. And so the Scriptures represent it. They speak of thirsting for God; and the Saviour said, "If any man thirst, let him come to me and drink."

Our associations with instinct may be low; but it is really a high and sacred thing. In it we see the Highest stooping to the lowest, and illustrating that care and guidance of which they may feel secure who follow the promptings of any nature that is unperverted, and as it came from his hand.

We now proceed to the Appetites. These are those cravings of the animal nature which have for their object the well-being of the body and the continuance of the race.

These are to be distinguished from a desire for those pleasures of the palate, for example, with which they become so intimately associated that they are seldom thought of separately. The craving is purely instinctive, and, as such, has in a healthy state the infallibility of instinct, both in indicating and measuring the wants of the system; but the pleasure of eating and drinking will be according to the quality and condiments of the material taken. This pleasure may be perpetuated far beyond the point at which the craving is satisfied; and the modes of causing it may be reduced to a system and a science. The science of cookery will be useful as it fits substances to satisfy the craving, and so for assimilation; it will be injurious as it merely stimulates the palate. If the substance stimulate the palate slightly, or not at all, as water, the craving is simply satisfied, and there is no danger of excess; but the more stimulating the substance, either to the specific sense connected with the appetite, or to the nervous system generally, the more danger there is of excess from confounding the excitement of the sense, or the nerves, with the demand of the system.

According to Stewart, the appetites are distinguished by three circumstances. 1st. They take their rise from the body. 2d. They are periodical. 3d. They originally imply an uneasy sensation, afterwards, upon experience, a desire for their appropriate objects.

The appetites are usually said to be three, — hunger, thirst, and the appetite of sex. But there are tendencies and cravings that may more properly be classed with the appetites than elsewhere. These are the craving for air, for exercise, for rest, and for sleep. These all take their rise from the body, are periodical, and originally imply an uneasy sensation; afterwards, upon experience, a desire of their appropriate objects. They also require to be regulated on precisely the same principles as those commonly ranked as appetites; and it may be well to place them here, as bringing them nearer the conscience, since all concede that the regulation of the appetites is a duty.

The necessity of the appetites for the accomplishment of their immediate ends is well stated by Reid. "Though a man knew," says he, "that his life must be supported by eating, reason could not direct him when to eat, or what, how much, or how often. In all these things appetite is a much better guide than reason. Were reason only to direct us in this matter, its calm voice would often be drowned in the hurry of business or the charms of amusement. But the voice of appetite rises gradually, and at last becomes loud enough to call off our attention from any other employment."

As they are means of sustaining the body and continuing the race, *the appetites are the condition for all that is above them.* But besides the direct objects thus immediately secured, they are also closely related to industry and the social affections. The craving, which is the radical and constant element in the appetite, is related to industry, and the pleasure, the incidental and variable element, is related to the social affections.

When we observe how busy a scene this world is, and what human labor has accomplished,—the forests it has cleared, the fields it has cultivated, the cities it has built, the ships it has constructed, the oceans it has navigated,—we are little apt to think how much of all this is owing to so simple a cause as the appetite of hunger. "All the labor of man," says Solomon, "is for the mouth, yet the appetite is not satisfied." Food is our first, and is a constantly recurring want; and probably the amount of labor for obtaining and preparing it is greater than for all other purposes. When the savage has plenty of food he does little but eat and sleep, and only the stimulus of hunger can goad him on to the labors of the chase. In civilized communities, those who turn the soil, and hew the wood, and lay the brick and mortar, are generally those who labor for their bread; nor is it probable that a less imperious motive would induce the effort. Nor is it bodily activity alone that is excited by this stimulus. Hunger, rather than any of the nine, has been the muse of some of the best poets.

This connection of the appetites with industry, which is so indispensable to force of character and to all good habits, shows that they were intended by God to be ministers of human virtue, and not the occasions of vice.

But the appetites are also connected with the affections. So naturally do our kind feelings rest upon those who share the same table with us that "to eat bread" with one, that is, to receive or furnish hospitality, has been regarded in many countries as a pledge of kindness and good faith. "He," says the Scripture, as if it aggravated the treachery, —"he that did eat bread with me hath lifted up his heel against me." It was from the connection of the appetites with the social feelings that the drinking customs of society derived much of their power and also of their danger. It was the *social* glass that led young men of generous affections to occasional excess, and the appetite was then cherished and justified on the ground of indulging the social nature, till the capacity for social enjoyment was diminished, and the man sunk into degrading habits of selfish, solitary, animal gratification.

It is from this natural and intended connection of the affections and virtues with the appetites that we are not degraded by them. We share them, indeed, in common with the brutes; but they so underlie our higher nature and may so blend with it as to become the occasions of some of its most beautiful manifestations, and when confined within the bounds of reason and religion are the occasion only of good. The man who eats that he may live and improve his higher faculties, and do good, is a *man*. But the man who lives that he may eat is a brute.

A course of indulgence of the appetites has been called a life of pleasure. But retribution reaches to the body, and there could be no greater misnomer. Every excess is sure to be punished. Besides the penalties of immediate reaction and specific disease, by the law of habit already noticed, the capacity for enjoyment becomes gradually less, and no object is more pitiable than a man who is beginning to taste the dregs of such a life.

At no point do the dictates of virtue and of an enlightened self-love more clearly coincide than in the regulation of the appetites. The proper notion of temperance with reference to them is not an abstinence from any particular thing, but such a control of all the appetites as will result in the greatest power and activity both of body and of mind, and as shall subject them most fully to our control. Anything short of this is criminal, and infallibly pernicious; and any use or enjoyment of the appetites compatible with this may be allowed.

From the above account it is most plain that the law of the appetites is to be found in their end. That end we have the capacity to see. We can also see the fitness of the appetites for its accomplishment, so that when we yield ourselves to the guidance of an unperverted appetite we are still governed by reason. It is reason committing the accomplishment of an end to a trustworthy servant, that can do it better than she. Let that end — the end indicated by the constitution of the appetites in their relative positions — be accomplished, — no more, no less,— and both reason and conscience are satisfied.

But besides the natural appetites, there are those termed artificial, or, more properly, unnatural, as that for intoxicating drinks, for tobacco, and for opium. In all these the principle is the same. An unnatural stimulus is given to the nerves, followed by a corresponding depression, and an uneasiness which causes a desire of repetition, and which often becomes a craving so importunate as to overmaster and control every other principle of action.

Between these artificial appetites and those that are natural there are four important differences.

The first is, that in the natural appetite the craving is an original part of the constitution, created by God with reference to an end intended by him. In the artificial appetite, the craving is wholly superinduced by man, and with reference to an end which God no more intended than he did murder.

The second difference is, that the objects of the artificial appetites are all violent poisons. They are incapable of assimilation with the system. Except as medicines they can contribute nothing to its health or well-being, and taken in any considerable quantity they cause death.

The third difference is, that the pleasure connected with the artificial appetites is purely and utterly selfish. It has no relation to the ulterior good of the man himself, or any other being. On the contrary, it lowers the tone of the system and the capacity for good; whereas the pleasure connected with the natural appetites has relation to the vigor which wields the axe and guides the plough, and even to the highest intellectual exertion.

The fourth difference is, that the artificial appetites have a tendency to increase. As the stimulus is continued, the quantity necessary to produce the desired effect becomes greater. It is this insidious tendency, this "facilis descensus averni," that has brought many gifted men to the verge of destruction before they were aware of it, and has prevented their return. The natural appetites have no such tendency.

Let no one, therefore, suppose that God has not given as many appetites as are for his best good, or that he shall be a gainer on the whole by attempting to reap where nature did not sow.

The wretchedness there is in the world from the abuse of the natural appetites, and from the expense and tyranny of the artificial ones, is so great that the purpose of God with reference to this part of the constitution is worthy of careful study.

We now pass to the Desires.

Of these the appetites are not only the condition, but they foreshadow and symbolize them. The desires are to the mind what the appetites are to the body.

Their negative characteristics are that they do not take their rise from the body; that they are not periodical, and that they do not cease after attaining a particular object. Positively, they are cravings which have for their object the well-being of the mind, as the appetites have for theirs the well-being of the body. They act in the first place impulsively and specifically with reference to particular objects; subsequently they are adopted by the reason, and through the operation of that and the generalizing faculty, their objects come to be designated by general terms, as knowledge and power.

What the original desires are, and how many, philosophers have not been agreed. This we may ascertain as we may what the appetites are. The ultimate appeal must be to consciousness; but if we can determine beforehand or by observation what is requisite for the well-being of the body, we can tell what the appetites will be. So with the desires. If we can ascertain what is needed for the well-being of the mind, we may know what they are. Towards those things we may be sure there will be instinctive tendencies or impulses which reason is to accept, direct, and limit, but which will not wait for the discovery by her of their necessities before they act.

The desires, like the appetites, imply appropriation, a gathering in, a use and assimilation of materials by ourselves. They are related to the affections, and are for the affections which are above them, and which imply bestowment, and giving out. As the appropriations by the appetites were not intended to be selfish or for their own sake, but for the giving forth of every form of physical and mental activity, so the appropriations by the desires were intended to furnish the material and groundwork for the activity of the affections and the will.

What, then, would be needed for the perfection of the mind itself, and that man might act most effectively through his affections for the good of others? He would need, —

1st. His own continued and secure existence. He would need property, that is, the possession of those things by which life may be sustained. He would need it both as a provision for himself, and as a condition of generosity to others. He would then need knowledge for his guidance; he would need power to reach the ends suggested by a regard for his own good and the suggestions of the affections for others; and he would need the good-will and esteem of others that he might coöperate with them, and they with him, and stand in such a relation to them as to be able to do them good. These he would need; they would be indispensable to his completeness in himself, and in his relations to others; and for each of these he has a natural and original desire.

The desires, then, which we shall consider, are, —

1. The Desire of Continued Existence.
2. Of Knowledge.
3. Of Property.
4. Of Power.
5. Of Affection, Good-will, Esteem.

Besides these, it has been said of late, and almost universally, that we have the desire of happiness, and the desire of society.

That the desire of happiness cannot be placed on the same footing with the other desires, is plain,—

1st. Because happiness is the result of the normal activity of each of the faculties. We know it only as such. But a desire, whose office it should be to receive the product of all the other faculties, would differ much from a simple desire that produces happiness. In other cases the desire is for a specific thing, and when that is met happiness is the result; but if we suppose an original desire of happiness, there can be no happiness back of the happiness desired, to be its result, and so its whole constitution must be different from that of the other desires.

2d. It does not seem either simple or philosophical to make a desire for knowledge, and a desire for the happiness resulting from that, each an original and simple desire. It would be more plausible to suppose, as some do, that the desire for happiness is the only original desire, and that the desire of knowledge, like that for books, is wholly secondary. But this will not do, because, if we had had no original desire for knowledge, we could never have begun to seek it, and should have found no happiness in its pursuit.

3d. In all other cases the desire goes directly to its own object. It finds that, and happiness is the result. But no man ever sought, or can seek, directly for happiness; he must have something else as his direct object, and find that indirectly.

4th. As each desire impels directly to its own end, and knows of nothing else, it may, in a measure, be its own guide; but, as happiness may result from different and often incompatible desires and faculties, there is far more need of a higher power than any blind impulsion to guide in its pursuit.

What, then, is the relation of this to the other desires? To me it seems to be the same as that of consciousness to the several specific faculties of cognition. Consciousness is not a separate faculty, but accompanies and pervades all the acts of each faculty. In the same way the desire of happiness is not a separate and specific desire, but accompanies and pervades each act of such desire. As good is the immediate product of the activity of our faculties, it must be given in the original act of consciousness. Every such act involves the conception, first, of being; second, of activity, since consciousness is activity; and, third, if the act be normal, of good as the result. But good thus known must be desired, otherwise it could not be conceived of as good. In this way it is that a desire of good enters into every specific form of desire, and that, as consciousness is the generic form of cognition, so the desire of good or of happiness is the generic form of all the desires.

For the existence of a specific desire of society the authority is high. That society is the natural sphere of man there can be no doubt, and it is surprising that the hypothesis of Hobbes, that the state of nature is a state of warfare, should have been deemed worthy of a labored refutation. "Man," it has been well said, "is born in society, and there he remains." The state of nature is a state of society.

But, while it cannot be doubted that man was formed for society, I yet esteem it rather a condition of his being than the object of a specific desire. He has desires and affections the exercise of which implies society, and it is, as it seems to me, the direct exercise of these, and not society itself apart from this exercise, that he desires. Take from him the desire of esteem, of power, of loving and being beloved, all those specific desires, and affections, and sympathies, which are mentioned by the philosophers separately, and which imply society for their exercise, and the residuum that would be left of a desire of society, as such, would be little or nothing. Observing a certain effect, the combined effect of all our faculties, they seem to have contrived a new faculty to account for it, extracting and compounding it from all the others. Certain it is that our delight in society arises chiefly from the exercise of other desires and affections which there find their sphere, and if any shall choose to say that there is, besides the effect resulting from the combined influence of these, an instinct or desire for society, I am content.

Though happiness and society are not inaugurated and guarded by a particular desire, yet the design of God in regard to them is even more clearly and strongly indicated than if they were. To me these seem to be, the one like warmth, and the other like the atmosphere, pervasive and enfolding conditions of our activity, and hence more intimately associated with it, and more fully cared for than any single principle of action. They are like the axioms in mathematics that are essential at every step in the reasonings, as compared with the definitions and hypotheses on which particular demonstrations depend.

I shall close this lecture with some remarks on the first of the desires mentioned, — that of Continued Existence.

This is often mentioned as the strongest of the desires. We say, "as dear as life itself." Yet it yields to that of reputation, and revenge, and sometimes gives way before mere weariness and ennui. Nor is the fact that there are so few suicides certain evidence of the power of this desire, since men often fear death greatly who desire life feebly, or not at all.

It is the object of this desire to guard life in sudden

emergencies, and to ensure for it our deliberate and rational care; and our present business is to inquire how far we should be governed by it.

This involves the question respecting a true courage, since a man is to brave danger and to die when required by that, and only then. Under no circumstances is a man to be a coward.

It is the grandest characteristic of man that he can deliberately look death in the face, and accept it rather than the alternative of spiritual degradation. On the earth there has been no nobler spectacle than that of those to whom this alternative has been presented, and who have chosen to die, to die in torture and in the midst of reproach. Required to renounce their integrity, or do violence to their affections, they have chosen to become martyrs. To die thus implies the conviction of an inner life far higher and dearer than that of the body, which no weapon can reach, and no flame scorch; of a liberty which no manacles can restrain; and of a will which all the might of nature cannot subdue; and the moment in which malice lifts its cry of seeming triumph over the destruction of the body of one dying thus, is the moment of the greatest possible triumph of fortitude and principle, and of liberty in its highest form. That man is capable of such persecution, is the greatest disgrace of our nature; that he is capable of enduring and triumphing over it, is its greatest honor. One such death, transcendent and perfect, the world has witnessed; it can never witness another. If *we* are called on to lay down our lives thus, we are to do it as best we may. To do this is true courage; not to do it is cowardice. In doing this we become martyrs; and no man has a right to do it, except as a martyr to truth, to righteousness, to liberty, or to humanity.

In imitation of this, but in striking contrast with it, is that common-place exposure to danger and death which comes from recklessness, and vanity, and a regard to the opinion of others. There can be no nobleness in blindfolding the eyes, or in suffocating the natural emotions. Rightly viewed, it is an awful thing to die. It becomes us to acknowledge this; but if required to testify to any great truth, or to sustain any great principle, it becomes us to have such a conscience, and such a trust in God, that we may die without fear, or even with welcome. This is true courage, and anything else in the guise of this is either stupidity, or cowardice and hypocrisy.

But the obligation to meet death with firmness, when called to it by truth or by duty, does not rest solely upon our individual interests and character; the interests of mankind are involved. Abstract truths and general principles often lie dormant till they are awakened into life by some powerful attestation. The attestation which the death of a wise and good man gives to the value of the principles for which he dies, has a voice that is startling to humanity, and will arouse it if anything can. If the existing generation do not hear it, as through interest or prejudice they may not, it will not be lost; it will be heard in after times. It is for this reason that the blood of the martyrs has been the seed of the church, and that the names of Hampden and Sidney have been the watchwords of liberty wherever the English tongue has been known. When such men die, death, in whatever form, does not come to them as to common men, whispering of terror or of hope for them alone, but —

"In its hollow tones are heard
The thanks of millions yet to be."

However strong, therefore, the desire of life may be, it

must yield when this is required by higher principles of action, by the affections, and the conscience. Mankind justify and applaud him who dies for his kindred, his country, his race, or to sustain his integrity. They disregard and despise him who dies, or exposes himself to death, from a desire of applause, or from the fear of a corrupt public opinion.

It only remains to notice the modes in which the intentions of God, as indicated by this part of our constitution, are plainly set at nought. These are chiefly four.

The first is, by any vicious indulgence which shortens life. The guilt and waste of life from this cause cannot be measured.

The second is from war. We need not inquire here whether men may expose their lives in war according to the principles already stated. That they may not on lower principles, is certain; and in the light of this truth, how dreadfully have the purposes of God in regard to human life been disregarded in war! So has it been in all wars of ambition, of passion, and of mere interest. The fact that mercenaries have been so readily found, who would espouse any cause, expose themselves to any danger, and do any amount of slaughter for the poor pittance of a soldier's pay, is among the saddest indications of the moral state of the race.

A third mode in which the purpose of God, as indicated by this desire, is set aside, is by suicide.

As this is a crime which cannot be punished, little can be done to prevent it except to point out and remove its causes. These are, — 1st. Insanity. With this we have nothing to do. 2d. The commission of crime and apprehended exposure and disgrace. 3d. Disappointment in the attainment of any object which has been regarded as the

chief good. 4th. Infidelity when carried to the denial of a hereafter or of human accountability. Not that infidelity has a direct tendency to induce suicide, but that, when men are tempted to it, it removes all obstacles. A thoroughgoing and unflinching infidel would feel himself at perfect liberty to choose nonentity rather than life if he should prefer it. Hence the levity with which this crime is spoken of by infidels, as Hume, who said that it was but the turning a little blood out of one channel into another. It is only by the removal of the causes now mentioned that we may expect that the frequency of this crime will be diminished.

A fourth mode in which life is wantonly shortened is by duelling.

In this we have a striking instance of the power of custom after the opinion in which the particular custom originated is entirely changed. Originally regarded as a species of judicial trial in which there was an appeal to God, a refusal to fight came in time to be considered a confession not simply of cowardice, but of cowardice on account of guilt. Then it was that the tyranny of custom and of public opinion commenced; and now, though the idea of an appeal to God, or of any adjudication according to merit, is utterly exploded, though the laws are against it, and it is known to be morally wrong, though the force of public opinion is in some regions entirely removed, and everywhere very much lightened, yet the custom still retains its hold, and the law of God is made void by the "traditions" of men in high places. This, too, is done when all the circumstances which once gave the combat eclat and dignity are entirely reversed. It was once sanctioned by law, and witnessed by multitudes who applauded the knightly bearing of the combatants. Now, those who fight shrink away to some place where the law may be evaded, the combat is witnessed only by the seconds and the surgeon, and there is no display of manly vigor, or of any other skill than that of a highwayman. The parties simply take pistols and shoot at each other. It was once an evidence of courage, and compatible with a sense of duty; now, whatever may be said of mere animal courage, it shows a pitiable want of moral courage, and is opposed to all the dictates of morality, of humanity, and of religion. Though founded in mistaken notions, it yet had, at its commencement, something noble about it, but like the Scylla of Virgil, whose head was human, it tapers off, as it comes down to us, into hideous and unmitigated deformity. In its present position, it is difficult to say whether this custom is more wicked or ridiculous.

LECTURE V.

DESIRE OF PROPERTY. — AVARICE. — DESIRE OF KNOWLEDGE. — DESIRE OF POWER. — INFLUENCE. — EMULATION. — DESIRE OF ESTEEM. — DESIRE OF GLORY.

After the desire of life, which we have already considered, that of property was mentioned.

As life is the condition of all the desires, so also is the possession of that which is necessary to sustain life. In common with the others, this desire has its root in the tendency of all life to appropriate to itself whatever is necessary to its own perfection and manifestation. So it is with the appetites as they are related to the perfection and power of the body. There is a point where they are identical, and whence they branch off in search of different objects necessary for such perfection and power, and so become different specific appetites. So, also, it is with the desires. There is a point where they, too, seem identical in their relation to the perfection and manifestation of mind, and whence they branch off in the directions mentioned as constituting the several specific desires. If, therefore, the ownership of something, possession, property, be essential to such perfection and manifestation, then this general tendency will be in that direction, and will become a specific desire.

But ownership, or property, is thus necessary. It is through this that we have security for ourselves, and a chief means of manifesting our individuality to others.

What is not our own we have no right to use. We have a right to use the fruit that grows wild only because, when we pluck it, it becomes ours. And, as this sense of property is the condition of our using anything for ourselves, so is it for our giving anything to others.

We may, it is true, conceive of a state in which the whole enjoyment of man, and perhaps an adequate one, should arise from what could not, or need not be appropriated, as the air and the sunlight; but, in his present state, if he had no material thing which he could use as his own, and none which he could give to others, he not only could have no security, but would lack scope for the activity of some of those essential faculties by which he is made in the image of God. If God had no ownership, he would not be God, and if man had none, involving dominion, he would not be in his image.

That the desire of property in the sense and to the extent above indicated is a natural desire, we can scarcely doubt, if, in addition to the considerations just adduced, we notice how early and distinctly it is manifested by children; how it stimulates industry; and how essential property is to the very existence of society. Doubtless, the natural desires often interpenetrate, support, and modify each other, but there seems to be no more reason for referring this desire, as some have done, to that of power, than for referring the desire of knowledge in the same way, since knowledge has often been said to *be* power. Holding such relations as property does, we might expect that God would indicate his will by giving a specific desire, and that he would make that desire, as he has all the others, the basis of a right. If God has given us a desire for property, then, within limits to be fixed by other considerations, we have a right to property, and when we look at the extent and validity of the right of property, we can hardly suppose it to be founded on anything but a natural desire.

This desire, then, being, in the true and original sense of that word, natural, cannot be wrong. Nor is it too strong in itself, for there is not too much honest industry or self-denying frugality. The doctrine holds here, that has already been stated in regard to those principles of action which relate to the material interests of the individual and of society, that the stronger they are, provided they be kept properly subordinated, the richer and better substratum of individual character and of society do they form. Those who have done the most for our public institutions, and done it most nobly, have been men with a strong desire of property, who knew the worth of what they gave; generally men who had accumulated it by their own industry, but who gave, nevertheless, cheerfully and gladly, in view of great interests to be promoted, and of the subordinate place which this desire holds as the purveyor of God, and the appointed servant of principles higher than itself. If an alabaster-box of precious ointment is to be opened, the perfume of which is to fill society, the box must first be filled. Only as we recognize the legitimacy of this principle can giving have its true merit and dignity, or indeed any merit or dignity at all. As men now are, it is far better that they should be employed in accumulating property honestly, to be spent reasonably, if not nobly, than that there should be encouraged any sentimentalism about the worthlessness of property, or any tendency to a merely contemplative and quietistic life, which has so often been either the result or the cause of inefficiency and idleness.

But while the legitimacy of this desire is not to be questioned, it is not to be forgotten that it is specially liable to excess and perversion.

The appetites have a material limit, but, like all the desires, this has none, and, unchecked, it grows, and becomes insatiate by its own activity. It is like an elastic receiver which could not be stretched beyond its capacity, but which would grasp the more tightly its contents the fuller it should be made. To the strength of natural desire there is added the power of habit; and then, in our state of society especially, there is everything to foster it. With no law of entail, with a form of government that stimulates every faculty, with unprecedented openings for enterprise from the newness of the country, with no order of nobility, and, with the exception of high talent and transient office, with nothing but wealth to give position and distinction, it is not strange that it should be sought with peculiar eagerness and unscrupulousness. More than any other it is the national passion, and, what with dishonest and injurious modes in the getting, and folly and luxury in the using, there is danger through it of national ruin. It is not merely on the protection of the right of property, essential as that is, that the material prosperity of a nation depends, but also on the prevalent modes of getting and using it. Gambling, lotteries, theft, fraud, are modes of gaining wealth, but are mere depredations on society; pandering to hurtful and vicious appetites is still worse, and when these are prevalent, implying as they do modes of spending money corresponding with the modes of getting, there can be no prosperity.

The perversions of this desire appear in covetousness and avarice. These have in fact the same elements; but covetousness, even to unscrupulousness, in getting property, is not incompatible with profusion in spending it;

while avarice refers more particularly to the grasp with which it is held. This grasp may be so strong as not only not to be relaxed at the call of public spirit and natural affection, but even for the supply of the most pressing personal wants.

It is here that we find, and are called upon to account for, that strange phenomenon in our nature, — a miser. A miser is one in whom this desire is so strong as to defeat all the ends for which it was given, one who suffers the very wretchedness which the desire was given to prevent, through an excess of the desire given to prevent it.

As it is money that is especially sought by the miser, it has been usual to say that as that is the representative of value, and stands for everything which it can command, we transfer, through the association of ideas, the regard we have for those things to that which represents and can command them, and so come to attach a high intrinsic value to that which has little value in itself, and none at all so long as it is hoarded. That something of this occurs almost universally, cannot be doubted, and if we combine it with unusual outward temptations, or with peculiar constitutional tendencies, or both, it may be sufficient to account for many cases of miserliness. Doubtless there are those to whom this is naturally a besetting sin. But there are cases for which it does not account; especially those in which persons who have been prodigals in youth have subsequently become misers. This has often been the case. It was so with the noted miser mentioned by Foster in his Essay on Decision of Character. But of all men we should suppose a prodigal would be the last to associate money with value. Brown, therefore, founds avarice, not so much on feelings of pleasure at seeing constant additions to a heap that is never to be used, as on the permanence of money compared with the transient pleasures of the prodigal, and on feelings of regret at having spent that which can never return. If a man purchase a house, though his money be gone, yet the house remains, and being constantly useful to him, he looks back upon the parting with his money without regret. But if he had expended the same sum for a palace of ice, though he might be pleased for a time with its glitter, yet, when it had melted away, he could not fail to reflect how much that was valuable he might purchase with his money if he then had it, and look back upon his parting with it with regret.

Let, then, a young man spend his money foolishly till he becomes embarrassed, or perhaps in utter want; let him be stung at the same time by what is, or what he conceives to be ingratitude, and every instance of such expenditure will haunt him, and a permanent and deep feeling of regret will be the consequence. If he again acquire money, he will regard it not so much as the representative of any particular value, as a guard against the perplexity and trouble into which he had previously fallen. As he formerly reflected afterwards how many things he might have purchased, so now his money seems to him, not the representative of the value of that particular thing which he may wish to purchase, but of all those things collectively which might be obtained by it. As it was from parting with his money that his regret formerly arose, so now, when he would part with any, whether the sum be great or small, and quite as much if small if it was by small sums that he lost his money, the same feeling presents itself and debars him, till at length penurious and miserly habits are formed.

This theory I deem correct, and bring it forward for the practical moral consequence which it involves. It is often thought an indication of spirit in young men to have a certain profusion and recklessness in their way of spending money. They think it essential to their position to spend upon trifles of fashion, and the demands of what is called good-fellowship, but what is too often fellowship in folly and vice, sums which neither they nor their friends can well afford. If, then, instead of being considered a mark of spirit, this profusion were regarded by the young man and his friends, as it truly is, as a mark of want of judgment and of genuine independence, and if in the prodigality of to-day they could behold the parsimony of future years, much evil would be averted.

In our cities and public institutions there are many young men who depend on a hard-working father, or a poor and widowed mother, or on self-denying sisters, who are liable to be drawn into associations with those whose means of expense are above their own, to incur obligations of what they call honor, and to engulf, if not in vice, yet in what is purely conventional and useless, the scanty earnings of their home. It is pitiable to see those who do thus, greedy of money whenever they can get it, evading small bills, and those of poor people; disappointing, alienating, perhaps ruining those who love them; losing their own self-respect, and incurring the contempt of those who care little or nothing for them. From such the public has nothing to hope. But from one who will deny himself, and rely for his position upon industry, integrity, and transparency of character, and who can respect himself in honest poverty, and look down upon meanness anywhere, if *he* shall succeed, the public may expect much. He will have an open hand for somebody.

In general, if we have been accustomed from our youth to spend money so that we have not regretted its loss, if we have given it for the necessaries and the conveniences of life, and especially for the gratification of the benevolent affections, we may expect to continue to part with money, — that is, if we have it, — if not nobly, yet usefully, and without regret. But if we have spent our money aimlessly, or with that mixture of meanness and profusion which those often exhibit who spend money only for selfish pleasures, we must beware lest the reckless expenditure of twenty become the avarice of sixty; lest the young man, flattered and praised by sycophants for his generosity, become in age a niggard and contemptible miser.

From the desire of property we pass to that of knowledge.

By the first we appropriate to ourselves whatever may be useful to us that is material; by the second, so far as that is possible, whatever may be useful that pertains to the spiritual world.

That this is a natural desire need not be proved, because it is not disputed. This was known to Solomon. "Through desire," says he, "a man having separated himself, seeketh and intermeddleth with all wisdom." Like him we give our hearts "to seek and search out by wisdom concerning all things that are done under heaven." It may be "a sore travail," but "this," in giving this desire, "hath God given to the sons of men to be exercised therewith." The desire has for its object the only element in which man can walk without stumbling. It is as the light by which we see, and so is indispensable to the intelligent exercise of any of the faculties.

It is not to be supposed, however, that all knowledge is gained under the stimulus of this desire. The desire is found existing in the light of consciousness and of the primitive ideas and truths of reason. These, which have been said to be —

"The light of all our seeing,"

are essentially the same in all. They are involved in the exercise of all our faculties, while this desire of knowledge, or the principle of curiosity as it has been called, may exist in different degrees, and with reference to different objects.

So far as the desire of knowledge is impulsive and involuntary it has no moral character. In this respect it is on the same footing with all the impulsive powers. They respect objects which are indifferent in themselves, that may be used for either good or evil, and moral character is manifested as we reject or adopt and control these impulsions. An angel and a fiend may have equal knowledge. Their character is shown by its use.

Of this desire the direct and proper stimulus is knowledge itself, and for itself. To the mind that can feel it there is in knowledge a power to charm as there is in music. It is a high attribute of man through which he can find in the works of God, and in the relations which he has established, an excellence so attractive as to be in itself a sufficient motive to their contemplation and study. In this is the root of the true enthusiasm for science. It is among those who have this that we find the mathematicians, who, like Archimedes, can spend days and nights in the contemplation of abstract theorems; the sages, who, like Socrates, can remain absorbed in thought four-and-twenty hours without changing their position; and without much of this no man can be expected to distinguish himself greatly in the walks of science.

But besides this primary motive, the desire of knowledge finds a natural and legitimate support in the esteem in which those are generally held who are distinguished by their attainments; in the direct and obvious utility of many branches of knowledge, and, from the wonderful and often unsuspected connection of its different branches, in the incidental and possible utility of all knowledge.

But even with such support, the desire of knowledge has often too little relative strength in the contest with indolence. In order to induce study, the best of men have therefore thought it necessary to admit and to sanction in our public institutions the far inferior and sometimes pernicious motive of emulation, but they have done it reluctantly, and only as polygamy was allowed to the Israelites, "because of the hardness of their hearts." It is to be hoped that the time may come when the adjustment of forces shall be different, and there shall be found in knowledge and in its necessary and legitimate results sufficient motive for its pursuit.

Like the appetites, the desire for knowledge may become artificial, and take directions that are capricious. It may also be in excess. It is always relatively so when the acquisition of knowledge has no respect to the attainment of mental power, and the use to be made of it. Knowledge is the food of the mind. And as food may overload and enfeeble the body, and is to be received only as there is a capacity of digestion and assimilation, and with ultimate reference to action, so knowledge may overload and enfeeble the mind, and should be received only as it can be reflected on and arranged, and so incorporated into our mental being as to give us power for action. Here, as elsewhere, the receiving is to have reference to a giving, but not wholly. If the thing received were not valuable in itself, there would be neither worth in the gift nor merit in the giving.

We now proceed to the desire of power. The idea of power is inseparable from that of will. The very act of willing, or, as Hamilton calls it, conation, gives the conception; but this is fully realized only in the passing of the conation into its results. Personal power is in the idea of a will; but the idea of power is implied, and would be given also in the spontaneous exercises of any of the faculties. A faculty and a power are the same thing. It may even be said that in all receptivity there is power. There is the power of receiving; but in the sense now contemplated this would not be a power. In all power exerted there is an origination of activity.

The idea of power, then, enters into our very conception of ourselves. We cannot exist except as powers. The consciousness of being, and of power, can hardly be said to be two things. We can neither know nor rejoice in our being nor its enlargement except through a consciousness of power, and of the enlargement of power. Doubtless there is a high pleasure as we make experiments upon our faculties corporeal and mental, and ascertain the effects we can originate through them, and the more striking the effects the greater the pleasure; but in that we are merely finding ourselves out, and the desire of power no more respects, as has commonly been supposed, that power which enters into the conception of ourselves, than the desire of knowledge includes the light of consciousness and the intuitions of reason. The very desire of power is itself a power, and it is absurd to say that a desire desires itself. In examining man we must take him as possessed of all that makes him man. We find him to be a power, and also to possess the desire of power; but, as the desire of knowledge implies a primitive knowledge which the desire does not respect, so the desire of power implies a primitive power which that desire does not respect. We must either adopt this mode of viewing the subject, or resolve all our desires into that of power, since there is in all of them an exertion of power and an enjoyment proportioned to the power exerted.

But all this is very different from that control over nature and men which we may gain by our own skill and exertion, which may be put forth in different directions, or not at all, and the desire of which may exist in different degrees. It is this, and chiefly the desire of controlling our fellow-creatures, that we mean by the desire of power.

Having made this distinction, it may be well to indicate, at this point, the difference between the desire of power and that of liberty, as the latter is often made a part of the former. Liberty has no particular connection with the desire of power as just defined, but has respect to the putting forth, within their legitimate sphere, of any of those faculties by which we are men. It is the condition of the manifestation of our being in any direction we may choose; but I did not class it with the specific desires for the same reason that I omitted the desire of society and of happiness. A free bird does not desire freedom. It was hatched free. Freedom is the general condition of all its activity. So men are born free, and God has given no natural desire to meet a condition of things induced by wrong. It is, therefore, no specific desire, but the whole nature, that rebels against unjust restraint; and freedom can be crushed out only by the degradation of the whole man.

Hence liberty, society, and happiness, the first two being general conditions of our activity, and the last a general result of it, are more intimate to us, more essential and sacred, than the object of any specific desire.

But to return. The power of man is from his will, and the extent of it he learns wholly by experience. If the movement of mountains had followed his volition from the first as uniformly as the movement of his limbs, it would have seemed to him, and would have been, no more strange. But experience shows him that his direct power extends only to the voluntary muscles of the body and to the voluntary faculties of the mind, and that even here his power is not absolute. Probably no man ever gained the full control either over his muscles or over the faculties of his mind. To give such control is one great object of education. In this is discipline. Here is the first sphere of power, the only one that is direct. Here lies the greatness of him who ruleth his own spirit.

But between this power, which, though direct, is so narrow in its range, and that indirect power which man may exert over the elements and over nations, the contrast is marvellous. It is this latter power that men chiefly seek, and all mechanism, all practical sciences, all forms of government, are but means for its exercise. They are means, more or less facile, for connecting the will of man with remote results; and nothing more indicates the superiority of man's nature than the extent to which this may be done. An animal can do nothing at a distance from itself in space, and nothing worthy of mention, except in the present, in time; but the will of a single man may find expression in a few words that shall set in motion armies and navies, and the echo of what was at first but a few feeble vibrations of the atmosphere shall come back from distant continents in the roar of cannon and the groans of the dying. The thought and feeling of one man may find expression in words that shall be repeated through all time, and work like leaven in transforming society.

The control of man over nature can never be arbitrary. "Nature is conquered only by obeying her laws." But while nature cannot be broken down by force, the will of man may be. Hence, in governing his fellows, instead of making, as he should, the method he is compelled to follow in nature his model, and governing men in accordance with the laws of their rational and responsible nature, man has employed arbitrary power. It is in the tendency to this that the danger from this desire is found. To a corrupted will the taste of it is like that of blood to the tiger. Under its influence man sets himself up as independent of authority, rejects moral restraint, and in passing to his selfish ends disregards the rights and the miseries of men. The larger part of history is but a record of the deeds of men under the influence of this desire thus perverted.

But whatever the perversions and abuses of this desire may be, there can be no more doubt of its legitimacy than of that of knowledge, since the great use of knowledge is to be a condition for the right exercise of power. If the results of its perversion are terrific, it only shows the uses to which it may be put when rightly directed. The element that rages in the conflagration is the same that enables man to mould to his will the most refractory substances in nature, and which may be made so much the more energetic in its usefulness, as, when uncontrolled, it had been destructive and awful. It is the same atmosphere that, in its condensed energies, forms the tornado, that wafts the ship, and kisses the leaf of the violet. Every creature of God is good; but it is to be used not only "with thanksgiving," but in accordance with his laws.

It is this arbitrary power that kings, and especially tyrants, have sought and possessed. In the early stages of society it was natural that such a power should be attained, and, once attained, that it should seek to perpetuate itself. But men have found the trust too great. They are, therefore, seeking to divide the power, and, by putting it into the hands of the people themselves, to bring interest in to the aid of principle. It is creditable to man that he can maintain a republic, but it would be more so if monarchy could be well administered. If democracy trusts the people to a certain extent, it yet proceeds upon a distrust of man. By adopting as its maxim that "eternal vigilance is the price of liberty," it declares that man has no moderation in the desire, and is not to be trusted in the use of power.

But besides arbitrary power backed by force, there is another which we call influence, not less effectual, and often not less extensive, which is exercised, not by coercion, but in compatibility with the laws of mind and the freedom of others. This is the power of the wise, of the eloquent, of the good man; and as it always implies the possession of qualities respectable in themselves, and generally beneficial, it is to be sought by every honorable means.

Power and influence are not incompatible, but, as contrasted, they differ in several respects. Power interferes with freedom; influence does not. Power stands above those whom it controls, and issues its commands; influence elicits and directs the individual energies of those upon whom it bears, and thus enlarges the sphere of their agency. Power keeps itself aloof as an object of fear and admiration; influence mingles in with the agencies which itself has set in motion, and is often so lost in them as to be forgotten, as the kindling spark is forgotten when the flames begin to spread. Power, especially if it be hereditary, depends upon accident; influence upon personal qualities. Power is maintained by pageantry, by chicanery, by brute force; influence by the cultivation of those commanding qualities from which it first arose.

While, therefore, we reject, as the object of desire, all arbitrary power, we cannot too earnestly desire those means of influence by which we may lead others freely to their own good.

Emulation, or the desire of superiority, is classed by Stewart and others among the original desires. By others it is regarded as a modification of the desire of power. So I regard it. At least I hardly know where else to place it, though the desire of esteem often seems to be involved in it, quite as much as that of power. If the contests in which emulation is excited were not public, and the results were never to be known, probably the emulation would be but slight. My reason for not classing it with the original desires will be found in the principle already stated. I do not see that it would be necessary to the perfection of the mind.

Of this as a principle of action much has been said, and moralists are not agreed respecting it. This may be, in part, from some ambiguity in the term. There can be no emulation unless a man pursues an object in common with others. Here other principles are brought in, and we need to discriminate.

There is in many animals an instinctive feeling that produces in them the effects of emulation. It may be seen in two horses drawing together, or attempting to pass each other. This feeling has in it nothing malignant. It is probably a modification of their social instincts.

In man there may be something of the same instinct, joined with the higher influence of sympathy. Of sympathy the influence is so great that Adam Smith made it the foundation of his moral system. If we see others laugh, we are disposed to laugh also; if they are in grief, our feelings and countenance conform in some degree to their emotions; and whatever feeling may be vividly expressed, if it does not shock our sense of propriety, we have a tendency to enter into and sympathize with. This is natural and right. If, now, in a class of young men studying together, and doing as little as possible, we suppose that one of them should wake up to a love of knowledge, and to a sense of his responsibility, and enter independently upon a course of work, it would be strange, since we sympathize with almost every other feeling, if something of his spirit should not be transferred to others. So far from being wrong in them to feel it, it would imply a baseness if they did not, and if this feeling should pervade the class, it would be a blessing to all. It would be simply a manifestation of our social nature in one of its higher and better forms. That there is in it nothing of malignity or personal feeling is clear, because the same feeling may be excited by reading the lives of those who are dead. What was it that brought tears into the eyes of Julius Cæsar, when, at the age of thirty-two, he saw the picture of Alexander the Great? What is it that causes the bosom of the young missionary to burn when he reads the lives of Brainerd and of Martyn? And if we may be thus stimulated by those who have gone before us, how much more by those who walk with us. It is in this effect and propriety of sympathy that we find not only the benefit of social study and work, but the obligation of setting a good example. If any deny the propriety of being stimulated, not merely in view of the thing to be done, but also in view of what others have done, they destroy the obligation to set a good example. This principle is recognized in the Bible. "Consider," says the apostle, not simply the excellence of the end, but "one another, to provoke — yes *provoke* — unto love and good works." "I speak not this," says he, "by commandment, but by occasion of the forwardness of others." He says, too, by way of commendation, and as what he rejoiced in, "And your zeal hath provoked very many" — not to do more than others, but what they could.

Thus, when we pursue an object in common with others, our motives are mixed. We have some love of the thing itself, we have some sympathy, some desire of the esteem connected with distinguished success, and we may also have a desire of superiority for its own sake. It is this last only that is properly emulation. So it is defined by Butler, and Reid, and Stewart, and Whewell; but in supposing this to be an original part of our nature, and in their discussions upon it, I cannot believe that they wholly separated it from the elements above mentioned.

That this love of superiority, taken by itself, is either a natural or a justifiable principle, I cannot suppose. It does not contemplate our doing what we can, which is all that is required of us, but more than another, and involves our unhappiness if we do not. It is nowhere commanded in the Bible that we should be above others. To desire to be above him simply for the love of it, is incompatible with loving our neighbor as ourselves. It is a pleasure gained at his expense; but there is no legitimate pleasure that is necessarily at the expense of another. God has not so constituted his creatures. It is closely, though perhaps not necessarily, associated with pride on the one hand

and envy on the other. It cannot blend with that love which is the fulfilling of the law. To suppose one person to be endeavoring to love God more than another is preposterous.

It is supposed by some that emulation is forbidden in the Scriptures, because "emulations" are classed by the apostle Paul with "wrath, strife, envyings, murder," etc. But in the Scriptures language is employed with the same latitude as in common life. The term is found in them but twice, and in the other instance is used by the same apostle as that which he was desirous of producing. "If," says he, "by any means I might provoke to 'emulation' them which are my flesh, and might save some of them." There is, therefore, an emulation to be commended as well as one to be condemned; and, doubtless, men often dispute on this subject, who, if they would be careful to understand each other, would find themselves perfectly agreed.

We have now considered, in its various forms, the desire of power. The vanity of those pursuits to which men are impelled by it, when in excess, is a common topic with moralists. Doubtless, the objects of it are less valuable when attained than they appear in the distance. The elevation is apparently smooth and inviting, but the way to it is hazardous, and when reached it is often found barren and comfortless. That those who enter upon this pursuit should be deceived is almost a necessity. By men who are in power, and have wealth, while they seem to have everything at command, their care, their weakness, their misery, are carefully concealed. They often spend more thought and labor to appear to be happy than to be so. Than our judgments respecting the happiness of others nothing can be more uncertain. The evils that we do not see we readily suppose not to exist, and often envy those who are far more wretched than ourselves. The impression of pain is much more vivid than that of pleasure, and a man apparently happy may have his life embittered in a thousand ways which we do not suspect.

But, laying aside the evils common to all men, power and wealth have cares and troubles peculiar to themselves.

"The needy traveller, serene and gay,
Walks the wild heath and sings his toil away;
Does envy bid thee crush the upbraiding joy?
Increase his riches, and his peace destroy.
Now fears in dire vicissitude invade,
The rustling brake alarms, and quivering shade,
Nor light nor darkness brings his pain relief, —
One shows the plunder, and one hides the thief."

" For heaven's sake let us sit upon the ground
And tell sad stories of the death of kings;
How some have been deposed, some slain in war,
Some poisoned by their wives, some sleeping killed —
All murdered, — for within the hollow crown
That rounds the mortal temples of a king
Keeps Death his court, and there the Antic sits,
Scoffing his state, and grinning at his pomp,
Allowing him a breath, a little scene
To monarchize, be feared, and kill with looks,
Infusing him with self and vain conceit,
As if this flesh which walls about our life
Were brass impregnable; and honored thus,
Comes at the last, and with a little pin
Bores through his castle-wall — and — farewell king.
Cover your heads, and mock not flesh and blood
With solemn reverence."

If these and similar evils of wealth and power are more than compensated by peculiar advantages, the balance in their favor is but slight. What is most to be desired and most to be dreaded in life is common to all men. The light of heaven, the air, the earth, the heritage of the senses, the play of the affections, the treasures of a good conscience, may be possessed by all. From the loss of friends, the encroachments of disease, the disorder of the passions, the forebodings caused by sin of an awful future, and from death, none are exempt. Where, then, there is so much in common, the difference of enjoyment that mere wealth or power can give is so small that if it must cost much struggle it will generally be found that the "play is not worth the candle," that we have sacrificed ease and independence to imaginary advantages.

It only remains to speak of the desire of esteem.

For this the other desires are, in a measure, the condition, since esteem is most fully reached through the use we make of property, knowledge, and power. It has reference not only to our own happiness, but to our coöperation with others, and is an indispensable condition of the social results intended by God. It is less stirring than the desire of power, and often requires us to forbear action as well as to act. With the desire of arbitrary power it is incompatible. He who would employ the means requisite to gain that, and would use it when gained, must forfeit esteem. Napoleon is reported to have said of his brother Joseph that he was too good a man to be a great man.

That this is a natural desire, is not now questioned. It appears in children before they are able to speak, and with many is stronger than any other, even than that of life itself or of a good conscience. Men will sacrifice life for the good opinion of others, and will lie that they may not be thought liars. Its opposite, scorn, contempt, ridicule, are among the things we most dread, and it requires the sternest principle and the greatest independence of judgment to stand before them. To do this is a higher form of heroism than to stand before the cannon's mouth. Few will not remember the impressions from first reading Milton's description of the faithful angel with whom —

> "Nor number nor example wrought
> To swerve from truth, or change his constant mind,
> Though single. From amidst them forth he passed
> Long way through hostile scorn, which he sustained
> Superior, nor of violence feared aught;
> And with retorted scorn his back he turned
> On those proud towers to swift destruction doomed."

From the legitimate influence of this desire the benefits are equal to its strength. The danger also is in the same proportion. This arises from the want of coincidence between the desire and the conscience in others and in ourselves, and will be in two directions.

In the first place, we may be desirous of doing right, but be tempted to violate our conscience in order to please others. This we are never to do, either by evasion or compliance. Those who do this are a kind of inverted hypocrites, seeming worse than they are. In matters of indifference we are to be ready to comply with the inclinations, and even the prejudices of others, but if we violate our conscience we not only incur guilt, but are generally despised by the very persons whose good opinion we seek. Besides, it is not to the good opinion of men only that we should have respect. Many things that are highly esteemed among men are abomination in the sight of God. This often causes a fearful conflict, but there must be no faltering.

In the second place, we may suppose others to be pleased with good qualities, and be tempted to make a pretence of those we do not possess, thus violating our conscience by acting a lie. This takes two forms. If admiration be sought, it will be affectation; if confidence and friendship, hypocrisy. In both we act a lie, but the one is a ridiculous lie chiefly hurtful to ourselves, while the other is a lie of the darkest hue. Affectation and hypocrisy! To how much light satire and spleen, to how much deep distrust and dark misanthropy, have they given rise! How have they given to human life, in which such momentous interests are involved, the appearance of a masquerade and a farce!

Has any one, then, principle? Let him abide by it. Would any one seem to be anything? Let him *be* that thing. This is the freest and safest way, and quite as easy as to preserve a state of forced and dangerous concealment. Regarding these two cautions, we need not fear being too much influenced by a regard to the good opinion of those around us.

The esteem spoken of hitherto is that of those whom we know, and with whom we have intercourse. But we also desire the good opinion of those who are remote from us in space and in time, whom we never expect to see or to have intercourse with. We desire fame, and, what is the highest form of it, glory.

By some this form of the desire of esteem has been ranked as a separate desire, but without reason. By others it has been greatly ridiculed, also without reason, since it is a natural form of the desire, and one justified by the Scriptures. "The righteous," they say, "shall be had in everlasting remembrance;" and Christians are those who seek for "*glory* and honor," as well as for "immortality."

Of glory as it is commonly conceived, Cousin has given the best account I have seen. That I propose to give in substance, and then make some remarks upon it.

And first, we are to separate glory from notoriety. The passions and feelings of one man are common to all, and mankind are always aroused by any vivid and startling exhibitions of their common nature in any of its elements or forms. If this exhibition be of the darker and fiend-like passions, they will utter a cry of execration which is at once *notoriety* and *infamy*.

We must also distinguish glory from reputation. This implies something praiseworthy to a certain extent, but may be gained by almost any one who pleases. Mankind, from education, taste, prejudice, are divided into parties, sects, coteries, the members of which are valued, not for their common humanity, but for the elements of difference by which that party or sect may happen to be distinguished. This is their common point of sympathy, and the man who embodies most fully, and expresses most strongly, the peculiarities of the party, will have reputation, will be the great man of the party. But the very cause of his reputation cuts him off from sympathy with the race, and he must pass into oblivion. Such are the party men of the day, who flourish because they are party men, and for that reason, so far as they are party men, must fade. Such are the zealots and sectarians, whether in politics or religion, who are distinguished by anything which is not connected with the great interests of truth and of duty. The possession, in an uncommon degree, of any quality, as wit, humor, memory, will confer reputation. It may be gained by contrivance and trick, by collusion and bargaining.

But with glory it is not so. It has been said already that the elements of humanity are common to all, and that it always recognizes and responds to any vivid portrayal of itself. We are all conscious of indefinite workings of our minds, of undefined and shapeless feelings, and when these are brought out into perfect expression by the touch of genius we are delighted. We admire, and are grateful to the man who can give us new aspects either of nature or of ourselves. It is the glory of all great poets and philosophers, of those who represent, and of those who analyze nature and man, that in whatever age or country their works may be found by man sufficiently cultivated to understand them, they meet with a recognition and a response. This master minds alone can accomplish. Chance has nothing to do with it. Artifice and pretence are futile here.

In the same way military glory arises from the relation of those who gain it to the permanent interests and universal feelings of man. What gives interest to a battle is not that it is a theatre where brute force contends, but one where different interests and principles are arrayed against each other. It has often seemed to depend upon the fate of a single battle whether liberty or despotism, civilization or barbarism, should be prevalent in the world. When the rights and destinies of men are thus at stake, he who is most perfectly under the control of the master idea that animates all, and most fully represents it, naturally becomes the leader. It is not in him as an individual that we are interested, it is in the principles of which he is the representative, and of which his acts are the manifestations. If by exertion and sacrifice he cause those principles to prevail, we feel that he is the benefactor of mankind, that he is our benefactor, and the cry of admiration and gratitude which mankind utter towards such a man is glory.

It is, therefore, only by producing some great result that glory can be obtained. To receive glory from mankind we must put ourselves in relation to them, must affect their destinies, must make some striking exhibition of talent, or of those emotions and passions that are had in admiration among men. The man who can do this may be a fortunate man, but he must be a great man.

Of this account of glory, in which we find the rationale of modern hero-worship, I remark,—1st. That as a motive of action it can apply to but few. Few, comparatively, can, by any possible exaggeration of self-esteem, suppose they can produce results that shall put them in relation with the mass of mankind. 2d. That if this glory could be a motive to many, it would be attainable by only a few, and so must lead to disappointment. Mankind are so much engrossed in their own concerns that there can exist but a certain moderate amount of admiration at the same time. The young aspirant for fame, when he has written or done something which he thinks extraordinary, is surprised and vexed on looking around and finding every man minding his own business. 3d. The opportunity for acquiring this glory often depends on causes that are beyond the control of man. At this day Washington could not reproduce himself. 4th. This glory depends on success, which is not proportioned to desert. Mankind judge by success. In the race for fame misfortune is a crime which they never forgive. 5th. The admiration of mankind is often given to qualities that do not deserve it, and withheld from those that do. It is not, therefore, always a safe guide to our conduct, or a certain criterion of goodness, without which there can be no true glory.

Can, then, this be the glory spoken of in the Scriptures? Or is it all an illusion? Neither. Our constitution does not deceive us. Its tendencies need guidance, but not eradication. This part of it is a striking indication of the greatness of our nature, and of its capacity of being put into relation with vast numbers, and with great interests. The approbation of God, and of those who judge in accordance with him, is no unsuitable motive for any. It is such an one as an apostle thought worthy of being presented. After enumerating a long list of the worthies of former times, he represents them as resting from their own conflict, and watching the progress of those who have succeeded them. "Seeing, therefore," says he, "we are compassed about by so great a cloud of witnesses, let us run with patience the race set before us." What we need, then, is to illuminate the desire of glory by the revelations of Christianity. Regarding ourselves, not merely as citizens of this world, but of the universe, and knowing that God is over all, and that there is somewhere a vast assembly of the good to whom our conduct either now is or shall be known, we may give to this principle of action free scope.

Such is the theatre on which we are to contend for the true glory and honor, and we are to do it in the only way in which success is possible, "by a patient continuance in well-doing." In this race the success of one does not prevent that of another. All may enter the lists, and all may gain the prize.

LECTURE VI.

THE AFFECTIONS. — NATURAL AND MORAL. — BENEVOLENT. — DEFENSIVE AND PUNITIVE. — ORIGIN OF MALEVOLENT AFFECTIONS. — FORGIVENESS. — HOW SUBJECT TO WILL. — THE INTELLECT. — LOVE OF TRUTH.

In the last lecture we finished the consideration of what are usually termed the desires. These have no moral character. But desire is not excluded from the sphere of morals. It will go with us not only as an element of the affections, but in its own proper form; for there are really both natural and moral desires, as well as natural and moral affections.

The desires we have considered imply no previous exercise of the moral nature, and have for their object things without us; the moral desires imply a previous exercise of the moral nature, and have for their object our own moral states. A paramount desire for virtue is a virtuous desire, and a similar desire for holiness is a holy desire. The object of the one class of desires is that we may *have* something, of the other, that we may *be* something. In either case, however, the desires respect not merely the well-being of the individual, but his capacity to minister to others through the affections; and it is to the consideration of these that we now pass.

As the appetites have for their end a perfect body, and the desires a perfect mind, — perfect up to that point, and as a condition for something higher, — so the affections, though ultimate to the individual, have, as a further end, a perfect society. They are that part of the constitution of man by which he is so put in relation with his fellows that society becomes possible.

And here we find the first difference between the affections and the desires. The object of the desires is things; the object of the affections is sentient beings, chiefly those that are rational and moral.

The affections differ from the desires, also, because they are disinterested. The desires receive and appropriate their objects to themselves. Their whole business is appropriation, whereas the affections flow from us. We bestow them and they appropriate nothing. There can be no interested affection.

A third difference is, that the affections are more complex. Affection is desire, and something more. It is impossible to have an affection for any one without having involved in it, and a part of it, a desire for his well-being. The affection itself, as distinguished from this desire, cannot be defined, and can be conceived only by being felt. It is among the ultimate and highest forms in which our humanity expresses itself.

But in analyzing the affections we are not to destroy them. This Brown has done. He makes no such class as the affections. The specific feeling of love, for instance, he classes with immediate emotions, and our wish for the happiness of those we love, with the desires. But this is like treating of oxygen and hydrogen separately, and then denying that there is such a thing as water. Water, which is one thing, is neither oxygen nor hydrogen, but the two united; and pity, which is also one thing, is neither a vivid emotion in view of distress, nor a desire to relieve it, but the two united; and neither can be regarded practically in any other way.

But we must notice here a peculiarity of that desire which is an element in love. As it is our own desire, its gratification must be a source of happiness to us. As it is a desire for the happiness of others, it must lead us to promote that, and it is impossible that we should thus promote the happiness of others without promoting our own. Hence, some question the possibility of disinterested benevolence. We desire, they say, the happiness of others for the sake of our own. It is true that we are made happy in making them so, and an admirable provision for mutual and extended happiness it is; it is also true that we may exercise and cultivate this desire, or rather the affection of which it is a part, as we may any other, with the knowledge that it will thus make us happy; still the desire is for the happiness of others, and the moment it ceases to be that, — that disinterestedly, — the affection itself is gone, and with it the very source of our happiness. A desire for our own happiness cannot be an element of affection, and when, for the sake of that, we pursue towards others such a course as affection would prompt, the whole source and character of our happiness, if we gain any, is gone. It may be from self-love and selfishness, but the pure happiness of affection it cannot be. The gold is become dim, or rather dross, and the most fine gold is changed.

The affections, regarded as a whole, further differ from the desires in being, as has been said, ultimate for man himself. They refer to society; but there is nothing within the man that is higher than they to which they minister. So far they are ends and not means. We rest in them. They react, indeed, on the inferior parts of the constitution, but do not serve them in the same sense in which they are served. Love, as involving not merely constitutional affection, but rational choice, is the highest form in which our nature can manifest itself. There is in it a synthesis of affection and of will.

From these differences it is plain that in passing to the affections, taken as a whole, we enter another region and group, where we find elements that are wholly new. We come to that in the intelligent world which answers to heat and electricity and magnetism in the physical world, or rather to the one agent of which these may be but the varied manifestations. Heretofore, all has been appropriation, and has looked towards self. Here self is not forgotten in the arrangements of God, but must be by us. The desire that enters into love retains its power of good to us as a desire, but by thus entering loses its capability of being abused into selfishness. As an appropriating desire it is wholly lost. In becoming a desire for the good of others, it becomes disinterested. Of this, the possibility, as I have said, has been doubted by some. They do not believe that a son, knowing that he should inherit a large estate on the death of his father, dependent on his assiduity, could attend upon and cheer him through his final sickness purely from affection. They are in the same position as the heathen, who cannot conceive that the missionaries should come with the simple object of doing them good, whereas the whole glory of the missionary work is in its unselfishness. When that departs, it is shorn of the locks of its strength, and becomes like any other cause. But in this structure and action of affection we simply find the paradox of our Saviour that he who would find his life must lose it. That is not peculiar to his religion. It has its basis in our nature. It is the condition on which any higher life of the affections is to be found. It is by losing all thought of himself that a man finds his own higher self. The ultimate happiness and good for man is something more than the happiness from desire, as found in affection. That is there the inferior and weaker element. It is from a union in sympathy, of which desire knows nothing, from a mutual love; it is in a glow, and ardor, and exultation ineffable in view of the high powers and qualities of other beings to whom we are united by an unalterable affection,—an affection springing from the very depths of our rational and voluntary nature, and through which we find relationship and kindred dearer than any other. Here again the Saviour understood our nature, and hence condensed all the natural relationships into one to express that of moral affinity. "For whosoever," said he, "shall do the will of God, the same is my brother, and sister, and mother." The blessedness from a sympathy and love where there is perfect moral complacency, who can estimate? Who can estimate the repercussion and multiplication of joy when each one shall not only have joy in himself, but shall also rejoice with all that do rejoice? How shall the whole principle and method of selfishness be reversed, when, instead of looking on his own things, every man shall look also on the things of others, not with envy or jealousy, but with the greater delight as the gifts and endowments are greater, and shall feel that he owns them all in a far higher sense than he who can enjoy it owns the landscape!

In affection it is the union in sympathy that is the electric element, and this may pervade society as if it were a living organism, and so that whatever is felt by one shall be felt by all. From what we see of the power of sympathy in large bodies of men, in nations engaged in a common cause, where there is yet much selfishness, and the means of communication are imperfect, we may imagine what it would be if there were no selfishness and the means of communication were complete. With these conditions, the "joy in the presence of the angels of God over one sinner that repenteth" would follow, of course.

Not only do the affections, as has been said, point towards society, but they are the only social element. The appetites and the desires both appropriate. They are not, in their own nature, and of necessity, selfish; but they have a primary reference to self, and become selfish when they so act as to encroach upon the sphere of the faculties above them. If a man so indulge his appetites as to encroach upon his desires,—if the love of eating overmaster and dwarf the desire for knowledge,—there is selfishness as well as sensuality in the act, because the man dwarfs his higher nature, and so unfits himself for the good he might do to others. So, too, though the desires, acting within their own sphere, are merely manifestations of our nature having reference to self, but not selfish; yet if they encroach upon the sphere of the affections, they immediately become selfish, and it is one of the common and prominent forms of selfishness for them to do this. With only appetite and desire, the whole object of man would be appropriation to himself, and he would use his fellow-men as things, simply for his own convenience. Men would care no more for each other than the player does for his nine-pins. Association there might be, but no society; and the association would have about it no charm, no beauty, no warmth, nothing disinterested or noble. But let now the affections come in; let friendship, and gratitude, and pity; let sympathy and love in its various forms, as conjugal, filial, and fraternal affection, appear, and they make a new world. They are like the angels from heaven descending among men. They come, and mere forms, and conventionalisms, and hypocrisies and overreachings, give place, and disappear like birds of night before the light of day.

That the affections are the only social element, it is desirable to notice, because it shows us precisely what we are to cultivate to make society perfect; and also how it is chiefly liable to be corrupted, or rather perverted. This is by the coming in of the desires where the affections ought to rule. The affections, as I have said, cannot be interested. A true friendship cannot be so, and hence its beauty, — a beauty scarcely paralleled on earth. But if we suppose those acts which seemed to be prompted by friendship, to be really prompted, not by affection going out towards the person, but by the *desire* of some benefit from him, the beauty will vanish in a moment, and contempt and detestation will take the place of complacency and admiration. In married life, and in all preliminaries to it, there is beauty as the affection is pure, not only from sensuality, but from all desire of property, or of any incidental advantage. There is an expression employed by some, — that of using one's friends, — that was always offensive to me. The displacement in society of affection by desire is bad enough, but the shameless avowal of it is worse. Here is a chief ground of the hypocrisy noticed in connection with the desire of esteem. Nothing can be more annoying or chilling than to be in a community where there is a universal tendency to gratify some form of desire under the profession and appearance of affection, and especially to boast of success in this as an evidence of smartness and of a knowledge of human nature. This it is that gives to fashionable life, when the people who are in it understand each other, as they generally do, its heartlessness, and lays it open to the shafts of satire. Let its polished but meagre conventionalisms be filled out with a hearty affection, and it would be like the resurrection and free motion of a corpse that had simply been galvanized. The same is true in all the relations of life. The corruption is, that appetite and desire, and so sensuality and selfishness, have usurped the place of the affections; and the great thing needed in society is that these should assume their due prominence, and rule in their own sphere.

In what has been said hitherto no distinction has been made between the natural and the moral affections. That distinction we must now draw, for in strictness it is only the natural affections that should be spoken of here.

The character of an affection is determined by its origin and its object. The natural affections are those that spring up impulsively as do the appetites and the desires, and are such as we share in kind with the animals. They do not spring from the moral nature, and have no regard to the moral character of their object. They have, therefore, no moral character in themselves, but, like the appetites and the desires, are purely instrumental, and are good and evil solely as they are controlled. They are good in their place, and for the purpose for which they were intended, but are not morally good, and do not become so by being brought under moral control. The moral affections spring from the moral nature; and it is upon moral beings, as such, that they rest.

This distinction seems plain, but may, perhaps, be made more so by a reference to the language of the Scriptures. In them the term "Heart" is used to signify the affections, but not the natural affections. In the expression, "My son, give me thy heart," we feel at once that, while the affections are meant, there is yet an entire exclusion of anything like the natural affections. That expression carries us at once into a region that is wholly moral and free, and when God is the object of affection there is in it the highest possible form of activity. A supreme love, as that of God must be, if it be at all, involves the choice of a supreme end, and that was shown in the second lecture to be the highest act of a rational being — the outgrowth of his whole personal activity. From what was said at one point it might be supposed that the will, as distinguished from the affections, would be the highest, but in this love there is a coalescence of will and affection such that the love may be said to *be* the two united. There is in it a rational preference which belongs to the will as free; there is in it benevolence and the highest complacency and delight. These are not there as separate elements, more than the ultimate elements of the flower, the oxygen and hydrogen and carbon, are separate in that. They tend to make up the one love, which, as the joint product of the highest faculties of man, thus becomes the one "consummate flower" of his existence. Not unlike is it to the flower of those plants which put forth but a single one at the top, and which is the product and highest expression of their whole life.

But while the line between the natural and the moral affections is thus theoretically distinct, it is many times both difficult and important to distinguish them practically.

It is difficult, because they so conspire together, and seem to permeate each other. They are often, we may say generally, in exercise at the same time, and with the same person for their object, and the whole result becomes so blended into one as to be inseparable. When the two conspire there is a perfect complacency and satisfaction, but we cannot tell how much to attribute to each; when they conflict it is often difficult to say how far each should prevail.

It may also be important to separate the natural from the moral affections. It may not. What nature gives us together we may receive together. We may eat the pudding with no attempt, even in thought, to separate the sugar that pervades every particle of it from that which forms its basis; and that is the pleasantest way. Still, if we would judge accurately or even fairly of men, the line which separates the two forms of the affections must be drawn. The reason is that the natural affections are liable to be mistaken for moral character. In all that pertains to the natural affections the differences of endowment by nature, and with no reference to moral character, are as great as they are with reference to the intellect, or strength and beauty of body. In some these natural endowments are rich and free and beautiful in their spontaneous action. Such are said to be, and they are, amiable. Others are the reverse of this. It is no fault of theirs; it is an infelicity. One is the rose, and the other the nettle; one is the smooth, and the other the rough-barked tree; and nature has made the difference. Still, it is not uncommon to find the richest gifts of the natural affections as well as of the intellect associated with the deepest moral corruption. To this there seem to be even some special tendencies. It is the smooth-barked hickory that bears bitter nuts. Nor, on the other hand, is it uncommon to find from those less happy in natural endowments moral manifestations that surprise and delight us the more on that very account. They are as the good nuts from the shag-bark hickory; they are as the beautiful flowers from the prickly and angular cactus.

While, therefore, we recognize all there is in this part

of our nature of beauty, and of desirableness for social life, we are not to confound gifts with virtues, nor natural kindness of heart and amenity of manners with moral principle. We admire the natural affections, we regard any great lack of them as a deformity, we are apt to censure it as if it must have had a moral origin; still, if the moral nature be withdrawn, there remains in them but the foreshadowing and prophecy of something yet higher.

The distinction now made is indispensable; but, in treating of what are called the natural affections in man, we are not to suppose we are treating of them alone. The light of the moral affections constantly shines through them, and gives them a radiance not their own. In what shall be said further of the affections, this distinction, therefore, need not be particularly regarded.

By most writers the affections are divided into the benevolent and the malevolent. But the term malevolent is unfortunate. Perhaps it would be better to designate them with reference to their end rather than their origin, and divide them into those intended to make others happy, and those for self-defence and punishment. We should then have for one class what we must still call the benevolent affections, and for the other the defensive and punitive. Affections strictly malevolent are not to be presumed, but self-defence and punishment are each necessary and proper, and we might expect there would be affections that should indicate these and support us in them.

In inquiring after the number of the original benevolent affections, for these come first in order, we are to be guided in the same way as when we were inquiring respecting the desires. Consciousness must be the ultimate test; but if we can ascertain what affections would be necessary to the upbuilding of a perfect society, we may be sure we shall find just those, and no more. The provisions of God are always adequate for their end, with nothing superfluous.

The first will, of course, be those that belong to the family as a divine institution into which man is born. He does not originate it, but is born into it. Here we have the conjugal, parental, filial, and maternal affections, and where these exist in their purity and proper power, a family is as the garden of God. It is worthy of being his institution. It is the centre of the affections, the home, the sphere of the purest and best earthly happiness, and the germ and source of all civil institutions. But besides these we have "the special and distinguishing affection of man towards woman, and of woman towards man, which tends to the conjugal union. This is expressed by the word love, without any epithet." We have also sympathy, pity, gratitude, friendship, patriotism, and general benevolence, or philanthropy. These may all be included under the word love, as their opposites may be under the word resentment.

Of the benevolent affections generally it may be said that the pleasure already noticed as connected with them may be regarded as an expression of the approbation of God, and as an invitation to us to cherish them. It expresses the wish of Him who made us that these affections should prevail, and evinces his benevolence, since they are at once happiness in those who exercise them, and productive of happiness in those towards whom they are exercised.

We are also fond of seeing excess in these affections rather than deficiency; and if duty be called upon to control them, we choose it should be for restraint and repression, rather than excitement. It is the excess of these affections, the preponderance of the natural element over that which is moral, which gives rise to what are called amiable weaknesses. Through these our respect for a man is diminished more than our love. The tenderness of a father for his child may be a little laughable, yet we easily forgive it, and prefer it to the least want of affection.

We have thus a double provision for the encouragement of these affections, — their effect upon our own happiness, and the sympathy of others.

The terms above given may indicate sufficiently the various forms of affection to enable us to speak of them intelligibly, but those affections are constantly differing from each other and from themselves as their objects differ. What it is to love can be known only by loving, and to appreciate the different shades of affection we must ourselves have felt its nice and varying adjustment to its varying objects. A feeling of responsibility, of anxiety, which is a mixture of hope and fear, of protection and of peculiar tenderness, is blended with parental affection. Filial affection is modified by gratitude, confidence, respect, and reverence. If the graver and sterner virtues enter largely into the character of our friend, we feel for him more of respect; if he be of the softer mood our affection partakes of that character.

Of the particular benevolent affections mentioned it would be pleasant to treat particularly and at large, but they are so far of one general character and object that that will not be requisite. Like the appetites and the desires, they are to be controlled with reference to their end, and will be most for the happiness of the individual when they are so controlled as to build up the most perfect home, and the most perfect civil society.

I will only add, that as society originates, and finds its

beauty and blessedness in these affections, so it will react upon them. That form of society and those habits of life are, therefore, to be preferred which give to these the best theatre and widest scope. Especially is it to be said that the breaking up of the home for any system of communism or socialism must be equally opposed to the intentions of God and to the highest happiness of man.

But besides the benevolent affections there are, as has been said, those that have been called malevolent. Concerning the origin and character of these there has been great diversity of view. There still is. But the part they have played in the history of the race is so conspicuous, and they are so difficult of control, that they ought to be well understood.

Concerning these, two remarks may be made, the opposite of those made concerning the benevolent affections.

The first is, that this class of affections, at least so far as they are malevolent, are painful to those who exercise them, thus indicating the will of God that they should not be indulged in.

The second remark is, that mankind are pleased to see these passions repressed and moderated below their natural standard rather than suffered to rise above it.

As, then, we found a double provision for the encouragement of the benevolent affections, — our own satisfaction and the sympathy of others, — so now we find a double provision to repress these opposite affections, — our own pain and the disapprobation of others.

Since the time of Butler a distinction has been made between "sudden," as he called it, or, as it has since been called, instinctive resentment, and that which is deliberate. The first is the guard appointed by nature against any sudden attack. It is the assertion by whatever is, of its right to be, and confers a promptness and energy which reason could never bestow. This is purely the work of nature, and cannot be wrong. It is only concerning deliberate resentment that there can be a question.

And here my wish is, by tracing its origin, to vindicate this part of our constitution from the charge of anything malevolent, properly so called, and to show its propriety. This will give us the key to its proper use.

Let us then suppose two moral beings, one perfectly good, the other perfectly bad, to meet together. It is clear that they could have no coincident wishes, but would naturally array themselves against each other. "What communion hath light with darkness?" If now the evil being should exert a particular act of injury towards the good, what would be the feeling of the latter? It could not be the same that he would have towards a being perfectly good. What will you call that necessary opposition, that sense of repugnance, of dislike, of condemnation, of abhorrence even, which the good being could not but feel?

It is this opposition of virtue to vice, of holiness to sin, that is the proper foundation of resentment, and that becomes the only resentment that is justifiable when vice exerts itself towards us in a definite act. In this view of it, resentment is nothing more than a sense of ill-desert where it really exists, and a desire to punish it so far as is necessary; and so far from being opposed to goodness, in the wide and proper sense of that word, it is a necessary part of it. The hatred of vice is the opposite pole to the love of virtue, and the positive cannot be evolved without the negative side. Of necessity, the strength of the one is the measure of that of the other. Moral purity, virtue, holiness, whatever we may choose to call it, is not a mere passive, undiscriminating quality. Nothing can be more positive, active, and uncompromising. Against whatever is opposed to it, it arrays itself in a conflict that can know of no cessation and of no compromise till one or the other is completely triumphant; and this opposition cannot be malevolent, since precisely as it prevails happiness is extended, precisely as it fails misery bears sway. If this were not so, there could be nothing venerable or awful about goodness. It would not command our respect, or be worthy of the throne of the universe. This is what is termed in the Scriptures the anger of God, without malice, without revenge, without respect of persons except as good or evil; and it will be the misery of those who shall be finally opposed to God, that they will be opposed to Infinite Goodness, and that Infinite Goodness will be opposed to them, not because it is malevolent, but because it *is* Infinite Goodness. Here we find the source of all penal law. Without this, there could be no security, punishment, or redress. It is this feeling, which, on the perception of wickedness and ill-desert, if the injury be ours, we term *resentment;* if it be upon others, *indignation;* but the principle is the same, and is entirely different from malevolence. This was no part of the human constitution as made by God.

When we speak of the opposition of virtue and vice, it will be remembered that these are mere abstractions. Strictly speaking, there are only virtuous and vicious persons, and hence the punishment of vice must involve the infliction of personal misery, though without malevolence.

But it will be asked, If there be in man no other malevolent principle than this, how shall we account for the jealousy, the envy, the hatred, the malice and revenge that fill and disfigure the earth? They may, I think, all be traced to the perverting influence of selfishness on the original and natural principle of resentment. To be satisfied of this, a brief reference to each will suffice.

Jealousy is an affection which has direct and sole reference to self. We are jealous of no one who is not or may not be a rival. It is when interests are likely to conflict that selfishness, without provocation, stirs up that form of ill-will which we call jealousy. The same may be said of envy. Indeed, envy and jealousy are the same affection towards persons differently situated. That which is jealousy towards those who we fear may surpass us, becomes envy when once we are fairly distanced in the competition. In witnessing a contest, we feel no envy. Envy is the dislike of those who are above *us* because they are above us, and a desire to pull them down to our own level. It is, therefore, directly to selfishness that these two evil affections may be traced.

But jealousy and envy are apt to become settled hatred. Hear those who are, or have been competitors, speak of each other, and you will find the reason. You will find that they impute the success of their opponent to unfairness in him or others,—to some cause which will justify them in showing resentment. Their self-estimation will not permit them to think otherwise. With her jaundiced eye selfishness can convert even the excellences of others into faults, and then, having something that she supposes she can fairly blame, she usurps the place of conscience, and calls upon resentment, which in this unholy alliance becomes malice, to pursue them. Hatred does not spring up naturally from the relations in which we find ourselves in society, as do the natural affections, but requires as its condition some injury real or supposed. So with revenge. By its very nature and definition it implies previous injury, and it is nothing more than the natural feeling of resentment exaggerated by selfishness, and abused into a settled and inveterate passion.

The extent of these passions, and the slight occasions on which they are permitted, are indeed wonderful, but they may all be traced to the combination of selfishness with the natural and necessary principle of resentment. If we distinguish between actions that are simply injurious but not malevolent, as when a robber plunders another, not from any hatred of him, but from a love of his money; and if we make due allowance for the operation of a perverted and perverting selfishness on the natural feeling of resentment, we may see how far man may be said to have originally affections that should be called malevolent.

Here, as elsewhere, evil is from the perversion of that which was good. That part of our constitution from the perversion of which these affections arise, we vindicate. It is essential to goodness itself. It guards our highest interests; it is the basis of penal law, keeping crime and tyranny lurking in their lair; and no character which cannot, and, if need be, will not reveal itself as opposed with the force of the whole being to moral evil, can command our respect.

But while we thus vindicate this part of our constitution as it was originally given, we utterly condemn all jealousy and envy, all hatred, malice and revenge. They are not a part of our original constitution, and were never made by God. Jealousy and envy are not only among the basest, but are the meanest, of the passions. They are indulged in only by those who are conscious of inferiority, and are not only malignant, but are a confession of that degrading consciousness. These, as well as malice and envy, bring their own punishment with them. They bring it in the disquiet which they necessarily cause to their possessor and in the detestation with which they are viewed by mankind. We cannot, therefore, too sedulously stifle these double curses, curses upon ourselves and others, and which have so filled the earth with discord and misery.

In opposition to these, I cannot forbear to mention that beautiful trait of Christian morals, the forgiveness of injuries. How infinitely superior is this to all recrimination! Revenge places us, at best, upon a level with those who have injured us, — forgiveness elevates us far above them. And then how fitted is it to the condition of man! If, as all experience shows, there must be mutual forbearance in the end, why not exercise it before suffering the miseries of mutual recrimination? If we all need forgiveness from God, how suitable that we should forgive each other! To make an offence unpardonable simply because it is against ourselves, is the arrogance and blindness of selfishness, and involves a principle that would preclude all forgiveness. Forgiveness and placability are not meanness or pusillanimity, — they are that attitude of humanity in which it most resembles God.

In considering the affections in connection with morals, we next inquire how far they are subject to the will.

There are those who suppose that the affections and passions are enkindled and drawn from us by a fixed law, as electricity flashes from one cloud to another, and that we are therefore not responsible for them. But the voice of mankind is that men are responsible for their feelings through the whole range of the emotive nature, as well as for their actions. They judge that men can govern their passions, not only by restraining those external acts to which passion would excite them, but also by moderating and subduing the feeling itself. This is correct. Men are responsible not only for the feeling they have, but also for not having the feelings they lack; and yet no man can, by any direct act of the will, cause any one feeling, affection, or passion, to exist. Throughout its whole range the emotive part of our nature is excited by an object adapted to excite it, and not by a direct act of the will. No man can feel pity simply by willing to feel it. He must have a view of poverty, sickness, distress, in some form, and it will arise in view of these. No man can feel gratitude except in view of a benefactor. No man can feel love or respect for one of whose character he is ignorant. These must arise in view of excellence real or supposed. Not on a direct act of the will, nor on the object as it is in itself, but on the object as viewed by the mind, will the feeling depend. A lover may suppose that he sees perfection where another would not see it, and where possibly it does not exist, but the feeling will be the same. Here the feelings and affections called moral are governed by the same laws as those that are not. Were a person commanded to feel the emotion of beauty, as he may be, and is, to feel the affection of love, he might shut his eyes and say that he had no control over his emotions, but not thus could he escape the obligation. Before he could do that, he would be required to seek out some fair face, or beautiful form, or exquisite work of art, or to find his way to some commanding eminence whence he might cast his eye over mountain and valley, the cultivated field and the winding stream, and then if he should not feel the emotion of beauty he might be absolved from the obligation.

But as men have different degrees of feeling on viewing the same object, it may be asked, What should be thought of one who should give his best attention to an object adapted to produce a given feeling, and not have it? What should we think of a man who could thus see distress but feel no compassion? That would depend on his previous history. If he had gone through no hardening process, I do not see that he would be worthy of censure. Such a case we should regard as unnatural, as monstrous, as we should a natural deformity, but it would simply indicate the want of an original capacity. To most persons the feeling of pity on meeting suddenly with a scene of distress is as unavoidable as the feeling of surprise on meeting with one that was unexpected; but as the spontaneous presence of a feeling without the intervention of the will is not a virtue, so its absence, where the susceptibility is wanting, is not a fault. This, however, is not the hardness of heart which mankind condemn. That comes from the over-mastering power of some cherished and selfish passion. A man who has given himself up to the love of gold, when he pays his visits to his poor tenants on the very day their rents become due, can see nothing, and hear nothing, and think of nothing but money. His mind is so absorbed by that, that there is no room for any other feeling. It is not that he has no susceptibility, but that an absorbing selfishness has closed up the avenues to his heart. Seeing, he sees not. His finer susceptibilities fall into desuetude; a current gets its set in his soul which undermines and washes away everything beautiful, and then, indeed, by wrong action long indulged, comes that hardness of heart which the world justly condemns. It is by a process like this that the priests and the Levites are formed who pass by on the other side. They know there is misery in the world, but they not only do not seek it out, they avoid it, lest it should disturb their selfish quiet.

In what I have said hitherto, the object which was to awaken feeling has been supposed present to the senses, but this is not necessary. Mental representation and thought will do as well. It is thought that is the condition of feeling, and governs it. As we think of a man so do we feel towards him. But that the mind has a control over the thoughts, can dismiss some, and dwell upon such as it prefers, can study one subject and not another, none will deny. If, then, any choose to let vain thoughts lodge within them, they must not complain that their affections are disordered; and if any choose to regulate their thoughts, they will thus indirectly regulate their affections also. Our control over the affections is, therefore, though indirect, yet efficient, and such as to render us fully accountable for them. A man can determine the kind of affections he shall have in the same way that he can the kind of knowledge he shall have, or the kind of feelings that shall be produced by the food which he eats. After he has taken food the will has no power to modify the effects, but by his power over the taking of that the man has indirectly a power over his bodily feelings and general health. A man may disorder his affections as he may his body, and be as responsible for the one as for the other, and that not by directly willing it, but by doing that which he either knows, or might know, would produce that effect.

But feeling, it may be said, reacts upon thought, and in turn governs it. True, but this is not the natural order. If we have become subject to a wrong governing passion everything will be seen in the light of that, and no person who shall stand in the way of the gratification of that passion can be viewed as he really is. Here we find the difference in their effects between a governing principle that is legitimate and one that is not. A legitimate principle can create no interest in the mind to prevent it from viewing everything as it is. It originates in light, and seeks the light. But no man can adopt a supreme end that is wrong, and be willing to come to the light. Having adopted his end, whatever shall be opposed to the attainment of that will be viewed with prejudice and regarded with hostility. This would be required by the demand of every rational nature for consistency with itself, and in this we find the origin of all criminal prejudices, and of much of the malignity there is in the world.

The affections, then, and the feelings generally, being thus controlled through the power of attention, how intimate must be the connection between the character and happiness of a man and the objects to which he habitually turns his thoughts! It is not only habits and associations of thought that are thus formed, but also of feeling; and thus the whole character is reached. He whose course of reading and meditation presents only what is pure, and generous, and noble, lives in a world wholly different from that of him who pursues an opposite course.

It is to be observed, too, that that system, aside from any consideration of its truth, which presents the noblest objects to the intellect, must also be most favorable to high and noble feeling. Hence atheism, which takes away the conception of an infinite and perfect God, or rather renders it inoperative, must wither the feelings and debase the character, and any system which shall present the Godhead as shorn of any possible perfection must have proportionately the same effect. Hence the vices and degradations of heathenism are naturally associated with idolatries. It was when men "changed the glory of the uncorruptible God into an image made like corruptible man" that "God gave them up unto vile affections."

This doctrine that we are responsible for the affections, and particularly for the natural affections, has special need of enforcement at the present time. Always there have been those who have justified lawlessness here on the pretence that the feelings were irresistible. They have even gloried in it as indicating the warmth and richness of a nature of superior endowments. It was not for them to be cramped by the rigidity of rules. How could feeling be brought under law? What had they to do with the sternness of principle? *That* they left to colder natures. They have had no conception of desire sanctified by affection, and strengthened and regulated by principle; but under the pretence of affection, in the sacred name of the heart, they have cherished selfish and licentious desires; and, as wolves in sheep's clothing, have crept into and desolated the fold of domestic peace. But never, perhaps, has this been so common as now. Now, on the ground of *affinity*, or the want of it, the most solemn vows are violated. Husbands desert their wives, and wives their husbands, and even their children, and doctrines are openly taught, claiming sanction from the spiritual world, that would subvert the most sacred institutions of society, corrupting it at its fountain-head, and that would obscure and defile those pure relationships in which its beauty and strength now abide. As constituted by God, with its origin in the family, society is a soil congenial to the natural affections, and, unless checked by the selfish passions, they will spring up. These selfish passions men can repress. They can have some degree of consideration in forming the conjugal union; they can substitute principle for passion as a controlling power, and can dwell on those aspects of character that would excite affection. They can control many circumstances and conditions that bear on the affections, and will be sure to foster them; they can perform the external acts which the affections require, and form habits of them, and these will react on the feelings; they can regard the higher interests of those with whom they are associated, and cause the LAW OF LOVE to take the place of those capricious emotions which have nothing in common with it but the name. They can thus vindicate the supremacy of the moral nature, and, instead of a sweltering and chaotic mass of moral corruption, tending to a corruption still deeper, can cause society to present the order and beauty of the planetary spheres.

In our division of what were called the instrumental powers, the powers that are to be governed, that are for an end beyond themselves, we made one class of those that indicate ends, and another of those in the light of which ends are pursued. The first class we have now considered, and a few words will suffice for the second.

These may all be comprised under the one term Intellect; but will include only those faculties and operations of intellect that may be modified by the will. It will include all those faculties by which we arrive at truth by a process, and will exclude those that are intuitive.

In a system of psychology it would behove us to consider these powers before those of emotion, since something must be known before anything could be felt. But we are now considering ends, and the initiatory step towards an end is not, as has been said, in the intellect, but in some tendency or craving, some feeling of want or apprehension of excellence. For this the intellect is indeed a condition; but it seemed more accurate to begin with our fundamental conception, and the powers which give us that, and then to regard the intellect as simply instrumental. This, however, is a mere question of arrangement, and is not particularly important. What is important is that we should apprehend fully the connection of truth with the rational pursuit of ends, and our responsibility for a knowledge of the truth.

That the intellect, as now defined, is simply an instrument, there can be no doubt. It is difficult for us to separate wholly the operation of knowing from ulterior results; but when this is done we see that it cannot be an end in itself. Knowing is in order to feeling and action, and without these would be wholly barren. The law of the intellect, therefore, like that of the powers already considered, will be from its end. That end, as we now contemplate it, is not knowledge to be acquired promiscuously under the stimulus of curiosity, but practical truth, as the first condition of wisdom. For this the intellect was given. It was intended for this, as the eye for seeing, and the true dispositions required in the conduct of it are earnestness and candor.

Of these, earnestness will secure that self-denying labor, that careful analysis, and patient induction, and comprehensive research, which the Scriptures imply when they say, "buy the truth and sell it not;" and candor will secure us against all biases from interest, and, as was said under the affections, from our having already chosen a wrong supreme end. This is the same as that singleness of eye spoken of by our Saviour, through which, if a man has it, "his whole body shall be full of light." It is a disposition — and this shows the philosophy of what was said by our Saviour, and cannot be too strongly enforced — a disposition which is impossible to any man who has chosen a supreme end that is wrong. On some points he may be candid, but not in reference to those persons and things which would thwart him in the attainment of that end. No man can be wholly candid who has not chosen the right supreme end, and so has no interest that he conceives to be supreme, to be otherwise. It is not that candor cannot exist where it is opposed to interest, but only to that which is regarded as supreme. In this case a man cannot consistently come to the light. To do so would be death to him in that which he counts his dearest interest, and so his very life. But he who has chosen the true supreme end and pursues it in simplicity, must see all things truly. There can be no refraction in his mental vision, and his whole body will be full of light. This is the only position we can take in which the light that God sends will not be refracted. Without this we shall see some things falsely; more or less we shall "walk in a vain show."

On this subject we concede that there are laws of evidence. Nay, this is the very thing we assert, and it is just because there are such laws that we hold men responsible for their opinions. Without them they could not be. If there were no certain road by which a man could reach a given place, he would not be responsible for not getting there. But if there were such a road, and he should be too careless and self-confident to inquire for it, or should think it too difficult or disagreeable for him to travel, he would be responsible. So here. Truth is one. It corresponds to the mind as light to the eye. It was intended to be seen, and if the laws of evidence, the fixed condition of our receiving it, be fully complied with, it will be seen as in a pure white light, and, so seen, "will make men free." If not, the mind is wrongly constituted in its relation to the objects of knowledge, and the constitution of man is hopeless. What should we think of a man who should hold a prism before his eyes, or shut himself in a room with windows of colored glass, and then complain that he could not see objects in their true color, because there were fixed laws and conditions of vision? Let there but be earnestness and candor, and nothing can prevent the truth from being both seen and received. But for earnestness and candor we are responsible. This none will deny who admit of responsibility at all.

The truth is, we are so endowed and so placed as to be capable, not of all knowledge, nor of freedom from mistakes, but of knowing the truth so far as it bears practically upon our highest interests. This we cannot do by any direct act of will, but through fixed conditions, which will ensure it, and to comply with these conditions is among our very highest and most sacred duties. To love the truth is here the first and great commandment; to tell the truth, which is like it, and a corollary from it, is only the second. It is, however, a duty that has been too much overlooked. In our current treatises on morals, truthfulness has had a large place, while this primal and higher duty of knowing the truth has been scarcely noticed. To this the time permits me simply to give, as I have now done, what seems to me its true place, and in doing so I bring to a close the consideration of those powers which require to be governed, and whose chief end is out of and beyond themselves.

LECTURE VII.

THE MORAL NATURE. — REASON. — IDEAS OF DIFFERENT ORDERS. — HAVE AN ORDER OF DEVELOPMENT. — FREE-WILL. — PERSONALITY. — ACTION TO WHICH RESPONSIBILITY ATTACHES. — ALL MORAL PHENOMENA IN CONNECTION WITH THE CHOICE OF A SUPREME END. — CONSCIENCE. — THE MORAL NATURE DOUBLE. — THE HIGHEST GOOD. — COINCIDENCE OF NATURAL AND REVEALED LAW.

INSTINCTS, appetites, desires, natural affections, intellect, — mere intellect, or understanding, — these are all subordinate and instrumental. They are not, for man, governing powers; and however they may be, in whole or in part, a condition for the moral nature, they are no part of it, and may be conceived of as acting wholly without it.

In passing upward in the scale of being we reach, as I have said, points of transition where there is no longer merely gradation, but a leap, and the introduction of something wholly new. We come to a difference, not in degree, but in kind. So we find organization in a variety of forms, and in great perfection, before a nervous system is introduced. That, as endowed with sensation, is wholly new. It supposes antecedent and auxiliary organization into which it may be put, of which it may take possession, and which may minister to its ends. There is much in every vegetable that simulates, and seems to anticipate a nervous system, but *it* is not there, and when, with its filaments and centres, it first pervaded an organization adapted to it, and responded consciously to the stimulus of the external world, it was as if there had been a new star set in the heavens. There was a new order begun; there was an animal. From that point all was gradation till a *moral* nature was introduced. Then there was another leap. Then man was made, and, if a little lower than the angels, yet in the image of God. Then organization became the abode and instrument of a spiritual and responsible being. It is concerning this moral nature that we are now to inquire.

And here I observe that whoever can tell what that is that is put into the animal nature and uses it, as a nervous system might be put into a vegetable organization and use it, so that there shall be a *person* of which the animal nature shall become the subordinate constituent, can tell what the moral nature is, for man is no further a person than as he is moral. Here it is that we find the ground and necessity of that threefold division of man into body, soul, and spirit, which the Scriptures seem to recognize, and which philosophy will be compelled to adopt. To this division our use of terms conforms but imperfectly; but as thus used the soul will include those powers of intelligence which we share in common with the brutes, and the spirit those higher powers which we now seek, and in which personality is found.

It was said in the third lecture that the special difference between man and all that is below him is, that he chooses his own end, or rather that he may either choose or reject the end for which God made him. If this be so, the powers to be added must be those in virtue of which he does this. According to distinctions already made, they must be directive and not instrumental. The nature thus added must be ultimate, that is, it must minister to nothing within the constitution above itself.

Nor will the addition of such powers be a slight step

upward. The transition from dead to vitalized matter cannot be greater. It is as a new morn risen upon the high noon of animal existence. In the powers thus given must be those for comprehension, for control, for wisdom, in distinction from mere devices and cunning. A brute has not merely instinct, but some degree of understanding, by which it may vary means, and adapt devices often showing much cunning, for the attainment of ends; but the end itself of an animal is the outgrowth of its organization, and admits of no alternative. But man is capable of knowing the difference between good and evil, and of choosing between ends that he may adopt as ultimate and supreme. He can either adopt as supreme the end proposed by reason and sanctioned by conscience, or follow his propensities. He can either serve "the flesh" or "the spirit," and one of these he must do. It is in his manifoldness, for which the capacity is thus given, that his greatness is seen. It is in the choice of the right end that there is the supreme wisdom, even though the best means may not be chosen; while, if the wrong end be chosen, though there be the utmost skill in the use of means, there is yet supreme folly. So is it that we have singleness of eye; so that the open and straight path of wisdom differs from the tortuous course of the serpent; so that "the children of this world are wiser in their generation than the children of light."

What, then, are the powers needed that man may choose his own ends? How can there be, not only impulses from behind that may impel, but also an end before that may be yielded to and adopted? What are the elements of personality, and the *a priori* conditions of a moral act?

Of the powers thus sought the first is *Reason*. In common language man is distinguished from the animals by saying that he has reason. Of this the correctness is not to be questioned if we mean by it that which gives origin to the word rational, rather than to the word reasoning. No one supposes animals to be rational, while many contend that they have some power of reasoning. By reason in this sense, we indicate that in every man by which he is necessitated by his constitution, and as the condition of his being a man, to have certain ideas and beliefs, so that there is in every man a certain amount of mental furniture that is common to all. These products of reason have received different names. They have been called "first truths," "elements of human reason," "laws of belief," "principles of common sense," but in all the same thing is meant. Perhaps a better name than either, as applicable both to ideas and beliefs, would be rational intuitions.

These ideas and beliefs are not innate, but the capacity for them is, and in such a way that they will infallibly appear in every human being when the occasion for them shall be given. The ideas are given at once, but the beliefs and judgments are not at first given in their general form, but immediately assume that form through a particular instance, and not from a process of generalization. They have a history and an order partly natural, and partly in accordance with the history of the individual and the process of his development. To say nothing of comparison, and of the ego and non-ego given in contrast, as stated by Hamilton, the first act of consciousness must involve, first, the idea of being; second, of action, since consciousness is an activity; and, third, of the results of the activity as of a thought or a feeling. Each of these must, in the order of nature, be given before the idea of personal identity, and this must be before that of causation. In regard to these we judge others by ourselves, and have a right to. We believe that every event must have a cause; we know that others believe it also, and have a right to treat them as if they did, even if they should deny it.

The ideas and beliefs which come to us thus may be divided into first, mathematical ideas and axioms. These are at the foundation of the abstract sciences, having for their subject quantity. In the second division are those which pertain to mere being and its relations. Upon these rest all sciences pertaining to actual being and its relations. The third division comprises those which pertain to beauty. These are at the foundation of æsthetical science. In the fourth division are those which pertain to morals and religion. Of these the pervading element is the sense of obligation or duty. Of this the idea necessarily arises in connection with the choice by a rational being of a supreme end, and with the performance of actions supposed to bear upon that.

Here, again, as formerly, we find gradation. According to the principles then laid down, abstract science is lower than that of being; that of being, considered simply, is lower than that of being in its beauty; and this is lower than that of being self-directed and seeking its end under a sense of duty. In the science of being abstract science is implied; in the science of beauty that of being, and the highest beauty is possible only in connection with duty done. Here each higher implies the lower, but not the reverse.

Of ideas and beliefs thus given, those that are moral are so peculiar that philosophers have properly attributed their origin to what they have called the moral or spiritual reason. This is reason, and something more, else it would not be moral. This something more comes from its complexity as higher than mere primitive cognition or rational intuition. In the first two classes of intellectual products above mentioned, the intellectual element is almost sole. In the third there is the synthesis of a rational product with that of sensibility. But here, not only intellect and feeling are involved, as in the mere contemplation of the beautiful, the will is also reached. The idea of obligation is nothing except as there is in it not only feeling, but a requisition upon the will. As a product of the moral reason is an idea, there is in it intellect; as it is an idea of obligation, there is in it feeling; and as this feeling is that of an imperative upon the will, it is clear that in a normal state the activity of the moral reason would involve that of the whole man. It is as nearly a synthesis of intellect, feeling, and will, as is possible, and leave the will free. Between ideas of the moral reason and others there is the same difference as between a cannon-ball that is heated and one that is not. They do not lie still and cold, but respect action, and are of such a nature that we cannot be indifferent to them.

This coalescence of ideas and affections, this fusion and blending of them so that it is possible to give them but a single name, together with their immediate proximity to the will, is a characteristic of the moral nature that has not been sufficiently noticed. In it we have moral ideas and moral affections interpenetrating and moulding each other, and thus a combination, as of light and heat, that is the highest possible. As the product of the moral reason, these ideas and the accompanying feelings arise necessarily in all men; if they did not, we should not have a moral nature; and because the moral reason is reason and something more, it raises us, according to our principle of classi fication, to the highest grade of earthly, and, indeed, of conceivable existence. It will thus be seen, too, that moral science must find its basis, not in any considerations of outward utility, or perception of external relations, but in the deepest and most fundamental intuitions of our nature.

The power by which moral ideas are thus originated, originated by necessity, so that they spring up from the depths of our being, together with the emotion that accompanies and forms a part of them, is an essential element of personality. It is not something which the person may use, but which being withdrawn, personality would remain; it enters into its very framework. This is that by which we are especially made in the image of God. It is the organ of rational and spiritual intuitions. It is not exhausted by those ideas which all men must have that they may be men, but being held in right relations, it is capable of receiving, and in the progress of the man is necessitated to receive, new and higher ideas, still having the same characteristics of universality and necessity for all who reach the same point.

We saw in the third lecture how man is connected with all that is below him, through the laws that govern all below, and extend up to him. We now reach the point at which he is, or has the capacity to be, connected with that which is above him. As rational and in the image of God he must have, in kind, the capacities of the very highest creature, and be subject to every fundamental law of the spiritual world. The laws of that world reach down to him, as those of the world below reach up.

After reason the next element of personality and condition of moral action is a Rational Will, — a Will in Freedom.

Without freedom of some kind, connected with an act at some point, all are agreed that there can be no obligation or responsibility. A man is not responsible for the movement of the earth in its orbit, because it has no connection of any kind with his will. To awaken a sense of obligation in regard to anything which has thus no connection with the will, direct or indirect, proximate or remote, is impossible. When, therefore, we see a man perform an act that we call moral, the element of will and of choice is presupposed.

By some, by most indeed, this element of will is supposed to be the chief one in personality, and there are those who regard it as the only one. Others again think of it as the executive of a person already constituted. To me it seems that the moral ideas that are given by reason, in the light of which we choose and act, through which, indeed, the will is a rational instead of a brute will, are quite as necessary to personality as the power of choosing and acting, and that both are indispensable.

But with these two, — reason and free will, including moral ideas and affections, and so conscience, — whatever we may think of the part that belongs to each, we have the *a priori* elements of personality, and so the power of doing a moral act.

I have spoken of personality as composed of elements. It seemed necessary to speak thus; and yet I am inclined to think that our idea of a person is simple. A person is something more than reason and will. We get misty and lose ourselves by always using abstract terms and the names of attributes. A person is a substance, a *being* that has reason and will. Here we reach an agent, and the true point of responsibility, — the man himself. It is the man himself, the person, the self, the ego, the me, whatever you please to term it, that we hold responsible and praise or blame. It is this mysterious — mysterious as all things are that are simple — this mysterious and inscrutable person, this self-conscious, thinking, comprehending, electing being, — it is the man himself that we approve or disapprove. Aside from their origin in him, actions have no moral quality. Constitutional tendencies, desires, affections, have no moral character till he adopts them, and consents, or elects that they shall move in a particular direction.

Of a person thus constituted the three characteristics are that he is rational, free, and moral. Such a being may perform acts merely instinctive; but as the moral reason, with its necessary products of moral ideas and affections, enters as an element into the conception of personality, it can never be optional with him whether he will have a moral character. He must have one involving the very essence of his being, and his only option is whether it shall be good or bad.

We have now the powers prerequisite to a moral act. But there is another condition. A moral act must be also rational, and as such must have reference to an end. This necessity which a rational being is under of acting with reference to an end, so that his doing this is a test of his rationality, would seem to imply that his conception of an end is the fundamental one for man as an active being. As has been said, the ideas of reason have a history and an order. For man, as speculative, the idea of existence is first. It is implied in all assertions respecting identity and causation. In the same way, the idea of an end involving a good is implied in all acts of rational choice. As a will, rational and free, is essential to morality, so must everything be that is a prerequisite of the action of such a will. But to a free and rational act of willing, the conception of an end is necessary. The moral sentiment, or conscience, is evolved only in connection with the action of free will with reference to an end. This may, therefore, be considered as the fundamental and primitive conception of man as active and moral.

But if reason would act reasonably it must not only know an end, but its own end. Would, then, a rational being naturally know his own end, or what he ought to choose? If not, he would be *lost.* Without a capacity for this, such a being would be an absurdity. The gropings of a baffled instinct would be nothing in comparison with his blindness and helplessness. This end may be known, either from the insight of reason, or from revelation; but however known, there must be a capacity in reason to recognize its own end; and the test of such an end as adequate must be that it shall always suffice to call forth the highest normal activity of the highest powers. In anything short of this a want would be felt. In such an end, if we consider the capacities, the worth and grandeur of spiritual being, there may be an infinite good. There may and must be that which should cause it to be adopted by the whole energy of the will.

We have now the prerequisites for a moral act. We have a *person knowing his end.* But a rational being knowing his end cannot but know his law, since the law is revealed in the end. Thus, and thus only, can he become "a law to himself." It is in the apprehension by a person of his end that the moral nature manifests itself in the immediate and necessary affirmation of obligation to choose that end. This is the moral law, and the whole of it. It is wholly spiritual, simply requiring choice. Lying in immediate proximity to the will, it cannot become a rule; no means can be used; and nothing but a want of will can prevent its being obeyed. Obligation to choose the end is affirmed in view of it as *good;* and such a choice is approved as *right.*

It is here that we find the point of coalescence between intuitional or *a priori* systems of morality, and those that are inductive. At some point these must come together, for it is impossible that the great thinkers in either line should be wholly wrong. The intuitional element here finds its sphere in the immediate recognition by reason of its own end, and in the necessary affirmation of obligation to choose that end. The practical nature, asking, "Who will show me any good?" is also satisfied, because the end thus chosen is a good, and *the* good; and because there is in all questions of right a constant call for the activity of the inductive powers.

By some beings it may be that their true end alone is seen and embraced. They may know no other as possible, and so never be tempted. But for others there is an alternative so presented that there must be a choice between this end and its opposite. Let now the true end be chosen, and the star finds its orbit; there is moral order, there is peace, there is "joy in heaven."

Choosing thus his end, with an apprehension of the worth of spiritual being, with a consciousness of worthiness in having thus chosen, such a being would move on in peace, — not the peace of quiescence, but of a tranquil and deep joy, — till there should arise from within or from without some disturbing influence that might come between him and his end. Then, in proportion to his sense of the worth of the end, and of the obligation to choose and seek it, must be his abhorrence and condemnation of an opposite choice, and his opposition to anything that would divorce him from his end. Hence virtue is necessarily bi-polar. As such, it becomes holiness. This is reason vindicating its right to attain its end. It is personality expressing its sense of the value of its end, now in complacency with it, and with all that would promote it, and now in indignation and opposition towards all that would oppose it. From the evolution on the one side comes all that is mild and winning in virtue; from that on the other all that is stern and awful. It is by the term holiness — that is, wholeness — that this double aspect, and so the completeness of virtue, is best expressed.

That the above may not seem opposed to our consciousness, it may be well to state that in choosing a supreme end it is not necessary that we should know or choose it abstractly and formally, but simply that our individual and specific choices should involve it, and be instances under it. So it is that we know and act under the idea or principle of causation, and so under mathematical axioms. The act of a child may involve the axiom that the whole is equal to the sum of all its parts, and yet the child may never have heard of the axiom, and in that form could not comprehend it.

In thus choosing a supreme end, if that end be the good of others, we reach the highest significance of the word love. This is an act both of the affections and the will, and carries every faculty and choice of the soul along with it. In it the man disposes of himself. It lies back of specific choices and volitions, and determines character. Springing from a synthesis of the rational sensibility and the will, it is the highest product of our highest powers, — the consummate flower of our existence.

From what has been said above, we shall readily see what that form of activity is to which responsibility ultimately attaches. It is not volition regarded simply as an executive act; it is preference. It is that immanent act of preference in which we dispose of ourselves, and on which character depends. It is this that gives its *set* to the current of the soul, and determines the character of subsequent specific acts of preference and volition under it. It is an act of will, as distinguished from the feelings. It is either that impartial love which is commanded by the moral law; or a giving up of the soul to be governed by the propensities. It is at this point that we find moral freedom. That the ultimate point of responsibility must rest here, appears from the effect of such a preference in controlling the thoughts and modifying the feelings, and, as thought and feeling act and react upon each other, in changing the very principles of association. Nothing is so cunning of fence as such an underlying preference when anything would interfere with it. As already intimated, it may so control the laws of evidence as perceived by us, that a man shall really believe and act upon a lie, and mistake the reality of such belief for that genuine sincerity and coming to the light of which our Saviour speaks. Hence it is that a man may verily think that he is doing God service while he is persecuting his people, and doing his utmost to overthrow his cause in the earth.

The word "intention" is often used by moralists to indicate what is ultimate when they would reach the source of morality; but it does not do this. Intention refers to specific volition, and implies an opportunity, real or supposed, to carry out the intention. Hatred of a person whom we were sure we never could reach would not be an intention, nor would it give rise to any intention of injuring him. All intentions that indicate character spring from some form of settled preference, which may multiply itself in such intentions without number or exhaustion.

Hence this preference, which in the Scriptures is called the heart, is compared to a fountain.

At this point there seems to be a general agreement among writers on morals on three things: —

The first is, that man is responsible for his preferences, his choices, the acts of his will generally, — for these and their results, — and for nothing else. It will be found that those writers, as Edwards, who speak of man as responsible for the affections or heart, either regard these as synonymous with will, or as a part of it. Says Edwards, "The will and the affections of the soul are not two faculties; the affections are not essentially distinct from the will." There are, indeed, some whose language might lead us to suppose that they hold to an inherent moral quality in affections that are purely spontaneous; but on reflection it will be found impossible to attach responsibility to a being incapable of rational preference, and so of the choice of an end.

It is agreed, in the second place, that there is a broad distinction between what is called, sometimes an immanent preference, sometimes a governing purpose, sometimes an ultimate intention, and those volitions which are merely executive, and precede specific acts under such a purpose.

In the third place, it is agreed that character is as the governing preference or purpose — that it consists in an original and thorough determination by a man of himself with reference to some end chosen by him as supreme.

In connection with the choice of a supreme end all the phenomena of a moral life are evolved. In view of the end there arises, as has been said, a sense of obligation to choose it. From these two arise the idea of moral law; for moral law is the affirmation by reason of the obligation to act rationally. A divine law is the same law proclaimed by the authority of the Infinite Reason, and accompanied by sanctions. So is it that while the man is a law to himself, the divine law is recognized at once as the law of the inner life; and so will its full revelation, if the inner law has become obscured, be but as the clear light of day after the dim twilight. It will not be a thing wholly new and strange, but homogeneous, and but the increase and fulness of "that light that lighteth every man that cometh into the world." It is into this light that men may come more fully and walk in purity, or they may withdraw from it, and walk in darkness.

After the ideas of obligation and of law, must arise those of merit or demerit, of self-approbation or of self-condemnation, as the true end, or its alternative, has been chosen. Merit and demerit are supposed to arise chiefly in connection with something done outwardly, but if the end be chosen with a paramount affection, as a supreme end must be, outward acts according with the choice will follow of course. These simply indicate the strength of the inward principle, and in that is the only merit.

Again, in a sense of merit or demerit there is not only a present satisfaction or dissatisfaction, but a promise or a threat for the future, and these may become elements of great power. We thus get the notion of reward and punishment, and through these of responsibility, for, if there were no reward and no punishment, there could be no responsibility. It is at this point that the moral nature of man is connected with the government of God as outwardly revealed. If there were no consequences of acts in the way of rewards and punishments through the *will* of another we could not be under the government of that other, or responsible to him; and if those consequences should have no reference to merit or demerit, the government could not be moral.

Thus do we find, in immediate connection with the choice of a supreme end, the ideas of obligation and of moral law, of merit and demerit, of reward and punishment, and of responsibility. We find also the ideas of right and wrong. Properly these are always relative, expressing either fitness or unfitness, and having reference to an end. As such they are secondary; but they imply a moral quality when they indicate the fitness or unfitness of specific moral acts, or of the fundamental position of the heart with reference to the true and supreme end.

As the ideas and feelings just mentioned arise in our minds, a tribunal will be erected within us by which we shall be compelled to judge ourselves, and by which we shall also judge others in accordance with what we suppose to be the character of their radical choices. Without such a tribunal, and power and necessity of judgment, our moral nature would not be complete. There would be no answering of face to face, and we should not be linked in sympathy with the one great community of moral beings.

As illustrating the gradation and classification of ideas heretofore referred to, it may be well to say, at this point, that the highest forms and ideas of beauty and sublimity are also evolved as subsidiary, in connection with the choice of a supreme end and its results. In all working of unconscious and involuntary powers towards their end, and the facile mastery by them of the material to be used and the obstacles to be overcome, there is beauty. Virtue is the same thing when the powers are conscious and voluntary. Hence their deep affinity. There is no beauty of a ship with every sail set, speeding its way over the subject element to its haven, that can be compared with that of the organized powers of man acting in harmony, — those ruling that ought to rule, and those serving that ought to serve, and all conspiring to their destined end; nor is any storm in nature so sublime as the conflicts that may arise when temptation and opposition come between a true-hearted man and the attainment of his end.

It is somewhere in connection with the central act of choice now spoken of that conscience must be found. Of the discrepancy there is in the views respecting conscience, I spoke in the first lecture. This discrepancy cannot be removed at once, if at all. It arises from the intimate blending there is in this higher nature of the powers of knowing and of feeling, so that we may and do call the product indifferently an idea or a feeling. Thus we say, the idea of obligation, and the feeling of obligation. Hence some have regarded, and probably will continue to regard, conscience as comprising the whole moral nature. "The moral nature of man," says Dr. Alexander, of Edinburgh, in a learned article recently published in the Encyclopædia Britannica, — "the moral nature of man is summed up in the word conscience. Moral nature and conscience are two names of the same thing. The analysis of conscience, therefore, will unfold man's moral nature." I prefer a view which makes the operation of our moral nature more analogous to those of the other departments of our complex being. In all of them there was original provision for the right performance of their work; for a recognition of the character of that performance as normal or otherwise; and in that recognition for a sense of satisfaction or the reverse, which may be regarded as reward or punishment. So with the moral nature. It was intended that it, or rather the person, should work in accordance with his law. If he does so, there is in it a testifying state that is not only recognition, but approbation and reward. If he does not, there is also a testifying state that is disapprobation and punishment. Conscience, then, will involve a recognition by the person of the moral quality of his own acts or states, and the feelings consequent upon such recognition. It may be defined as that function of the moral reason by which it affirms obligation before the act, by which it approves or disapproves after the act, and by which it indicates future reward or punishment. Here, high as it is, we still see in it an analogy to appetite. In that, as in hunger, there is both impulse and discrimination, and there is subsequent pleasure or the reverse. To the prophetic power of conscience, however, appetite has nothing analogous. Conscience will then reveal itself as, 1st. Obligatory. 2d. Judicial. 3d. Prophetic. There will be, first, the affirmation of obligation before the act; second, the excusing or accusing by one another of the thoughts after the act; and, third, a promise or threat that becomes, on the one hand, a hope of eternal life, or, on the other, "a certain fearful looking for of judgment."

By many, by most, conscience is regarded as a separate faculty, and, as has been said, the whole of the moral nature. I prefer to say, as above, that it is a function of the moral reason. Besides affirming obligation to choose the true supreme end, the moral reason is that in the light of which it is chosen. It is that by which that end is recognized as supreme. The affirmation of obligation, as above stated, is what many mean by the apprehension of an ultimate right.

On this subject writers generally begin by assuming that there are actions having a moral quality, and regard the conscience or moral nature as that by which we perceive and become affected by that quality. But whence came the moral act? From a moral being certainly; and we should naturally suppose that those capacities by which a being could originate an act having a moral quality would be the leading part of his moral nature, rather than that by which he should perceive and become affected by the moral quality after it was originated. Is our moral nature that only by which we approve and condemn? Or is it that also by which we originate and do the things that we approve and condemn? We love God. By an act of our moral nature we approve ourselves in so doing. Is it by an act of our moral nature that we love him? I suppose it is. We do not love God because we are under obligation to, except as his worth and worthiness impose the obligation. We love him impartially because of his worth, and complacently because of his worthiness; and such love is from our moral nature, but not from conscience. If the states or forms of activity judged did not have a moral quality they could not be approved or condemned, and they belong to our moral nature in virtue of their having a moral quality. That also by which we judge belongs to our moral nature because it judges of moral quality.

In the order of nature there must be a moral being before there can be a moral act. But, as we have seen, a moral being is a person having moral reason and the moral ideas and affections necessarily originated by that, together with free will, which is implied as a condition for the formation of those ideas. In these is personality and a moral nature — the capacity of doing a moral act. But these are not conscience. That becomes possible only when there is a question respecting the conformity, future or past, of a being, already moral, to what either is, or is supposed to be his law.

A moral act is one that respects the supreme end. Any act which a man may either do or leave undone, and still stand in precisely the same relation to his supreme end, is not a moral act; and the moral nature will comprise, as I have said, all that is ultimately directive — the moral reason, the will, the personality, the man himself, that which does the moral act, as well as that which judges of it.

We may, then, regard the whole moral nature as consisting of those powers whose activity gives the moral quality, and also of those which judge of the moral quality and are affected by it; and it would conduce to perspicuity if the term conscience could be confined to the latter.

Of the moral quality itself which conscience presupposes, our notion is simple, as of color or extension. We perceive it immediately as belonging to certain states of mind, as selfishness, envy, malignity, on the one hand, and benevolence, generosity, and kindness, on the other. Relations may be needed to evolve the acts, but it is from no perception of them. It is from no sense, but is an immediate knowledge, by the spirit, of the quality of its own states and acts. We know a moral act as moral precisely as we know an intellectual act as intellectual. We know an intellectual act to be intellectual because it is an act of the intellect; and what an act of the intellect is, and that it is intellectual, every being having an intellect must know intuitively on the exercise of his intellect, and he could know it in no other way. Here is primitive knowledge, without which no definition could give the first elements of the knowledge of anything. It is in the same way that a moral act presupposes a moral constitution, and is known to have a moral quality.

In the definition of conscience the prophetic element requires special attention. It is important not only practically, but as proving the being of a personal God, and as connecting us with his government. Not only would it require a God with will and freedom, and an apprehension of moral distinctions, to originate a creature endowed with these, but without such a being as a rewarder and punisher, the idea of reward and punishment other than that which is natural and immediately inflicted, is nugatory. Without such a being it would be a practical absurdity — an eye without light, a part in nature without its counterpart, a falsehood in the very sanctuary of the moral nature of man.

In strictness I suppose the office of conscience to be to take cognizance of our own moral acts, and that a decision respecting those of others should be referred to the judgment. That this is its proper sphere appears from the fact that conscience was not originally, in our own language, and is not now in some others, distinguished from consciousness. It was consciousness *par eminence;* but on a subject like this, whatever may be thought of Hamilton's view of it, consciousness can respect only what passes within ourselves. In the common definitions and descriptions of conscience, powers are assigned it, as that of impulsion, and of rewarding and punishing, which must have reference solely to our own acts. This, too, would seem to be the scriptural idea. Paul says of the Gentiles, "Which show the work of the law written in their hearts," — that is, in their moral nature, — "their conscience also *bearing witness*, and their thoughts meanwhile accusing or else excusing one another." In all this there must have been reference solely to their own acts.

In thus finding a moral nature, and so a person, with the

power both of doing moral acts and of judging of them, we reach the highest form of created being. It is, doubtless, the highest possible, since there is in it the image of God, who is himself a person. We reach that for which all else is a condition, and which has, therefore, over all else, as below it, a natural supremacy. By a natural law "all sheep and oxen, yea, and the beasts of the field, and the fowl of the air, and the fish of the sea," are put "under the feet" of such a being. In the same way everything in his own system that is physical, or animal, or merely intellectual, must either be in subjection, or in disorder and rebellion. We now reach a form of activity that is a condition for nothing within the system, above itself, which has in itself and in its results not only *a* good, but *the* good, and the supreme good for man, and which can, therefore, be subject to no law of limitation.

In the exigencies of the present life it may happen that there shall be not only limitations, but exceptions to the laws of every subordinate portion of the system. The laws on which the welfare of the body depends may be disregarded, because the welfare of the body is not the highest good. There may be virtue, and even heroism, in disregarding them. But the laws of the moral nature cannot be thus disregarded. Than the end and good which these laws would secure, there can be nothing higher; there can therefore be no law to which these can give place; they can be subordinate to nothing, are always binding, have no exceptions, and the activity under them can never be in excess.

Having thus reached what is highest in man, we must, in accordance with our previous discussions, here find his true end and good. And here we do find it in the activity of the personality according to its law. What then is that law? The law of the subordinate faculties is, an activity for each upon its appropriate object up to the point at which it would interfere with some higher form of activity and good. Now, however, there can be no interference with anything higher. The law, therefore, of the highest faculties will be their highest possible *form* and *degree* of activity upon their appropriate objects. What, then, is the highest form of activity of which we are capable? By a fair analysis this has been shown to be *love*. What are the appropriate objects of love? They are God and our neighbor. What is the highest possible *degree* of this love? It is the love of God with all the heart, and of our neighbor as ourselves.

Here, then, do we have, after as full and fair an examination as I could give it, the human constitution itself uttering the substance of that law which was spoken in thunder four thousand years ago, and uttering, because it is impossible to find those more appropriate, the very words of Him who spoke as never man spoke, when he gave a summary of that law. Wonderful is it that his words should be the exact formula for the expression of the highest possible activity of the highest powers.

Thus, as in a former lecture we found that the teachings inwrought into the whole frame-work of nature were in perfect harmony with the constitution of man, so do we now find that the teachings of that constitution are themselves in perfect harmony with those of the revealed word of God. So is it that "deep calleth unto deep." So is man the connecting link between that which is lowest and that which is highest.

We have now answered the three questions put in the second lecture. The first was, What ought man to do? The answer was, To choose and seek the end for which

God made him. The second was, Why ought he to do it? The answer was, Because of the intrinsic good there is in the end. The third was, How ought he to do it? The answer is, By the highest activity of his lower powers according to the law of limitation; and by the full activity of his highest powers upon their appropriate objects. Does any one inquire more especially what this activity is? The answer is, Since we have shown the moral affections to be higher than the intellect, and since God is the highest and only adequate object of the affections, that it can consist only in the supreme love of God, and the impartial love of man.

LECTURE VIII.

RELATION OF VIRTUE TO HAPPINESS. — QUANTITY AND QUALITY OF GOOD. — MORAL AND NATURAL GOOD. — REGARD FOR OUR OWN GOOD. — CONNECTION WITH BENEVOLENCE. — ENJOYMENT FROM APPROBATION. — THE TRUE END OF MAN. — CONNECTION BETWEEN MORAL AND NATURAL GOOD.

The identity which we found in the last lecture between the teaching of the constitution of man and the law of God was not sought. The result was reached because the analysis would go there. I was myself surprised at the exactness of the coincidence. The formula we reached for the end and good of man was the highest possible activity of the highest powers upon their appropriate objects. Love has been shown to be the highest form of activity; and how readily and perfectly the law of God takes the form of the above expression will be seen if we observe that no love of him can be greater than that with all the heart, and no love of our neighbor can be greater than that we should love him as ourselves.

It is a grand and beautiful thing thus to begin, as we have done, at the foundation of this lower creation, and to follow it upward as its stories rise one upon another till they culminate in man, and then to hear from his constitution an articulate utterance identical with an utterance from heaven that comes down to meet it. So is man fitted to be a being, as Milton says, —

"Commercing with the skies."

The teachings of the constitution, or of natural law, being

thus identified with those of the revealed law, it would now be in order to go on and evolve the specific duties that would flow from this law as applied in the various relations of life. This might be done, as it generally has been, in the light of that disposition which would lead us to do good to all men; or, more properly, as more in accordance with the preceding course of thought, in the light of ends. The duties of man to himself and to God would then be determined in the light of his end as a creature of God; his duties in the family in its various relations would be determined by the end of the family, and his duties to society by the end of society. And this it was my purpose at one time to do; but that would be beaten ground; the time would not be adequate, and there are still speculative questions of interest, that are also practical, that require our attention. We need particularly just now to analyze this love with reference to certain general conceptions that have been formed, and their harmony with each other. We need to inquire after the relations to each other of holiness or virtue, and happiness.

The revealed law is practical. It applies its precepts directly to a person; it says *thou;* and it requires duties to be performed towards persons. The objects are God and our neighbor. But the mind forms necessarily certain general conceptions. These are represented by general terms having no reality or one thing in nature corresponding to them, but simply the notion as it is formed in different minds, and which may vary much, both in its content and in its distinctness. The general notion of property may be in some minds clear, in others indistinct; in some it may be represented by land, in others by stocks. These general terms, formed by abstraction, and thus varying in their significance in different minds, have been thrown into the arena of discussion, and bandied about endlessly. So will they continue to be; the terms, as we may hope and believe, becoming in the mean time more definite, the conceptions of men in connection with them more distinct, and their relations with each other better established.

Such conceptions, those too which have been the subject of much discussion, we shall find involved in the general formula already reached. Those to which I refer are the conceptions of holiness and of happiness. What is needed is that these should be uniform and distinct in the minds of men, and that their relations to each other should be clearly seen. There is a natural feeling that virtue, or holiness, and happiness ought to be united. Moral order seems to require this. In this world they appear to be often separated, and hence the strangeness of that state in which this world is.

That holiness and happiness can be identified as objects of pursuit is denied by Kant, and it is in their separation that he finds what he calls the "antinomy" of the practical reason. According to him "the connection between them is not causal." "Man is bound to pursue virtue; man cannot but pursue happiness; and yet neither are these identical, nor does the one lead to the other." Of old the doctrine of the Epicureans was that "to be consciously influenced by maxims that lead to happiness, is virtue." The doctrine of the Stoics, and the opposite of this, was, that "to be conscious of virtue is happiness." "The identification of happiness with duty," says Whewell, "on merely philosophical grounds, is a question of great difficulty." Possibly our past discussions may throw some light on this point.

In estimating enjoyment or good, regard must be had to

both quantity and quality. The quantity from any given susceptibility or power will be as its normal activity. The quality will be as the rank, according to the gradation heretofore indicated, of the susceptibility or power. There are, I know, those who say that the only difference in respect to enjoyment is in degree. So Paley thought. They say that the enjoyment of the glutton is just as excellent and valuable as that of the saint or angel. Do you believe this? Do you think that any amount of swinish enjoyment could be weighed against one hour of the clear comprehension of God and his works, and of sinless and fervent love? I greatly mistake if there be not in the common consciousness of men, as there is expressed in their language, a feeling of gradation in respect to enjoyments that corresponds substantially with the order of the faculties as heretofore explained. When, however, we come to the moral nature, as we there make a leap in respect to the order of the faculties, so do we in respect to the kind of enjoyment. As we now come to have faculties like those of the angels, and are made in the image of God, so do we become capable of enjoyments like those of the angels and of God. Between such enjoyment and that of an animal, or of our own animal nature, there is as much difference in dignity and worth as there is between an angel and an animal. Here only do we find moral and spiritual enjoyments; here approbation and disapprobation; here the consciousness of worth.

The above being premised, we say that the natural law and formula for the highest *enjoyment* is the highest possible activity of the highest powers upon their appropriate objects. We say, also, that the formula for *virtue* is the highest normal activity of the moral powers. But *the moral powers are also the highest powers*, and hence the highest enjoyment must be in and from the same activity in which virtue consists. If, then, they may not be said to be identical, they are inseparably connected by a natural law, as much so as the light is with the sun. It is one of the properties and characteristics of the sun by which we define it, and as God made it, that it gives forth light; and it is one of the properties and characteristics of virtue as we always conceive of it, and as God intended it should be, that it gives forth its own natural, inseparable, peculiar enjoyment. It is an enjoyment that belongs to it, and inheres in it, as the property in its substance; so that the Stoics were right in saying that "the consciousness of virtue *is* happiness."

This brings us to the distinction between what may be called moral good and that which is merely natural. Moral good is that which is immediately, and by a natural law, connected with the normal activity of the moral powers; natural good is that which comes from the activity of any of the susceptibilities or powers below those that are moral. They are alike in being instances under the general law that there is from the activity of each faculty its own enjoyment; and in that sense both are natural; but what I have called moral good is not only the product of the moral powers, — it has peculiarities well worthy of notice, and such as to fit it to be *the* good of the race.

One of these is its independence. By this I mean that it is wholly within the control of the man himself. This arises from the fact that moral good is from the direct activity of the will itself, and not from the activity of those faculties that depend on the will. Tyranny may fetter the limbs; want of discipline may render the faculties indocile; but virtue consists in the voluntary acts themselves, and in those voluntary dispositions which lead to the acts, that is, in the activity of the will. This is central to the man. It is the man himself acting, and nothing can come between him and it, together with its natural results. It is not these results that are meant when we say we will do right and leave the result with God. These we conceive of as included in doing right. It may even be doubted whether, moral beings existing, the results could have been otherwise. The dispositions and volitions are one thing, the command of the faculties through which these express themselves is another. In the one is character; in the other ability. Any object of our desires we may be prevented by external circumstances from obtaining; but no will of another, no violence or imprisonment, no external circumstance can come between a man and his voluntary dispositions, together with the blessedness there may be from their activity.

This puts the highest interest of every man into his own power. If he have confidence in God, it gives him a rational ground on which he can stand and be a martyr. Here is a citadel that can never be forced; if it surrender, the man himself must open the gates. In respect to this, the exhortation may be fairly given as against any external influence, "Hold that fast which thou hast, that no man take thy crown." It is in this power of man thus to resist, in his allegiance to virtue and to God, all solicitation and all violence, that his true greatness is found.

It is at this point, as the will is differently related to the grounds of its action, that moral beauty and moral sublimity arise. When the propensities and faculties yield themselves in ready and glad coincidence with the virtuous will, when other moral agents conspire with it, and nature is accordant, there is moral beauty. There is no temptation then, and the current of the soul flows on without a ripple. But when the propensities and faculties are refractory, when they solicit to evil, and would fain rebel; when example and authority are against us so that integrity would require resistance unto death, then, if the will remain firm, there is moral sublimity. In the one case the element is spontaneity, consent, and harmony of action; in the other it is force, struggle, victory. In both there is a sense of dignity, of freedom, and self-direction. There is the joy of the young eagle when he poises himself on his own pinions, and that something more which the eagle cannot feel that is involved in self-approbation and a consciousness of merit.

This leads us to a second peculiarity of moral good. It is that it is necessarily accompanied by a sense of approbation. This is an element wholly unknown till we reach the action of the moral powers. Up to this point we have a pleasure in all excellence; we admire it; but when we reach moral excellence, admiration becomes approbation. This gives a pleasure entirely distinct from that naturally connected with moral goodness. In the love of God or of man there is an enjoyment wholly distinct from the approbation. *That* is in view of the love, and subsequent to it. Love and hatred have in them respectively the elements of happiness and of misery, aside from any subsequent act of approbation or disapprobation. It is in these subsequent acts that we find a consciousness by the spirit of its own state as it is, or is not conformed to the law of its being, involving a feeling of self-approbation and hope, or of self-condemnation and of an indefinite dread. As virtue is in the states and acts of the will, so, if there be candor, the eye of conscience is directly fixed upon these states and acts; and so distinct at times do these sentiments of approval and condemnation become that they seem like the product of a second personality within us, recording our deeds, passing sentence upon them, and giving dim forebodings of a coming and more perfect judgment. This is, indeed, the great, and almost the only evidence from nature of a future retribution; at least, it is that without which no other would have any weight. Here, then, in connection with moral good, we have a new and striking element, and one which we should suppose could hardly fail to direct men to that as their chief good. This approbation is not, as is sometimes supposed, the good itself, but comes in as the accompaniment, the sanction and heightener of that good.

A third peculiarity of moral good is that in seeking it for ourselves we necessarily promote the good of others. We thus find a coalescence of what is called self-love with benevolence, and of interest with duty. In this perfect coalescence and harmony is the point of reconciliation between what have been called the selfish and the benevolent systems of morals. By some it has been held that all virtue has its origin in a regard for our own good; by some that it consists in a regard to the good of others. The true system is found in the coincidence of the two; and that becomes possible only from the peculiarity of moral good now mentioned.

This point requires attention, not only because different and seemingly opposite systems have sprung from it, but also because there has been in the public mind, to some extent, a wrong estimate of what has been called self-love, or rather of the right and the duty of every man to seek his own highest good. As indicating this right and duty, self-love has not been a fortunate term. It has not always been clearly distinguished from selfishness, and, if not positively wrong, has been supposed to be less noble and worthy than benevolence. Both the element of duty that is in it, which ennobles all things, and that of beneficence, which is also in it, have been overlooked. To exhort men to love themselves has been supposed to be a work of supererogation, if not positively wrong. We need, therefore, to say a word on this point, and then to show how the two coalesce.

If the terms are rightly understood, we need not hesitate in saying that a man cannot love himself too much. Does this startle any one who has been accustomed to a particular form of phraseology? I would ask him whether he thinks we can love others too much? If not, neither can we ourselves, since the love of ourselves is made in Scripture, as it must be by reason, the measure of our love to others. "Thou shalt love thy neighbor as thyself." Let a man then love himself as much as he will, only let him love his neighbor as much. Let him love his neighbor as much as he will, only let him love himself as much. This is the Bible doctrine, and in this equal and impartial love the good of the whole will be provided for, since both the individual and his neighbor are equal factors in making up the great sum of good.

Again, that it is the duty of the individual to seek his own highest good is involved in his structure. He would be a reproach to his Maker if it were not. It has already been seen to be the characteristic of a rational being to act with reference to an end. But an end can be sought rationally only as there is in it an apprehended good. It would seem, therefore, that the idea of good must be among our primitive and elementary ideas, as much so at least as that of an end. It will probably be found to result at once, immediately, and always, from any normal activity of the powers. Without a supreme good, man would be a contradiction and an absurdity. If there were no good for man he could do nothing for himself, and nothing could be done for him. Without a rational conception of good there could be no rational activity; and that which is thus at the basis of all action of the rational powers we may well suppose to be primitive. In the analysis by Cousin of our moral ideas, he says that those of merit and demerit, of justice and injustice, of right and wrong, must precede those of reward and punishment. This is true, but it does not follow that they must precede the idea of good in general. The idea of good certainly underlies those of reward and punishment; but since justice must consist in bestowing good and inflicting evil, it would seem that it must underlie that also, and that there can no more be a conception of justice and injustice in general without that of some end or good, than there can be one of commercial justice and injustice without that of an exchangeable value. But that the ideas of justice and injustice are natural and necessary, no one doubts.

In connection with this idea of good there must be some tendency towards it, or there could be no harmony in the being himself, and we could have no conception of him as acting morally. Towards the supreme good there must have been some constitutional impulse, as well as towards those that are lower, since it must have been intended for a motive, and for that mere comprehension would not suffice. It may indeed be doubted whether good could be conceived of as good, without such a tendency. This tendency may have become enfeebled, obscured, confused; but no philosophy of ends could be conceived of without it, and unless the nature be hopelessly ruined something of it must remain. For a nature thus ruined, all attempts at a philosophy of itself would be simple bewilderment.

This tendency is always implied both in speculation and in action. By many it has been called a rational instinct. Archbishop Leighton went so far as to use for it the term "*appetite.*" "Actual or formal felicity," says he, "is the full possession and enjoyment of that complete and chief good (that, namely, which most perfectly supplies all the wants and satisfies all the cravings of our rational *appetites*)." Of this tendency McLaurin says, "God has implanted in us that *thirst* after complete happiness which is the spring of men's actions; and since the above-mentioned faculty of reason shows where that thirst may be satisfied, the direct tendency of both, if duly approved, would be to lead the soul to the eternal fountain of all good." It was of this that the schoolmen were wont to say, "In beatitudinem fertur voluntas, non ut voluntas, sed ut natura"—"The will is borne towards happiness, not as will, but as nature." This is what was meant by the psalmist king, in whom this tendency worked in the light, when he said, "My soul thirsteth for God, for the living God." "My heart and my flesh crieth out for the living God." This it is which creates the restlessness of many,—a deep and underlying dissatisfaction, often cropping out at the surface, with every form of inferior good, and which makes the knowledge of God, in and from whom is the supreme good, like cold water to the thirsty soul. This it is the inspiration of which all feel at times lifting them mysteriously, like a mighty ground swell, and intimating a connection with that which is spiritual, infinite, and eternal. There is in this a commitment of each to himself, that each may work out in himself the great end of all.

If to this inherent tendency and native correlation to

good we add the provision made by God for it; if we remember that he wishes our good, and how strongly he has expressed that wish in giving us the capacity and making such provision for its gratification; if we reflect, too, that the very end of God in the whole will be defeated if his creatures decline the good for which they were made, we shall see how sacred is the duty laid upon every man to accept of all the good that God gives, and to seek for all that he provides. Has he indeed given us capacities for good, great capacities? Has he provided for their gratification? Has he made our acceptance and attainment of that good a condition of our benefiting others? Has he even offered himself as the correlate of those faculties, so that we may love him, and find our good in that love,— what obligation can be more sacred than to acknowledge our sense of his goodness by accepting all that he gives, just as he gives it, and rejoicing in it?

Having thus seen that it is our duty to secure our own highest good, let us see how, in so doing, we shall promote the good of others, as we have already seen how, in promoting the good of others, that is, in loving them, we promote our own. When the laws of God are observed there is no clashing of interests, but the reverse. It is a great principle, and the gain would be immense if it could be thoroughly incorporated into the minds of the people, that the highest good of each man or nation is more conducive than anything else could be to the highest good of all.

This results from the nature of the highest good, which is such that the enjoyment of it by one heightens instead of diminishing that of others. It is not like a feast, of which he who eats consumes that which might have been enjoyed by another; but rather like a musical concert, where each new performer, with voice and instrument accordant, adds something to the harmony, and to the joy of all. This it does, first, because, as the highest good consists in loving, and as "love works no ill to his neighbor," but all good, and good only, it will follow that there must be an identity of the two. The direct tendency and result of a virtuous love is the happiness both of the person loving and of those beloved. No one can truly love without doing good to those beloved; and no one can truly love without being made happy in so doing.

But, second, moral good can be sought only in and through moral goodness. But the more moral goodness there is in any individual, the more will others feel complacency in him, the more approve him, and the more will he be a source of light and a ground of joy. He who seeks his own good in moral goodness, not only lays a foundation for his own increasing good as his goodness increases, but also for the higher good of the whole system with which he is connected. There is no way of doing good so effectual as to increase our own moral goodness. We thus increase the material of happiness, and lay the foundation of that subtle and most efficient of all influences, an unconscious influence.

A distinction has been drawn between the enjoyment there is from a moral act, as love, and that from the subsequent approbation. This is here worthy of special notice. The enjoyment of the agent who does a good moral act is heightened by the approbation which follows it; but such an act is not approved by the agent alone. Whenever and wherever a rational and moral being may become cognizant of the act, he also will approve it, *and in approval there is joy*. Approbation — moral complacency — there are few higher joys than from these. In them is the foundation for the highest sympathy, and esteem, and friendship. Perhaps we do not sufficiently reflect on the immense change that is wrought in the character of our happiness, and in all our relations, by the addition to the natural good of good moral acts, of this of approbation. It is that by which moral beings have an interest in each other as such, and become a community, a society, instead of a herd. The addition of this element is like that of light to the heavenly bodies. We may suppose them hanging or floating in space without light. There could then be no recognition or watchfulness of sympathy. But let light be added, let an interchange of rays be passing throughout all space, giving to the heavens their beauty, and proclaiming momently how well each observes the law of its movement, and we shall have some illustration of the change wrought by the coming in of this element of approbation and moral complacency. If we suppose a new star to be lighted up in space we see at once that it will be in sympathy with the rest, and that the brighter it is the more light the rest must receive, and the more will they rejoice in it. And so it must be with moral goodness. The more there is of it, and so of moral good, in any one, the more material and ground must there be for the happiness of others. "They that be wise shall shine as the brightness of the firmament; and they that turn many to righteousness, as the stars forever and ever."

So do we, in adopting moral good as an end, harmonize and identify what has been called self-love with benevolence; interest with duty; the highest possible regard for our own good with the highest possible regard for the good of others.

From the above discussion it appears that moral good is broadly distinguished from all other, and that its peculiarities are such that it is fitted to be the highest good. It is, first, independent. It is wholly within the power of the individual. The world cannot give or take it away. It is beyond the reach of violence or fraud. In this it is strongly contradistinguished from all other good. Second, it is accompanied with approbation. This may be regarded as the voice of God expressing his wish that this good should be sought, and is in itself an entirely new element of good. And, third, the activity required for its attainment is identical with that which is required for the general good. In the pursuit of it the interests of the individual and of the community become one. To such moral good we say, in opposition to Kant, that goodness, or virtue, or holiness, does stand in a causal relation; and that it is the only possible cause, since it can be only in and from that specific form of activity.

Do we say, then, to close this discussion in the terms with which we started,—do we say that the end for man is happiness? No. The good here, the highest good, is from the normal activity of the moral powers. As such, that activity is obedience to the law of God, however revealed. It is all that can be commanded or directly willed, or that can be approved and honored. It is virtue; it is holiness. Do we, then, say that virtue or holiness is the end for man? No; for in this holiness there is a blessedness wholly distinctive and peculiar, higher, purer, nobler than any other; a blessedness like that of God himself, and as inseparable from the holiness as its light is from the sun. Not, then, in happiness without holiness do we say is the true end for man, for without that the happiness could not be; not in holiness without happiness, for without that the holiness could not be and be holiness, any more than the sun could be the sun without its light. But we do say that the true end for man is HOLY HAPPINESS, that is,

BLESSEDNESS. Not the oxygen alone do we need, not the hydrogen alone, but the water, — that living water of which if a man drink he shall never thirst.

Since, then, blessedness, as now defined, is the true good for man as man, and so for all rational and moral beings, it will be the end of man to increase the sum of blessedness; and virtue will consist in a supreme purpose to promote this impartially and in the highest degree.

The true end of man is not to be found wholly in his subserviency to others; and it is no more to be found in himself than the end of a stone, with its faces hewn and fitted to be joined with others in a building, is to be found in itself. The end of such a stone would be to be fitted in with others as a part of the building, and if the stone were rational it would seek as its end its own place, and would rest there. So man, being capable of comprehending and choosing the good of the whole as an end, is capable of choosing his individual happiness and end in harmony with that, as a part of that, and as being possible of attainment only in connection with that.

But it is only through *love* that man is so adjusted as to fill his place in harmony with others in a perfect society; for, in loving, that is, in choosing the good of the whole, man chooses his own good, and in choosing his own good as consisting in loving, he chooses the good of the whole.

The difficulty here has resulted from a false conception of interest. If this had always been conceived of as the highest activity of the highest powers, there would have been no supposed opposition between interest and duty.

The difficulty in indicating the full end for man by any single form of expression arises from its complexity. That he was designed to promote intentionally the blessedness of others there can be no doubt. This he is capable of doing from a rational estimate of it, and from love. As little doubt can there be that he was designed to be himself blessed; and he is capable of promoting his own blessedness for its own sake. Further, there can be no doubt that in doing these he was designed to glorify God. This, also, he is capable of doing intentionally, and this he will do just in proportion as he promotes the blessedness of others and is himself blessed, because the blessedness of the creature arises from that manifestation of the perfections of God which is his declarative glory. In aiming at either of these most would agree that man would act rightly, and that in promoting the three to the highest possible extent his whole end would be found. Are these then three ends? Perhaps we may say that; still the tendency and effort has always been to find a single form of expression that should include the three. This has been encouraged by the peculiar manner in which these are involved in each other, since no one can promote his own blessedness without promoting that of others, or can promote either except by glorifying God.

In the Bible form of statement the three elements are involved. The love of God and our neighbor is made most prominent, but when it is said, "Thou shalt love thy neighbor as thyself," there is implied the regard for self in just the right proportion.

In the form adopted by the Westminster divines we have also the three elements. "To glorify God, and *enjoy* him," are combined as one end. This is substantially right, since we can glorify God only by loving and obeying him, and since, in thus loving and obeying, we shall do what we may to secure the blessedness of all other creatures.

The form adopted by Edwards is, that virtue consists in

the love of being. This includes the three elements, and, if taken literally, much more.

In the same way we include the three elements when we say, as above, —

1st. That the end of man is to increase the sum of blessedness, and,

2d. That virtue consists in a supreme purpose to promote blessedness impartially, and in the highest possible degree.

3d. This being the end for which God made man, he is glorified just in proportion as man seeks that end.

Having thus placed moral good in its rightful supremacy as the highest good, and having found in it the point of coalescence for individual and general good, to complete the subject we need to see its relations to natural good. The two are not immediately and necessarily connected. As we have seen, moral goodness is the choosing by a free being of his true end, together with all subordinate acts and choices involved in that. Moral good is the enjoyment inseparably connected with such choice. It holds the same relation to the activity of the moral powers that natural good does to that of the other powers, and is in no proper sense a reward of moral goodness. There is in it that which is meant when it is said that virtue is its own reward. But, properly speaking, reward is natural good conferred by the will of another on account of moral goodness. On the other hand, moral badness, or wickedness, is the choice by a free being of any other than his true end, and the acts under such choice. Moral evil, or suffering (for it is here used for that), is the suffering inseparably connected with such choice; and punishment is natural evil inflicted on account of such badness or wickedness. These, that is, moral good and evil, follow moral goodness and wickedness as the shadow the substance. Between moral goodness and a certain joy and approbation and hope the connection is as immediate and inseparable as any under the laws of nature, and more so; between wickedness, the lie, the fraud, and a moral deterioration, a stain, a foreboding of evil, the connection is as immediate and close as between putting the finger in the fire and being burned, and more so. This effect of wickedness upon his innermost being no man can escape, and therefore no wicked man can be, in the highest sense, prosperous. But this effect is invisible, and in this life incomplete. It is possible for a man to conceal it in a measure from himself, and wholly from others; especially if there be in the mind, as there commonly is, such a perversion that moral good is comparatively disregarded, and the possession of natural good is made the standard of happiness.

There is here then no antinomy, to adopt the phraseology of Kant, between virtue and happiness. If that exist anywhere, it is between moral goodness and natural good. Here there is, if not an opposition, yet a want of harmony that has always given to this world the aspect of a moral enigma. External advantages, natural good, are often possessed by the wicked and not by the good, and the distribution of them is so far promiscuous as to jar upon our moral sentiments, and perhaps to lead us to question the existence of any moral government. In the oldest book extant the inquiry is made, "Wherefore do the wicked prosper, become old, yea, mighty in power?" More than a thousand years afterwards the complaint was, "They overpass the deeds of the wicked; they judge not the cause,—the cause of the fatherless; yet they prosper."

And the same is the complaint of to-day. Says Coleridge, —

> "How seldom, friend, a good great man inherits
> Honor and wealth with all his worth and pains.
> It seems a story from the world of spirits,
> When any man obtains that which he merits,
> Or any merits that which he obtains."

Such passages show what the mind naturally regards as moral order. It is that natural good should follow in the train of moral goodness and wait upon it everywhere as the satellite upon its primary. But this it does not. It is often the reverse. Often natural good becomes the tempter of man to lure him from virtue, and often he is compelled, if he would be virtuous, not only to renounce natural good, but to suffer the extremest natural evils, even the loss of life itself. Not only does moral goodness fail to produce natural good, — it often becomes incompatible with it.

To relieve the jar thus made upon our moral sentiments philosophy points us to the fact that each natural as well as moral law is independent, and that obedience to each gives its own separate and specific good. Be benevolent, it is said, and you shall have the rewards of benevolence; but if you violate the laws of temperance, your benevolence will not and ought not to prevent your paying the penalty. The view is that men get what they earn, and that if they do not choose to pay for a good, they should not complain if they do not get it. Says Mrs. Barbauld, in an essay upon Inconsistency in our Expectations, "We should consider this world as a great mart of commerce, where fortune exposes to our view various commodities, — riches, ease, tranquillity, fame, integrity, knowledge. Everything is marked at a settled price. Our time, our labor, our ingenuity, are so much ready money, which we are to lay out to the best advantage. Examine, compare, choose, reject; but stand to your own judgment; and do not, like children, when you have purchased one thing, repine that you do not possess another which you did not purchase. Such is the force of well-regulated industry that a steady and vigorous exertion of our faculties, directed to one end, will generally insure success. Would you, for instance, be rich? Do you think that single point worth the sacrificing everything else to? You may then be rich. Thousands have become so from the lowest beginnings, by toil and patient diligence, and attention to the minutest article of expense and profit. But you must give up the pleasures of leisure, of a vacant mind, of a free, unsuspicious temper. If you preserve your integrity, it must be a coarse-spun and vulgar honesty. Those high and lofty notions of morals which you brought with you from the schools must be considerably lowered, and mixed with the baser alloy of a jealous and worldly-minded prudence. You must learn to do hard, if not unjust things; and for the nice embarrassments of a delicate and ingenuous spirit, it is necessary for you to get rid of them as fast as possible. You must shut your heart against the muses, and be content to feed your understanding with plain household truths. In short, you must not attempt to enlarge your ideas, or polish your taste, or refine your sentiments; but must keep on in one beaten track, without turning aside either to the right hand or to the left. 'But I cannot submit to drudgery like this; I feel a spirit above it.' 'Tis well; be above it, then; only do not repine that you are not rich."

"The man whose tender sensibility of conscience and strict regard to the rules of morality make him scrupulous and fearful of offending, is often heard to complain of the disadvantages he lies under in every path of honor and profit. 'Could I but get over some nice points, and conform to the practice and opinion of those about me, I might stand as fair a chance as others for dignities and preferment.' And why can you not? What hinders you from discarding this troublesome scrupulosity of yours which stands so grievously in your way? If it be a small thing to enjoy a healthful mind sound at the very core, that does not shrink from the keenest inspection; inward freedom from remorse and perturbation; unsullied whiteness and simplicity of manners; a genuine integrity

Pure in the last recesses of the mind; —

if you think these advantages an inadequate recompense for what you resign, dismiss your scruples this instant, and be a slave-merchant, a parasite, or what you please."

There is good sense in this. Perhaps it is the best view that philosophy can take; it is substantially the view of Combe, in his Constitution of Man. But then there is in it no vindication of a state of things in which vice so often and so greatly gains outward advantage, and in which virtue and piety are not merely left destitute of what they may not choose to bargain for, — to which there would not be so much objection, — but are compelled, if they would remain virtue and piety, to submit to the loss of all things, and to suffer whatever the physical nature may be capable of suffering. Of such cases the world has been full, and for these philosophy has no solution. They point to the future. The constitution and course of nature, with the moral phenomena which it envelops and enshrines, does not furnish data for its own explanation. As the solution is not from itself, it can neither know of it, nor have organs to utter it. If the course of things were to go on forever as it does now, this world, in its relation to the moral constitution of man, would forever remain an inexplicable enigma. So far as I can judge, neither a moral government, nor a moral governor, nor the existence of any being worthy to be called God, could be proved. No; the solution can come only from the future. This Coleridge felt; for, while he recognizes the incompatibility just spoken of, and so assigns to the good great man only the natural rewards of goodness and greatness, yet the friends he gives him are such as to show that he did not suppose the solution of the problem to be here.

"What woulds't thou have a good, great man obtain?
Wealth, title, dignity, a golden chain,
Or heaps of corses which the sword hath slain?
Goodness and greatness are not means, but ends.
Hath he not always treasure, always friends,
The good great man? Three treasures, — love, and light,
And calm thoughts, equable as infant's breath;
And three fast friends more sure than day or night, —
Himself, his Maker, and the angel Death?"

This relation of moral goodness to natural good may doubtless be justified in a temporary dispensation. It brings new elements into the divine administration; it trains virtue as it could not be otherwise. It is at the basis of moral sublimity and heroism. The object is the enthronement of the moral nature. Let that be fully done, and there comes the subjection, and subordination, and right action of all the other parts of our nature, and consequently all possible natural good from that. Here, so far as natural good can arise from the harmony and right action of all the powers of the individual, do we find the natural, and, indirectly, causal relation between moral goodness and natural good. With the rule of the moral nature must come all temperance, all kindness, all harmonies of the individual system, and so all the good it can give. Here is no antinomy between moral goodness and natural good. Naturally there is none. The present relation and arrangement is clearly a derangement, and such an one that the moral nature can never be satisfied till the adverse influence of evil shall be eliminated and separated from the good, and till external nature shall be so re-adjusted that all her substances, agencies, laws, forces, influences, shall come into accord with the laws of a higher sphere, and shall offer themselves always and everywhere as the servants of goodness. This, and this only, is the natural relation between moral goodness and natural good, and thus do we harmonize the two.

LECTURE IX.

THE SPHERE OF MORAL SCIENCE. — RIGHT AND WRONG. — DEFINITION OF TERMS. — PROVINCE OF CONSCIENCE. — HOW FAR INFALLIBLE. — TWO SPHERES. — DIVERSITY OF MORAL JUDGMENTS. — CRISES OF LIFE. — RELATION OF CONSCIENCE TO OTHER PRINCIPLES OF ACTION. — COMPLEXITY OF MOTIVES. — AFFECTIONS HAVE A MORAL CHARACTER IN THEMSELVES.

HAVING now examined the moral constitution, we are in a position to discriminate more perfectly the true sphere of moral science.

In examining an outward act of a moral being and seeking to determine its character, we may either go backward to its source, or forward to its consequences. In one or the other of these we must find the sphere of the science; for though actions are often spoken of as if they had a moral quality in themselves, yet aside from their origin or their consequences this is not conceivable.

If we go back to the source of the act we find that moral constitution which we have considered. We find a person capable of doing moral acts, and of judging of them, and it is in some mode of his activity that we find the moral quality. In connection with this we find the terms virtuous, vicious, goodness, wickedness, morally good, morally evil. In connection with these there are invisible consequences upon the spirit itself which affect the character, and which we think of as necessary.

If we go forward to the outward consequences of the

act, we find a conformity or want of conformity to fixed relations, together with the terms utility, injuriousness, general consequences, and more generally, though they are, as we have seen, applied in the other direction, the terms right and wrong. An action is good because its source is good. "Make the tree good, and his fruit will be good." It is right because it is conformed to a rule or law based on a recognition of relations, and so, adapted to attain its end. But the terms right and wrong have often been so applied, now to indicate moral quality as belonging to a person, and now to indicate a conformity or want of conformity to fixed outward relations, as to produce much confusion.

Thus it is said in the most popular work on morals published in this country,* that "Moral philosophy takes it for granted that there is in human action a moral quality; that is, that a human action may be right or wrong." Here, for an action to be right or wrong, and to have a moral quality, is the same thing. Again, in another part of the work: "From these facts we are easily led to the distinction between right and wrong, and innocence and guilt. Right and wrong depend upon the relations under which beings are created, and hence the obligations resulting from these relations are, in their nature, fixed and unchangeable. Guilt and innocence depend upon a knowledge of these relations." . . "An action may be wrong; but if the actor have no means of knowing it to be wrong he is held morally guiltless in the doing of it. Or, again, a man may have a consciousness of obligation, and a sincere desire to act in conformity to it, and may, from ignorance of the way in which that obligation is to be discharged, perform an act in its nature wrong, yet, if he have acted

* Wayland's Moral Science.

according to the best of his possible knowledge, he may not only be held guiltless, but even virtuous."

Here, then, is an act that is virtuous and also wrong. Which, now, of these words expresses the moral quality of the act? Virtuous, certainly. All usage would show this; and we are also told by the same author that the moral quality of an act resides in the intention. Here we have the words right and wrong used to indicate moral quality, and we have also a formal statement that they depend upon abstract relations which have no necessary connection with moral quality; so that an action may be right and vicious, wrong and virtuous, at the same time. But an investigation of "intention," on which moral quality is said to depend, is one thing; and an investigation of "the relations under which beings are created," on which right and wrong are said to depend, is an entirely different thing.

Which, then, of these is it, or is it both, that moral philosophy investigates? It has sometimes been one, sometimes the other; but I suppose that moral philosophy properly stops where there is no longer any moral quality; that moral quality is found only in mind, and that the study of relations, and so of right and wrong as depending on them, can be useful only as furnishing guidance for the action of principles already formed. He who studies these relations that he may act in accordance with them, does it because he is already virtuous.

In a philosophy making the idea of choice and that of an end central, the term good becomes prominent, rather than the term right. "The True," "The Beautiful," and "The Good," says Cousin; not, as his own philosophy would require, The Right. Both words are indispensable, and both are liable to analogous ambiguities, so that it is difficult to use either in one uniform sense. Used as adjectives, and where no moral quality is implied, the general rule is that the term good is applied to things, and expresses that quality of the thing by which it is adapted to the use for which it was designed; while the term right is applied to acts, and expresses such a mode of using the thing as will accomplish the particular end designed. Thus, we say a good pen, meaning a pen adapted to write well; a good axe, meaning an axe adapted to cut. But of any use of the pen in writing, or of the axe in cutting, by which they fail to accomplish their end, we say that it is not right. Of any action not having moral quality, and adapted to accomplish its end, we say, that was right. This is the general rule, and those exceptions in which the word right is applied to things prove the rule. Thus a right line is that which is the most direct between two points; the right road is that which will take a man to the proposed end of his journey, though it may be as far as possible from being a good one. The right man in the right place is the man that will do the work of that place.

When moral quality is involved, and these terms are used as adjectives, good is applied to both persons and actions; right to actions only. We say, a good man, and a good act. But when we say a right act, having sole reference to moral quality, we mean the same as when we say a good act. More generally, however, even here, the word right, instead of looking backward to the source of the act, looks forward to its outward consequences, and often it is doubtful which way it was intended to look. Here is the ambiguity.

Used as nouns, good expresses some form of enjoyment; right is defined to mean "conformity to the perfect standard, rectitude, straightness;" that is, conduct adapted to attain the true end. With the article, as, "the Right," the term is hardly naturalized with us yet. Generally, when used as a noun in morals, the word right is employed in a connection wholly different, as when we speak of rights, and say that a man has a right to his estate, or speak of the doctrine of rights.

Having considered the source of moral actions, and thus the province of moral science, we next inquire after that of conscience.

And, first, the primary activity of conscience is not directly from the will, or what the will makes it to be. It is not, therefore, of the nature of virtue or vice, but from the constitution, as made by God. The fact, therefore, that man possesses a conscience has nothing to do with his character as good or bad. That he should have a conscience as a part of his moral nature is simply a condition of moral character of any kind. Plain as this may appear, the possession of conscience has often been supposed to be a proof of moral goodness.

We inquire, secondly, how far conscience is infallible, and so a reliable guide.

And here I observe that conscience is infallible so far as it is uniform in its decisions. This follows from its being a part of the constitution, or a separate faculty. That would not be the same faculty in all men, which, under similar circumstances, should give different results. Place two men with perfect eyes under similar circumstances and they will see alike, and see accurately. There must, therefore, be circumstances in which there will be a uniform and infallible action of the conscience. What are these? This will be when the conscience is unperverted, and the subject on which it judges is seen just as it is.

Under such circumstances all men would, all men now do, immediately discriminate between benevolence and malignity, as in themselves morally good and morally evil. Inseparable from this idea and feeling, all would have the blended idea and feeling of obligation, — that is, that benevolence ought to be manifested and malignity restrained. It is by the term *ought* that this idea and feeling of obligation is expressed, and when our own conduct is in question, there is in it an impulse towards the doing of that which we feel that we ought to do. This is sometimes called the impulsive power of conscience, and it differs from others as having *authority*. This is the characteristic of conscience so much insisted on by Butler. It is the proclamation within us of the moral law, carrying with it its own authority, which no man can deny without denying his nature. Let, now, this authority be obeyed in carrying out the principle of benevolence, and all men would feel approbation; let it be disobeyed, and all would feel disapprobation. In our own case these would become self-approbation or remorse. They would be the sense of merit or demerit heretofore spoken of, involving an indefinite promise and threat under the divine government.

So far, and under the above circumstances, the action of conscience would be uniform. To deny this would be to deny that man has a moral nature, and the possibility of moral science.

But if there be under any circumstances this uniformity, how do we account for the diversity of moral judgments there is among men, — a diversity so great that eminent moralists, as Paley, have even denied the existence of conscience as an original part of the constitution?

To do this we must look first at the different spheres in

which conscience acts; and, second, at its liability to be disregarded or misled.

And, first, we notice the two spheres in which conscience affirms obligation, and the different circumstances under which it is affirmed.

Here it is to be observed that conscience affirms obligation solely in view of the choice of ends, especially of the supreme end, and not of means, except as they are conducive to the end. Conscience responds to the moral law, and is satisfied when that is fulfilled; but the law respects only the choice of ends. "Love," says the Scripture, "worketh no ill to his neighbor, therefore love is the fulfilling of the law." In the exercise of supreme love to God and impartial love to man, the law is fulfilled, and the conscience satisfied. The means of expressing that love must be left to positive command, or to the judgment.

What is done, then, in connection with the choice of a supreme end is wholly in the spiritual sphere. It is in the immediate presence of moral law. There can be no action of a fallible understanding in estimating probabilities, and the affirmation of obligation is immediate and uniform. As between the good and the evil seen in themselves, it is impossible that the moral reason should not make the distinction, and that conscience should not affirm obligation to choose the good. To suppose otherwise would be to deny reason to be reason. It would be to deny the possibility of conscience.

But conscience not only affirms obligation as pertaining to the choice of a supreme end as good, but also to the performance of acts as right, that is, as conducing to the supreme end.

Here there is liability to mistake. We may, first, suppose that to be conducive to the end which is not, but the reverse, and so approve of it as right. In this case the act would be said to be subjectively right, but objectively wrong. Such an act is one respecting which conscience affirms obligation under an unavoidable mistake of the judgment. A man may do it and be innocent. He may also do such an act and be blameworthy, because he had previously failed to inform himself as he ought. But, second, an act may, on the other hand, be subjectively wrong and objectively right. A man may give poison with intent to kill, that may cure an inveterate disease. According to this, and as the word right is here used, a man may, first, intend to do right, and do it; or, second, he may intend to do right, and do wrong; or, third, he may intend to do wrong, and do it; or, fourth, he may intend to do wrong, and do right.

In the first of the above spheres, that of ends, so far at least as the supreme end is involved, the decisions of conscience are uniform. In the second, that of means, there is great diversity. Is this in the decisions of the conscience or of the judgment? If we suppose the decision honestly come to that a given means is indispensable to the attainment of the supreme end, the affirmation of obligation to choose the means will be as uniform as in the former case. The judgment may be at fault, but there will be no guilt. In such a case a diversity of judgment would seem to involve a diversity in the decisions of conscience, but it would not. One man would say the thing ought to be done, and would verily think so; another, that it ought not; but if the decisions of the judgment were alike, those of the conscience would be also.

It remains, then, to find the source of the diversity, and the guilt, in some dishonesty in forming the judgment —

in some failure to come perfectly to the light, that light which is presupposed in our being moral beings, and even in the remorse of the wicked.

How such dishonesty may and must mix itself with every activity of the man when once he has chosen a wrong supreme end, we saw in the sixth lecture. That this should ever be done is the mystery of sin. But being done, the end becomes, of necessity, the standard of action. To that, as supreme, everything must give place. Now there begins a moral twilight tending to thick darkness. In proportion as the conscience shall act, the man must be at war with himself, and henceforth, if he would have peace, conscience must be either evaded or quieted. Hence the infinite subtleties of self-deception; hence the agitations and conflicts when the conscience *will* speak. Under such circumstances it is not difficult to account for any perversion or delusion. The man is in a position wholly false either for action or comprehension. He acts in twilight, and studies astronomy from the planet Neptune.

Thus situated, men fail to form habits of moral reflection, neither considering nor regarding what is right. They are governed by sense, by desire, by passion, and conscience is held in abeyance. It is ignored. The tribunal is there, but the cases are not brought before it.

Individuals and communities have also the power to set up false standards which are in morals what the shrines of idolatry are in religion. By these everything is tested, and what they call conscience, and its vocabulary, are prostituted to the service of evil. The law is read falsely, and the sentence is according to the law as read. Let a man believe that the law of God forbids his eating meat during Lent, and if he eat it his conscience will reproach him as if he had committed a real crime; while the same man may, as the inquisitors did, torture and kill heretics, not only without remorse, but with self-complacency. There is no fanaticism, or bigotry, or folly, that does not become more cruel, or intense, or absurd, under the guidance of a perverted conscience. It is this element that has given their peculiar ferocity to religious wars, and that is apt to make religious disputes so acrid and virulent. Certainly men fail to come to the light, and they "put evil for good, and good for evil."

It is plain, from the above, that to do right will be a very different thing, as we mean by it the choice of a right supreme end, and the determination through that of all subordinate choices; or as we have reference to some subordinate standard, as of fashion or popularity, which we may have adopted. According to one meaning, to do right would be to fulfil all righteousness; according to the other, most men can say, as they do, that they "mean to do what is about right." This they may do in particular instances, and often, and yet their radical character be wholly wrong.

Of the diversity of moral judgments, then, great as it seems, we may say, first, that there are, according to what has been stated above, many supposed cases of such diversity that are not really such. From the complexity of the cases presented, and the limitation of the human faculties, men apprehend imperfectly, and so differently, facts and their relations. Of this difference in intellectual judgment a differing moral judgment is the result, but this implies no want of uniformity in the action of the moral nature. Nor, second, do the apparent vagaries of conscience when men are dishonest with themselves, imply any want of uniformity in its action. If men will put on spectacles with differently colored glasses, it is not the fault of their eyes if the confusion and disputes are endless. Let them take off their glasses and they will see alike. But, third, the law of use and of improvement by exercise applies to the moral powers, and under this there may be a real diversity to a certain extent. A conscience well trained will utter itself with greater promptness, and energy, and precision, than one that is not.

This diversity of judgment under one guiding principle we find in taste as well as in morals. Men are born with some natural power of apprehending beauty. Of this they judge; this they wish to produce. But when the question comes to be what is beautiful in any particular case, there are great differences of opinion. At this point it is that the practical questions arise. Will you build a square house or a gothic cottage? Will you paint it white or brown? Will you lay out your grounds regularly, or irregularly, or with a regular irregularity? To such questions no original faculty necessitating the idea and the emotion of beauty can furnish an answer. Taste must be cultivated in accordance with principles and standards; and such cultivation will make all the difference in decoration and in art between the tawdriness and finery of the savage and the perfection of taste. In connection with the study of these principles and the application of these standards, there will arise, as in morals, different schools of art, each having its own merits, and gaining a supremacy more or less wide and permanent.

We have thus, both in æsthetics and in morals, original capacities which act uniformly to a certain extent. In both there is an original intuition, but this was never intended to supersede the necessity for careful training. Especially was it intended that there should be in the highest department of conduct, that of morality and of duty, the highest possible combination of the intuitional element with the results of induction, thus giving the broadest practical wisdom. The intuitive element must be obeyed, but what does it say? In the one case it says, produce the highest beauty; in the other, do all the good you can. For these no consultation is needed with any one, and no advice. But when the practical question comes whether a young man engaged in mercantile business shall give it up to prepare for the gospel ministry, something more is needed. Here the inductive element comes in. It will depend upon his age, his talents, his means, upon those dependent upon him, or likely to be; and upon this he may properly ask advice. Of this kind are most practical questions. Nothing can be more trying than the suspense and nice balancings these often require; and when the decisions are made, they will be those of beings limited and imperfect, liable to mistake even where there is no sin. Respecting decisions of this kind men need much mutual forbearance in judging of each other. It is seldom that we can put ourselves fully in the place of another, and no general rule can be laid down. We can only say, with the wise man, that "wisdom is profitable to direct."

In connection with these two spheres of judgment, the intuitional and the inductive, I would call your attention to the two great crises in the life of every young man, — of most persons, indeed, who come to maturity, — and to the very different character of the elements and questions they involve.

The first and great crisis is that which involves the whole of duty and of destiny under the government of God. In the life of every one much instructed a point is reached when the question consciously arises respecting a supreme end. It is found that a wrong one has been chosen, — shall there be a change? The question here is between two things different in kind and utterly incompatible. It is one of giving and receiving. Shall the person give himself up in love to the service of God and man? or shall he regard God and men as means through which he may receive what he desires? The question may not be thus stated, but it involves this; and there are no balancings, and agitations, and suspense, like those often connected with its decision. Here the intuitional element and the will are alone concerned. The question is not one of means, but of ends. It is aloof from the relations of time. There is no place for induction or call for advice. Neither is there room for doubt. Intuitively, peremptorily, persistently, the conscience affirms obligation. It is now proximate to the will, and these are like two vessels grappled in conflict. They are the Monitor and the Merrimac. The question is one of simple obedience. Will the will yield, or will it not? Will the man come into harmony with himself and with God, or will he not? This question no one can decide for another, and the act required is so simple and elementary that no one can tell another how to do it. To attempt this, as is often done, is like attempting to define an elementary notion. This, if the question is to be decided once for all, is the crisis not only for this life, but for the whole of existence.

The second great crisis in the life of a young man comes when he is to decide on his profession, that is, on the particular form and direction of his activity under the general choice previously made. On this will depend not merely the amount, but the kind of good he will do, the books he will read, his professional friendships, the line of his thoughts, and the principles of their association.

The question here, it is often supposed, is to be determined by conscience; but if the previous question has been fully settled, conscience has, in strictness, nothing to do with it. The simple question will be, in one case, how we can do the greatest amount of good; and in the other, how we can best subserve our own private ends. These are questions of comparison and judgment involving many particulars. Men equally conscientious might decide them differently, and with them conscience has nothing to do, unless it be to secure for them a careful and candid attention. The process is like that by which we find the minor proposition of a syllogism. We inquire whether a particular proposition comes under another that is more general.

The distinctions above made will enable us to account in part for the confusion there has been in our moral philosophy, and particularly for the prominence given to right, and *the* right, as distinguished from the good.

The choice of a supreme end is generic. It is made once, in a sense only once. In a sense, too, it is made always, constantly repeated, since it is only under this that other choices are made. It is like the light of consciousness, and would naturally be the last thing investigated. Indeed, as consciousness is the generic form of intelligence, and the desire of happiness that of the desires, and love that of the affections, so the choice of a supreme end is the generic form of volition. It enters into all the others; they are made in its light and partake of its character. In respect to this the affirmation of obligation is not constantly repeated in any specific form, and may be scarcely thought of for years. But the affirmation of obligation as connected with right, or what is supposed to be so, is constantly made, as it is concerning that that practical questions and discussions constantly arise. Hence it has attracted the chief attention. The immediate question, and that on which the obligation would turn, has been one of right, and hence the idea of right in its relation to obligation has been supposed to be ultimate. It is ultimate only as the seaport is ultimate where everything is stopped, examined, exchanged, but which would be no seaport at all but for the ocean beyond. If there were nothing good, no end to be chosen, there would be nothing right. The only question is whether the right *is* the good.

We next inquire after the relation of conscience to the other active principles. How far should it be merely regulative, and how far a positive principle of action?

A philosophy of ends requires for the person that which we find in all nature below it, a good which shall result from the congruity of itself with that in which its good is found, and which shall come immediately from the activity of the one in its relation to the other. Everywhere there is duality. In vegetable life there is the living seed, there is moisture, air, and warmth, and there is growth. In sensitive life there is the eye, and there is light, and from these, vision. Not from the eye alone, or from light alone, does seeing come, but from the two in right relations. Seeing is not a thing, a being, but a product and result of vitality acting according to its laws. Of that inward constitution and congruity by which the eye and light are adapted to each other we know nothing. We only know the facts, and the conditions, or laws of the facts. So again in the appetites. There is hunger, and there is food. The enjoyment is not from the appetite alone, or from the food alone, but from both in the right relation.

In the mental world there is the knowing mind and the object known. Knowledge is not from the mind without the object, nor from the object without the mind, but is the result of the two in the relations intended by God. The same holds in the affections and the will. There is the love and the object loved, the will and the thing willed, the choice and the thing chosen, and the blessedness is not the result of the mind alone or of the object alone, but of the right relations of the two.

And here, as we reach enjoyment from love, I wish to notice a peculiarity, which, according to our previous principle of classification, must place that higher than any other, at least when it is in its fulness. It is higher, not merely as the product of our highest powers, but as more complex. It has the element of reciprocity. It is not simply because personal beings are higher and intrinsically more excellent than others, or that we can have affections for them specific and peculiar, that the activity of our faculties when they are the object can give us a higher joy, but because they are capable of the conscious recognition and reciprocation of that affection. Hardly less than the joy of loving is that of being beloved. Here we find the necessity of each for all, and of all for each, and the foundation for the highest good of all and of each. The highest conceivable good must be from a conscious and perfect accordance of the will and moral affections with those of a being of infinite excellence who should recognize and reciprocate the affection.

In all this it will be observed that the relation of the faculties and their objects is immediate and direct.

But with such a constitution in perfect adjustment it is plain that the office of conscience, if required at all, would be simply regulative. We have provision here for activity throughout its whole range, without the conscience. We are not to eat from conscience, else why the appetite? The affections are not to act from conscience, else they would not be original parts of our nature. It is not the office of conscience to supersede any of the natural principles of action, nor can it ever lead to action except as there are grounds for that action furnished by principles other than itself. In this respect it is analogous to self-love. Its office is to affirm obligation to choose in a particular way. The grounds of choice are presupposed. Hence the double function of our moral nature. As a condition for the action of conscience man has the power, in virtue of his moral reason and of the affections growing out of it, to apprehend the end which he ought to choose, and he is drawn towards the beings whom he ought to love. This end he apprehends and chooses, these beings he appreciates and loves, as a moral being, not merely from a sense of obligation, but from their inherent worth or excellency. Acting in the light of moral reason, from the play of the moral affections, and in the exercise of freedom, man is a moral being; but as there is an alternative, and he is liable to choose wrongly, the moral nature would not be complete if there were not an affirmation of obligation to choose the good apprehended by the moral reason, and towards which the affections were drawn. But conscience is that function of the moral reason by which it affirms obligation to choose primarily the good, and secondarily the right, from its apprehended relation to that. This is its function before the act. Subsequently there are evolved its rewarding and punishing, and its prophetic power.

We have, then, as a condition for the action of conscience in affirming obligation, not the mere perception by the intellect of external relations, but those primal acts of affection and choice which are involved in our very conception of ourselves as acting, and which spring from that which is deepest and most sacred in our nature. As means of fulfilling the obligations thus affirmed when actions other than the mere choice are required, we have the perception of actions as right, sometimes apparently intuitive, but often clearly the reverse, and in which we are liable to great mistakes.

We may now see when the action of conscience is required; when it is merely regulative, and when it becomes a direct impulse to action. Let a man, as has been said, eat from appetite. This is a sufficient reason for his eating. His appetite was given that he might eat. There will be no need of conscience here, except as assenting, or as there may be room for doubt respecting the quantity or quality of what is to be eaten. On both these points a man is bound to use his best knowledge, and if there be reason to suspect anything injurious, conscience will say no. It will become the veto power of the mind. Self-love may forbid it as opposed to individual interest, but conscience will pronounce it wrong as opposed to the great law of love.

If we might suppose the appetite so constituted as to crave nothing injurious, there would be no need of supervision by either self-love or conscience, and such need must be in proportion to the want of autonomy in the appetite. The above is the law for all natural appetites and principles of action that are sufficiently strong to induce all the action in their line that is required by their ends. The office of conscience will, then, be simply to say no, if there be a tendency to excessive or perverted action. But if any faculty or impulse, as the desire of knowledge, be not strong enough, then it may and should be put at work under the imperative of duty. Then conscience not merely says no, — it impels; it becomes a task-master. In such cases, however, we feel it to be unfortunate and undesirable that the action of conscience should be needed. The faculties do not work cheerfully, but as under a yoke. We prefer that a sense of duty should be required to restrain a boy from study, rather than to impel him to it. This holds true of all the instrumental powers. They have no moral character, except as the man accepts and directs them, and we prefer to see them full and redundant, rather than meagre. But when we reach the directive, and especially the moral powers, the relation is different. Here conscience does not come in as a power from without, standing above the faculty, but as part of a circle of activity that is necessary for the completeness of the whole. In all life there is a circle, every part of which implies every other. We may treat of respiration separately, but it involves circulation and digestion, and there is no life without each. So in the moral life. We may treat of the apprehension of good and the power of choice apart from conscience, but all are necessary to life. Hence, in a natural, that is in a right state, a sense of obligation will so coalesce with moral affection as not to produce constraint, but rather to heighten joy. It will be as the seal of a bond to which we set our names with an unwavering confidence and an ineffable delight. Between the affections and the conscience there will be full consent, and there is not a note in the harmony that goes up from the full action of the moral powers that is more pervading and would be more missed than that from an approving conscience. It is in a spring of affection, coördinate with the affirmation of obligation, that we have a marriage of strength and beauty, whose fruit is blessedness.

That the moral nature does not, like the other powers, work under a yoke in the presence of obligation, but simply finds its own completeness, it is important to see, because there is a prevalent impression that there is in all obligation something of constraint. It is an objection to the system that makes the right ultimate, that, as based on a mere abstraction, it furnishes no object for the affections, and moves us through its imperative by constraining and driving, rather than by attracting us. In our conception of a perfect being the law is not known as an outward and constraining force, but there is a coincidence with it of inclination and of will by which perfect obedience becomes perfect freedom. Love is free and directly from a view of its object; but "love is the fulfilling of the law."

Seeing thus the relation of conscience as a motive to the other active powers, let us look at the gradation and possible complexity of motives in human action. The gradation of motives will follow from that of the powers, and will be in accordance with it. Motives will be higher or lower as the powers are from which they spring, and both virtues and vices will be designated from the sphere of activity that is rightly directed, or abused. A man abusing the sensitive part of his nature is sensual; rightly using it, he is temperate. Abusing the desire for power, he is selfishly ambitious; rightly using it, he is beneficent. Throughout, both virtues and vices are designated by the activities employed. If there are not high vices, there are those that are low, and some virtues are higher than others.

Of the possible complexity of motives we may gain a

correct view if we suppose a father to command his child to get a lesson. Here there is, first, between the mind of the child and knowledge a natural congruity, and he may get the lesson from a simple love of the knowledge. It may be just what he would have done without any command. But the parent says further, — If you get the lesson it will aid you in getting a living; you shall have my approbation, and I will express that by a reward. If you do not get it you shall have my disapprobation, and I will express that by punishment.

Now, between the mind of the child and the approbation of the parent there is a congruity. It is right for him to desire that approbation. The reward itself may be one that would appeal to the legitimate desires and which it would be right to seek, and the reverse may be said of the disapprobation and the punishment.

We have, then, as motives, 1st. Love of knowledge for its own sake. 2d. A desire for it as useful in gaining a living. 3d. A desire of the reward. 4th. Fear of punishment. 5th. Regard for the authority of the parent. 6th. A love of his approbation. 7th. Dread of his disapprobation. 8th. The affirmation by conscience of obligation.

Of these each is legitimate, — is appropriate to a rational being, — is right. Each may take its turn, or they may conspire together; and if from any one or all of them the lesson should be learned the parent might be satisfied. Still, it must be remembered that the ultimate character of the mind in every movement relative to these motives will be determined by that generic act of choice under which they all take place. The motives may be objectively right, but the man not subjectively right in being governed by them.

If the preceding remarks, or indeed the general doctrine

of these lectures, be correct, they will go far to determine the question whether in order to be virtuous an act must be done from a sense of duty. On this point distinguished thinkers differ. Chalmers says this is essential, and, as is usual with him, reiterates and enforces the point in a variety of ways. "It is not," says he, "volition alone which makes a thing virtuous, but volition under a sense of duty; and that only is a moral performance to which a man is urged by a sense or feeling of moral obligation." Again he says, "Whatever cometh not of a sense of duty hath no moral character of itself, and no moral approbation due to it." This opinion of Chalmers is quoted with approbation by McCosh. On the other hand, Dr. Woods says, "It would be very easy to show that moral affection may exist in one who has at the time no distinct apprehension of its nature, and no present feeling of approbation or disapprobation." "I say, then," he continues, "it is not essential to our moral agency, or to the existence of moral good and evil in us, that we should at the time have a distinct consideration or conception of a moral law, or a sensible approbation or disapprobation of our feelings and actions."

This inquiry runs back to the constitution of the moral nature as involving any other element than that of right and of conscience, and to the question whether there is anything virtuous in the moral affections and the will when they act according to their own law, and directly with reference to their objects.

That there is something thus virtuous, McCosh, in opposition to his direct assertion, seems everywhere to imply. Thus he says, "Much of human wickedness is displayed in the ingenious schemes which are contrived to deceive the moral faculty and avoid its humbling judgments." This implies something having wickedness, and yet acting independently of the moral faculty. Again, he says, "Moral excellence is truly the whole powers and affections of the soul in healthy exercise, and in order to guard it there is a faculty with a train of corresponding feelings, presiding over all the other faculties and seated in the very heart." This implies excellence before it can be guarded. Again, he says expressly that "the moral quality is not given to the action by the mind contemplating it." "It is not our perception and approbation that renders a benevolent action good, but we perceive its excellence and approve it because it is good."

It is not to be supposed that moral actions are done except under moral law and some generic choice of good or evil. But as a vicious man does not do evil actions because of their viciousness, so neither would it seem necessary that a good man should do good actions because of their virtuousness; at least it cannot be implied, as it seems to be in the statement of Chalmers, that a sense of obligation is the only virtuous motive. It is the law of the affections that they are drawn out in view of their object. An interested love is impossible. Only from an apprehension of some quality in the being loved can love come. The love of God may imply virtue. It does so. But the love cannot be in view of its own virtuousness, or with the thought of that, but must be in view of either the worth or the worthiness of God.

LECTURE X.

RECTITUDE AND VIRTUE. — RELATIONS. — EXPEDIENCY, PRUDENCE, AND VIRTUE. — ORIGIN OF MORAL DISTINCTIONS AS RELATED TO THE DIVINE NATURE. — COINCIDENCE OF INSTINCT AND REASON — OF FAITH AND REASON — OF PHILOSOPHY AND RELIGION.

It will be remembered that in observing a moral act we went backward to its source. In so doing we found a moral constitution. That constitution we have examined, and have found its end and law. In doing this we considered those voluntary states of mind which are in themselves good or evil, virtuous or vicious.

We know immediately and intuitively that love is good, and malignity evil; and it is inconceivable that their nature should be changed by any will. They are opposites, as are light and darkness, hardness and softness; one may give place to the other, but can never *become* the other. This, I suppose, is what is meant by the eternal and immutable distinctions of morals.

It was then said that in passing outwards from a moral action we found right and wrong, utility, expediency, general consequences. It will be next in order to examine these, and to inquire how far their claims may be reconciled with those of virtue without confounding the two.

As has been said, right is often used as synonymous with virtuous, and wrong with vicious. *The right*, also, seems to be used as synonymous with moral goodness; at least if that be not its meaning I am unable to say what it is. But by right is also meant conformity to a rule or law, tendency to an end, accordance with fixed relations, and by wrong, the reverse. "Right and wrong," says Dr. Wayland, "depend upon the relations under which beings are created, and are invariable." In this sense actions may be right or wrong without reference to the character or intention of the agent. In the first sense they cannot, and the trouble has been that these terms have been used, now to indicate virtue as originating in will, and now to indicate a quality, sometimes called moral, that has no reference to intention. So far as they are used in the first sense we have already considered them, or rather that which they indicate; it is in the second sense that they now claim our attention.

Plainly the results of human conduct in this life are not determined solely by the dispositions and intentions from which they spring. We live under a natural as well as under a moral government, and the first is the instrument, frame-work, and prophecy of the second. We are surrounded by other beings, and by an external nature that is complicated, involving numerous substances, and forces, and laws. These beings, this nature, these substances, and forces, and laws, have a determinate constitution in accordance with which we may act upon them and they upon us, and this action, at least so far as nature is concerned, will not be affected by our state of mind as good or evil, or by any intention that may spring from that. Between us and external nature there are fixed relations, and the result will depend upon our acting or not acting in accordance with those relations.

A being wholly virtuous may act in entire accordance with the nature of the beings and substances around him, and then the whole result will be right and good. Again, with character unchanged, but ignorant of the relations in which he is placed, the same being may so act as to produce suffering to himself, or others, or both. He may intend to preserve his health, but be ignorant, and unavoidably so, of the effect of a want of ventilation, and in consequence may live for years in debility and suffering. Such a person would not act in accordance with "the nature of things;" or, as it has sometimes been expressed, with "the fitness of things;" or, as it has been expressed again, with "the truth of things;" or, once again, with "the relations in which he was placed."

From the very nature of man it is impossible he should act except in some relation. Hence the consideration of *relations* — not merely of things as they are in themselves, but in their relations — must always enter into our estimate both of propriety and of duty.

So numerous, indeed, and complex are these relations, and so intimately is their right adjustment connected with human well-being, that not a few moralists have supposed moral obligation, and so the whole science of morals, to be founded on them. "It is fit," says Dr. Samuel Clarke, "that man should obey God, and therefore he ought to obey him." It is true, according to Wollaston, that fresh air is needed for health, and he who acts as if it were not, acts a lie, and therefore does wrong. "The relation of parent and child," says Dr. Wayland, "is constituted by God, therefore men are bound to act in accordance with that relation." He asserts, moreover, that the sense of obligation arises immediately on the perception of the relation.

But it does not seem to be true, it may be observed here, that a child is bound to obey his parent simply because he is his parent. A parent may be an idiot, or insane, or intoxicated, or wholly abandoned to vice, and then the law makes provision for the guardianship of the child, that is, for placing him where he need not obey the parent. The sole reason why the child is to obey the parent is the presumption that the end for which God made him will be thus best secured. If it could be certainly known that that end would thus be defeated, the child would not be under obligation to obey, but the reverse. Relations cannot indicate what is good. They may, and do, what is right, but so far as they do this they may all be reduced to one, that is, the relation of any act which a moral being may be required to do, to his end. So absolutely is the will of God revealed in that, that it is inconceivable he should lay a being under obligation to do anything not in accordance with his highest end.

But while we do not find the foundation of morals in the nature, or fitness, or truth of things, or in any mere relations, we may not overlook the important part which a perception of these was intended to play in the regulation of human conduct. Not only, as has been said, may a virtuous man fail to conform to the nature of things, or to the relations in which he is placed, and thus suffer; but a man not virtuous may conform to them, and be rewarded. Beneficial effects will follow without respect to the motive. There is a sense in which an action thus conformed to the nature of things is right although the motive may not be good. It is, as we say, right in itself; it is conformed to the nature of things; it is fit, and suitable, and proper, and what ought to be done. Let a man be outwardly honest; let him pay his debts, and tell the truth, and though he may do it simply because he thinks honesty the best policy, and so not be virtuous, yet the acts are right in themselves, and the confidence of men in each other and the prosperity of the community will be promoted by them. On the other hand, from an imperfect apprehension of relations, a person may take the redress of his private wrongs into his own hands, or may buy and sell lottery tickets, or intoxicating drinks, or perhaps be a polygamist, and while the motive may be good, that will not prevent the disastrous effects of these acts as wrong in themselves. Sooner or later such acts will work out their own retribution.

It cannot, indeed, be too clearly seen that into the whole system of nature as related to us, into the human constitution in its very texture, into the constitution of society, there are not only inwrought laws of reward for conformity to relations and fixed laws, but also laws of retribution that seem to execute themselves. Violate a law of nature by stepping from a precipice, and you fall; violate a law of your organization by intemperance, and your punishment will be in proportion to the offence. And so of society. Violate the law of its organization as one whole so that portions of that whole are neglected and degraded, and that very violation will work out a sure retribution. In all this we see only the working of fixed law without regard to motives or character. A mistake is punished just as severely as a wilful violation of the law.

There is that in the working of these laws that is precisely as if there were a moral instinct in all these departments. As with instinct, let everything else be as it should, and these laws will work right, and produce only good; but let there be perversion and derangement, and then, like instinct again, they will work blindly and disastrously. They may not overturn, but will utterly disregard all moral distinctions.

If, now, we carry the working of these laws into the mind, we shall have the whole of what many believe to be the moral system of the universe. They believe there is no reward or punishment except from the operation of fixed laws, and know nothing of a personal being working within or through those laws. Especially do they know nothing of one working above them.

The difference between those who do, and those who do not recognize a personal being at this point is radical, and forms a dividing line, not only between schools, but between individuals in their habits of thought who know nothing of schools. To me the indications of a moral system in these laws are like the indications of reason in instinct, or rather lying back of it, and needed to account for it. Taken by themselves, they are a mute, imperfect, often baffled expression, not so much of the thing itself as of a yearning after it. They are the harbinger of the thing, a beautiful frame-work into which a perfect virtue may be fitted. But a system thus regardless of character, and as cold and remorseless as that of fate, can never meet the demands of either the conscience or the affections.

Of acts under such a system, whether right or wrong, the good and evil results may be calculated, because they are wrought out within and by the system, and will be the same, whether intended or not. But the results of virtue and vice cannot be calculated, because they depend immediately upon will, and involve the principles of a moral government that has an extent and bearings wholly beyond our comprehension. Here, as well as in the absence of approbation and disapprobation, is a great difference between this system and one truly moral. When a rational being *wilfully* goes against the laws of that being; when the child refuses to obey his father; when the creature *knowingly* disregards the will of the Creator, it is impossible to say what may be the results. Here we find, not merely a mistake, which is an intellectual crime,— not merely a want of acting in conformity with fixed and impersonal law, but *guilt*, — the most dreadful word and thing, and the only thing to be really dreaded, in the universe of God.

But while we cannot identify what is right with what is good, they are yet closely allied. Goodness is good in itself. Regarded as a fundamental choice conformed to moral law, it is also right, and must involve a disposition that would lead to the doing of all right acts. As tending, then, to produce right acts, goodness is *righteousness;* and if there be adequate knowledge, there will be in all its acts *rightness*, — that is, an entire conformity to all fixed relations, and so to all divine law. Nothing but sufficient knowledge can be wanting to effect a perfect coincidence of all virtuous and of all right action. An action will not be right because it is virtuous, nor virtuous because it is right. For the one we look backwards to its source; for the other, forwards to its relations and consequences; but virtue cannot be virtue except as there is in it a disposition to do right.

If, then, any contend for an absolute and ultimate right that is identical with goodness, we are content; but if not, it will devolve on them to show what they mean by it that is different from the above statement.

Having thus treated of right in its relation to virtue, we next inquire after the relation to it of utility and expediency. This has been a difficult point in morals; but those who accept the above statements will readily see what that relation must be. Whatever is useful or expedient must be so with reference to some end. Hence, utility and expediency always imply an end previously chosen. Here nothing will be chosen for its own sake, and all questions must respect the choice, not of ends, but of conditions and means. We have thus two classes of questions closely connected, but of an entirely different order. An ultimate end, so far as it is regarded as ultimate, — and a supreme end must be wholly so, — can have neither utility nor expediency. It is chosen for its own sake. In the choice of such an end character alone is involved. In that of means and conditions, character is always implied; but it is capacity that is chiefly involved.

And here it is to be observed that conditions and means can be rationally chosen only on the ground that they are adapted to the attainment of the end; and that, having chosen an end, it would be an inconsistency and folly not to choose those conditions and means that would be the best adapted to attain it. What else can a rational man do?

It is to be observed, again, that if the end chosen be the true supreme end of man, then any means in themselves adapted to attain that end will be right. This is not the doctrine that the end sanctifies the means, but implies the fact that this is such an end as can be obtained only by sanctified means. An inadequate and false end, chosen selfishly, may be attained by vicious means. If money be the supreme end, it may be attained by fraud. Power may be attained by violence and injustice. When a man has chosen a supreme end, if he be consistent, he will use whatever means may be necessary to attain it. The very fact that the end is supreme to him will render it impossible that anything should come between him and it. But no man can seek to promote *blessedness* by *sin*,— by any interference with the rights of others. It would be a contradiction.

In treating of the intellect, it was noticed how the wrong choice of a supreme end will pervert that. We now see how it is that it will pervert the heart; and how it is that no man can consistently stop at any wickedness necessary to the attainment of such an end. If the love of power be absolutely supreme, then the esteem of men and the favor of God must be relatively of less account, and must be disregarded. And as we saw how the choice of the true end would lead to candor and a coming to the light, so we may now see how it involves unselfishness in the choice of means. We here find deep and pervading laws of our constitution.

We may now see what the true doctrine of expediency and utility is, and how largely the consideration of these must enter into human life. In all secondary choices and executive volition they must govern every rational man. Does a man pursue his own ends by what he deems to be the best means? If not, he is blameworthy. But if he does, it ill becomes him to rail at expediency.

But may not expediency be opposed to right? A false expediency may; and hence the prejudice. The objections to expediency seem to have arisen, first, from the general choice of wrong ends, and measuring expediency by them. Two men have a quarrel. The object of each is to humble the other. One can do it by fraud. He says this would be expedient, but not right. Expedient for what? Not for the promotion of blessedness on the whole. And, second, objections have arisen because, even when the true end has been chosen, men have sometimes failed to see that they might not and never could promote it by interfering with the rights of others, — that means, to be means at all, must here partake of the character of the end.

This true doctrine of expediency some have failed to see; and in seeking, in opposition to that, for an abstract right, have fallen into a fanaticism not the less mischievous for its high pretensions, and the fair garb in which it has clothed itself.

We now pass to another distinction which belongs here, — that between prudence and virtue. Prudence does not furnish positive motives. It presupposes the choice and pursuit of an end, and its office is to guard against danger under the operation of fixed laws. "The prudent man foreseeth the evil, and hideth himself." Prudence has sole reference to our interest as under fixed laws, and not as under the rule of a personal being. In its perfection it is an acquired sagacity in regard to the laws, whether of matter or of mind, and a habit of shaping the conduct in accordance with them; and as such, it becomes to man in his sphere what instinct is to the animals in theirs.

As prudence regards only consequences from fixed laws, the moment we come to faith, and to suffering and martyrdom for adherence to principle at all hazards, its sphere is transcended. A man may purposely so act in opposition to fixed laws as to jeopardize or destroy his whole interest under those laws; and this he may do rationally, but in no proper sense of the word can he be said to do it prudently. The hero is not prudent. The martyr is not prudent. He is brought into a position where the rules of prudence are out of place, and where it becomes necessary to vindicate the supremacy of the spiritual nature and the majesty of virtue by an unconditional trust in goodness and in God.

Prudence may then be regarded as the appointed guardian of the interests of man in the present life, and under those fixed laws that are made known by experience. As such, it is, as Butler says, "of the nature of virtue." To study those laws, to heed them when we may, and to secure the good there is under them, is our wisdom and duty. Wantonly or heedlessly to disregard them is wrong;

but the highest life of man is not in them, or from them, or under them; and when the demands of that life require us to give up every interest under those laws, or even to lay ourselves down in their track to be crushed by them, it is to be done.

Right, expediency, prudence, are all found by tracing actions outwards, and have their basis in a nature of things, and in which some have placed the foundation of morals. Of this nature of things, there are some who so think as if it were something back of the will of God, and controlled it. So Dr. Dwight. He says, "It is, I apprehend, evident that the foundation of virtue is not in the will of God, but in the nature of things." And to this nature of things he supposed the will of God to be conformed. He says further, confounding, as it would seem, the nature of things with their tendency, that "virtue is termed good only as being the cause of happiness," so making the foundation of obligation to be in the tendency of things, and the will of God to be governed by that,—as if there could be either a nature or a tendency of things that did not have its origin in the will of God.

Others, again, supposing the nature of things, and so their tendencies to be originated by God, go back to the nature of God himself for the origin of these distinctions and the foundation of moral obligation. Here they seem to find the limit of all analysis, and of all thought, since nothing can be more ultimate than the nature of God. "Instead of any abstract fitnesses being the standard of the divine nature, the divine nature must itself," it is said, "be the origin and standard of all fitnesses."

On a subject like this it becomes us to speak cautiously and reverently. It may be doubted, however, whether this mode of speaking either originates in, or conveys a true conception of the nature of God. It supposes a nature in him that lies back of reason and of will, and from which impulsions come by which his will is necessarily determined. Because we have a nature that is distinct from our personality, and underlies it, it is imagined that God has. It may be, however, that the nature of God is nothing distinct from his personality, and that so he is wholly supernatural. It may be that the terms nature and natural, used as they commonly are to indicate something fixed, stated, uniform, and not made so by will, are without meaning when applied to God. So far as we can apply the term to God, it may be that it is his nature to be simply a *Person* determining his own will in the light of an all-comprehending reason, and in view, not of any intrinsic differences in a nature of things, but of the different character and results of different possible forms of his own activity. It may be that what we must reach in our ultimate analysis is a free personality, — a Person, with no nature, or fate, or fitnesses of things back of him, or above him; who is himself, by his own free choice, the originator of everything that may properly be called nature, and of all fitnesses of things. That this is not so, who shall say? Who shall say that this is not our only way to avoid that conception of God, so very general, that is equivalent to fate?

The confusion at this point may be largely due to the inadequacy of language for such a subject. Two extremes were to be avoided: one, the founding of obligation on mere will; the other, the virtual exclusion of will.

The difficulty arises from the eternity, and so the necessity, of the divine existence. But if it be said that God is a necessary being, it is also to be said that he is necessarily rational and free, and that what he is now he has always been. Go back as we may, we find simply a personal God, rational and free. As such, he is a law unto himself, subject to no necessity, except the necessity there is that reason should act rationally. Obligation is affirmed in him, as in us, we being made in his image, only with no danger of mistake, and with no possibility that he should be responsible to any one. This gives us, as the origin of all things that had an origin, character and will; and instead of a blind fate it gives us that moral certainty which accompanies the highest freedom. Something must be given. What we need is simply a person; and it is a mere abuse of language to convert that constitution of the Divine Being, by which he is a person, and capable of a rational freedom, into a nature the very idea of which excludes freedom.

But if this be so, then, as in our search backwards for the origin of being, the ultimate fact is the *being* of God; so, in our search backwards for the origin of moral distinctions, we shall find, not any nature of things, not any nature of God, not any necessary and eternal principles, but simply the *character* of God. It would be a grand consummation thus to find, standing at the termination of all our investigations physical and moral, as that beyond which nothing could be more ultimate, simply the being of God, and the character of God.

If this be so, then virtue or goodness, and rectitude, will, in God, be the same thing seen in different aspects. His goodness will be seen in his choice of ends, and his rectitude in the mode of attaining them; and there can be for man, and indeed for any creature however exalted, nothing higher, or better, or more ultimate than conformity to the character of God. It may be that, as all the natural teachings of the works of God are but indications and expressions of his natural attributes, so all their moral teachings, together with those of revelation, are but the expressions of his moral character; and that the end of all teaching, and of all influences, will be the formation by creatures made in his image of a character similar to his.

If we accept what has now been said, it will follow, as moral distinctions have their origin in God as a person, as his character is the standard of goodness, and his will is the expression of his character, that his will, however made known, must be the ultimate rule of moral action; it must be that to which the conscience will respond, not simply as will, but as the will of *God.* It was made to respond to his will because that is the expression of his *character;* and his character, as combining benevolence and rectitude, is the perfection and standard of moral excellence.

As we, then, find in the being of God the origin of all other being, so that without him there could be no other; so do we find in the character of God, and in his will as expressing that character, all that is ultimate in moral distinctions, and without that will and character those distinctions could not be. Thus do all our speculations lead us to God, not merely as the fountain of being, but of excellence, and as the Head and Governor of the moral universe.

We have now examined the human constitution as related to ends rationally apprehended and pursued. In so doing we have necessarily assumed that that constitution is, for our purposes, in a normal state. A true physiology is not morbid anatomy. We have assumed that from a study of the structure of man, physical and mental, some knowledge may be gained not only of his separate organs and faculties, but also of man himself as a system, and of his end. If he cannot know his own end there can be no philosophy of man, no comprehension, no satisfactory knowledge.

That man could, in his present state, know his end without revelation, does not appear. There is no philosophy in a ruin; and facts are against it. Where the Bible has not been it does not appear that man has either attained or retained a knowledge of his true end.

But if it were otherwise, so that the best minds of the race could reach such knowledge, or even if there were no moral ruin, yet for a race coming up to moral agency from the blankness of infancy, and through the long twilight of youth, it would seem that such knowledge could never be sufficient as a practical guide. Something more immediate and direct would be needed; and that we find in those two other principles, Instinct and Faith, in accordance with which it was said in the second lecture that ends might be pursued.

Having, then, found the harmony there is between the constitution of man and nature on the one hand, and that same constitution and revelation on the other; having shown the relation between virtue and moral good; between individual and general good; between moral and natural good; between right, utility, prudence, and virtue, it remains to find the harmony there may be between the pursuit of ends through these principles of Instinct and Faith, and by the method already considered.

In comprehending ends man is wholly a philosopher; in pursuing them he is a practical philosopher. His knowledge becomes power in the highest form, — the power of attaining his supreme end. But as an end may be attained by instinct and by faith, we need to see the relation of a rational philosophy to the attainment of an end by these.

If we mean by instinct that principle which directs animals without any comprehension or election of theirs, which seems, indeed, to be but a higher form of the same principle that causes the plumule in a plant to tend upwards and the radicle to tend downwards, with no relation to anything higher, then it does not belong to our subject. But if we mean by instinct that tendency of a rational nature towards its supreme end which must, as it seems to us, belong to it if rightly constituted, without something of which we could not conceive of an end, and which we may elect to accept or reject as our guide, then it does come within our range. Then does it become us to examine both it as a part of our frame-work, and the end it proposes, and to accept or reject both the end and the guide. If we accept both, and give ourselves up to the guidance of the instinct, or the impulse, or the nature, or whatever we may please to call it, then are we, in an important sense, governed both by instinct and by reason; and it is obvious that there will be a harmony of the two. It is the instinct that guides us, but we are not blind in following it. We trust ourselves to it willingly, as the muleteer who traverses mountain-passes knows that his wisdom lies in letting the mule plant his feet where he pleases. It would, perhaps, be possible for a person to eat by philosophy. Taking it for his end, an excellent end, to keep his body of the same weight, he might ascertain by experiment that there was precisely so much waste of the system in a given time, and of just such proximate elements, and he might gather and compound the materials chemically, and supply them by weight with no regard to appetite, as he would put so much meal into a bag; but if he were to do that repeatedly and find the result no better than when he left the whole business to appetite, and perhaps not as good, it would be rational in him to trust that. In everything relating to the body, to the preservation of health, and to its restoration, there is a wisdom of nature which the wisest regard most, and to which men constantly return after long vagaries of theory, and of what they call rational methods. Now it may be that what we call instinct here has not been sufficiently investigated. We hear men speak of the higher instincts, and of rational instincts. Are these, then, for the higher nature what the lower instincts are for the lower? As many view it, what is conscience but a rational instinct, a guide without comprehension, but rational because it reveals itself as the voice of God, which all instinct is without thus revealing itself? But if these instincts are the product of the higher nature, how do they differ from those intuitions which have been called the product of reason, and so of the highest form of intelligence? However we may answer these questions, there can be no doubt respecting the main point of our inquiry. . Whatever there may be of instinct higher or lower to guide us in the pursuit of a supreme end, must be perfectly coincident with the impulse to be derived from a rational comprehension of that end, and in accepting such guidance we may be wholly rational.

Having thus seen that instinctive morality, if such there may be, would be in harmony with a rational morality, we turn to the third mode in which an end may be obtained, that is, by faith, and inquire for the relation of that to a rational morality. Can a man be rationally governed by faith in precisely the same way as by instinct?

Of the term faith there are different shades of meaning,

but its general import is so well fixed that they will give us no trouble. It is distinguished from knowledge, certain or uncertain. And, first, from certain knowledge. This must come directly from the action of some of the senses or faculties. If we have not faculties that find their evidence in their own activity, we can be sure of nothing, not even of the being of a God. Our intuitions, those first truths of reason which are implied in all our other knowing, the legitimate results of the operation of any of the faculties, — tested as legitimate, the constitution being given, by their uniformity and necessity, — must be received as certainly known. When through these faculties we have once reached the being of a God, faith in him would assure us that faculties given by him could not be mendacious; still, in the last analysis, the evidence of their trustworthiness must be given in their own activity.

Faith is also distinguished from those beliefs which we gain from our own processes of reasoning. It is not by faith that we believe in the result of a mathematical demonstration, or, if we had never heard of the case, yet should understand the conditions, that we should believe the mercury in a barometer would sink if carried to the top of a high mountain. It is not by faith that we believe anything that we are required to believe by our constitution or by the laws of evidence, except as confidence in personal character enters into those laws.

Faith is also to be distinguished from uncertain knowledge.

It is mischievous, as opposing faith to reason, and as bringing religion into contempt, to make faith something mystical and obscure, and to which a man may resort when he is pushed in argument. Says Hamilton, "Faith — belief — is the organ by which we apprehend what is beyond our knowledge." "In this," he adds, "all divines and philosophers worthy of the name are found to coincide." Faith an organ! Belief an organ! As if, making them, as is here done, synonymous, belief were anything but an opinion not substantiated beyond all doubt. He might as well make opinion an organ instead of a product. If all divines and philosophers worthy of the name have believed this "the more's the pity."

It is also said that faith is that principle of our nature by which we apprehend the invisible. But what is an apprehension of the invisible but a form of knowledge or belief based on evidence? If there are principles of our nature through which we believe in the invisible, they must be common to all men; but "all men have not faith." Faith does, indeed, often imply a belief, or, if you please, an apprehension of the invisible, but that is not its distinctive element. Faith has always a personal element. It is confidence in a person with reference to anything for which he offers himself to us. If we believe what a man says solely because he says it, that is faith. If we believe it in the face of strong improbabilities from other sources, the faith is more signal. It is more signal still, if, on the mere ground of character, and when that stands in conflict with other sources of belief, we commit to another great interests. When Alexander the Great drank the cup presented to him by his physician, though he had been warned by a note that the physician intended to poison him, he did it by faith. A traveller who should himself know the way through a forest would walk securely and independently on the ground of his knowledge; but one who should know nothing of the way, and should commit himself wholly to a guide, would walk by faith; and if his faith were perfect, he would step just as firmly and securely as the other.

Now, from the condition and circumstances of man it is plain that faith was intended by God to be a great natural principle and guide of life. In the absence of instruction and comprehension, it is to creatures with reason what instinct is to those without it, and something more. It was intended to be to them not merely a guide, but a formative, an assimilative, and an elevating principle. It is to mere belief what the moral reason is to reason. It is belief and something more, and is therefore higher. By the element of belief that is in it, it guides its subject; and by that which is specifically the confidence, it assimilates and elevates him. It is the one great link, the magnetic link, between parent and child, by which the parent is enabled to raise the child to his own level. Take this wholly away, and not only would the improvement of the race be checked, but improvability could scarcely be affirmed of it.

That it is a natural principle, is obvious, not only from its being thus necessary, but because life is full of conditions and relations in which men act from it naturally, necessarily, and with no feeling of degradation. It is true universally of children, in their relation to their parents, and of men generally in their relations to each other as proficients in specific branches of knowledge, and that without regard to general superiority. An admiral may rationally entrust his ship to a common pilot, and a Newton entrusts his health and life to his physician.

But what is thus natural and necessary in the common relations of life, we might expect, if God be indeed a father, would be carried up into our relations with him, only with such modifications as would be demanded by his character and those relations. Here, obviously, reason would demand that the faith should be unwavering and absolute, stopping at nothing except that which would make God deny himself. This the very conception of God as possessed of infinite excellence would require. From what was said formerly of the identity of a moral and of the divine law, it will follow that man must be able to judge to some extent of anything claiming to be a divine revelation by its intrinsic qualities; and it may be conceded to the advocates of reason that if anything can be shown to be opposed to the final or highest end of man, it cannot be from God. He cannot require essential wickedness. So much seems to be conceded by the apostle in the case of Abraham; for he says that Abraham acted on the supposition that God could reconcile two revelations which seemed to him contradictory. "He counted," says the apostle, "that God was able to raise him up even from the dead." It is not that, the ultimate end being known, the insight of reason in regard to that as good can be shaken, for then would God contradict himself, but that, in respect to any prescribed means, or to anything short of the relinquishment of that, faith in God should be unlimited. At this point it must stop, because the denial of essential goodness and the denial of God would be the same thing. If God could command malignity and the hatred of goodness as such, he would not be God.

If, then, within this limit, it can be shown that God has made any communication to man respecting his end, — if he has either told him what that end is, or directed him how to attain it, — it will be wholly reasonable for him to receive implicitly what is thus communicated, and to rest his whole being upon it. Doing thus he is acting upon a natural and necessary, as well as an ennobling principle, and his tread may be as firm, and his assurance in regard to ultimate results as absolute, as if he comprehended the whole system of the universe from beginning to end and from centre to circumference. It would not indeed be philosophy by which he would be guided; but it would be reason rejecting as inadequate such philosophy as itself might be able to form, and trusting, instead, to the guidance of Him who is the author and source of all philosophy. It would be the mariner trusting his compass; it would be the child taking exercise or medicine by the direction of a father, without knowing the laws of his system. It would, in short, be man understandingly and rationally taking that place as a child in which is his dignity and his happiness. With sufficient ground of confidence in his father, a child holding his hand — which is faith — might rationally close his eyes and step where his father should direct; or, with his eyes open, he might step in opposition to what would be his individual judgment; and in these two cases, with the limit above given, we have the whole relation of reason and faith.

As connected with religion, faith has been the subject of much discussion, but as a great natural principle of action it is an illustration of the principle noticed in the first lecture, that what is the most intimate to us, and from the beginning wholly a matter of course, is the last to attract attention. When the term was first used in Christianity, nothing could have been more strange. It was unknown in philosophy, and it is a strong evidence for Christianity that it should have thus seized upon a principle which must act from the first moment of conscious existence, which is in society what gravitation is among the stars, and without changing its nature, but only modifying it according to the relations involved, should have transferred it from its all-pervading though unrecognized earthly uses to the higher uses of religion.

From what has been said it would appear that in pursuing an end from instinct, by faith, or with a full comprehension of both means and ends, we may be acting rationally, while it is only in the last case that we should be acting philosophically, because a system of philosophical action can be based only on a conception of ends and of means. But these three systems or grounds of action, the instinctive, the religious, and the philosophical, can have the common characteristic of being rational only on the condition that they conspire to a common end. That most clearly they must do. A system not based on the true end would be erroneous and not philosophical; an instinct or tendency in a being rightly constituted must prompt to the true end; and faith in God could lead only to that.

Thus does this philosophy of ends, in connection with the law of limitation, make provision for the harmonious operation of every active power in man. In whatever proportions instinct and faith and philosophy may be combined, there is yet full provision for the high prerogatives of man as personal and rational, and every power may conspire to lift him up and bear him on to his true end.

Having thus brought moral philosophy to a perceived harmony with those original impulses of the constitution which are of the nature of instinct, and with faith, which is distinctively and naturally the religious principle, it will need but a few words to show its harmony with religion itself.

It will, first, be a test of any system that may claim to

come from God, whether it be one of revealed law, or of a mode of restoration when law has been violated; and, second, of any such system that should really come from God it would be the adjuvant.

Moral philosophy analyzes the powers of man, and thus discovers the true end of each, and so of man himself. If, then, there be a revealed law, or what claims to be such, which would require the pursuit of the same end, moral philosophy must accept that law. It cannot do otherwise. Then the law is right and binding, whether revealed or not. If any law claiming to be from God could be shown to be thus wholly in harmony with the moral constitution of man, it would be conclusive evidence that it was from God. It would be a revelation in words of the same will that had been previously revealed in ends. And this is precisely what we claim for the Bible as a revelation of law. What we say is, that no fair and correct analysis of our faculties can be made that will not necessitate for them the same end and law that are revealed in the Bible.

So of anything that should claim to be revealed as a method of restoration. If it could be shown to be not only in harmony with the law as revealed in the end, but also to have in it an efficacy so to restore the man that he shall attain that end, it would be conclusive evidence that that too was from God. Here the problem would be double, and the difficulty increased. But as it is the object or end of the foot that we may walk, and as a rational physiology would accept whatever would restore a broken bone so that it should be as good as if it had not been broken, so, if the moral powers have been injured, a rational philosophy would accept and welcome any remedial system which it could be shown would enable them to attain their original end. Here is the test of any system claiming to be remedial, — harmony with law on the one hand, and the power of restoration on the other, — and, tried by this test, we have no hesitation in saying that Christianity must be received.

LECTURE XI.

RIGHTS. — THEIR ORIGIN AND KINDS. — ALIENABLE. — INALIENABLE. — SLAVERY. — RIGHTS OF PERSONS AND OF THINGS. — GIVING AND RECEIVING. — RIGHTS OF GOVERNMENT. — LIBERTY AS RELATED TO RIGHTS. — DIFFERENT KINDS OF LIBERTY — NATURAL, CIVIL, POLITICAL.

Of any correct system of moral philosophy one characteristic must be that the active powers will, in their movements, harmonize with each other. That they do this in connection with the system of ends, we have seen. Through the law of limitation each higher power is harmonized with the lower, while the highest is left to act freely and to expand in its connection with those infinities to which it is naturally related. This gives us a philosophical system for the *individual* which we may comprehend.

But not only may we comprehend both means and ends, and so seek them intelligently; we may also seek ends from a native tendency involving in it, if it be not instinct, the instinctive principle; and we may seek ends by faith. These principles may be combined in very different proportions. They must be, as persons are younger or more advanced, as they are ignorant or instructed; but it was one object of the last lecture to show that whatever the proportions might be, these principles might be so accepted and permeated by the rational nature that we should be rational in acting from them, and that they would be in perfect harmony.

But God does not regard the individual only. He has

instituted families, communities, nations. Of these he designed the well-being, and has provided for it in the organization of man. Would, then, this doctrine of ends, with its law of limitation, be an adequate basis for social order?

As an individual, man is to do right; as a member of a community he has rights. What it is on this system to do right, we have seen. Would there also grow from it a perfect system of rights? If so, there would be in it an adequate basis of social order, because of that it is the one condition that every man shall have his rights. If so, we may well accept a doctrine thus providing for the right ordering not only of the individual, but of the community.

On this system, we have seen that that is right which a man must do that he may attain the end for which God made him. Rights must, therefore, be based on the relation of those things to which we have a right to the attainment of our own end or that of others. A man will have a right to everything that is essential to the attainment of the end for which he was made. So a parent will have a right to everything which is essential to the attainment of the end for which God made him a parent; and society and government will have a right to everything necessary for the accomplishment of the ends for which they were instituted — just that, and no more.

An exclusive capacity, inherent or given in the order of nature, together with a disposition to confer upon others what is essential to their end, is the ground of rights over them. Hence the rights of God, of parents, and of governments. A necessity for anything essential to his end is the ground of a claim by the individual upon any who, in the order of nature or of providence, may have the exclusive power to meet that necessity. Hence the claims of children, of citizens, of the poor, of humanity.

We have here the general principle; and if it be correct, then will the basis of right and of rights be the same, only it will be viewed in different relations. We shall have, moreover, what is not a little desirable, in the distinction drawn between the higher and lower powers, a measure of rights as more or less important and sacred. Thus we shall have rights from the instincts, that is, those which would respect the attainment by instinct of its end; and rights of the appetites, or those which would respect the attainment by them of their end; and so of the desires, and of the intellect, and of the natural affections, and of the moral and spiritual nature. Certainly we may say that he who should be in no way so encroached upon or obstructed that he should be unable to attain in the best way all the ends indicated by these different active principles might be said to have all his rights; and if he were so encroached upon that he could not reach perfectly any one of these ends, he would not have all his rights. The truth seems to be that in the tendency of every active principle towards its end there is the voice of God; and that when, through the intervention of others, there is an obstruction to the attainment of its ends, that voice utters itself through the moral nature in the assertion of *rights*.

That this is the history of the idea and sentiment of rights — for it is not merely a sentiment — seems probable, because it is foreshadowed by what occurs among animals. That they have the perception of relations and the sentiment that we have, cannot be supposed, but practically they assert what seem to be rights, and what is analogous to them, on the same principle. Let an animal have an instinct, or an appetite, or a natural affection, as that of the parent for its offspring, and it will be found that it will be ready to resist and beat off all intrusion that would prevent it from accomplishing the end thus indicated, and the strength of endeavor will be proportioned to the importance of the end. So is it with man. He is prompted by some original impulse to the attainment of an end. This would imply struggle against obstacles, and the resistance of any interference that would prevent the attainment of the end. It is in connection with such promptings and resistance that the moral reason necessarily forms the notion of rights, and that the sentiment is felt; and thus that which with the brute is defended simply by force, comes with man to be guarded by the most sacred sentiments, and to be fortified by laws, and customs, and institutions.

From this view of the origin of rights it will appear that the idea of right is the primary, and that of rights the subordinate and secondary idea. A man has rights in order that he may do right. If there were no end, and so nothing right, there could be no such thing as rights. Hence rights, however real and important, may never be defended at the expense of right. A man may be deprived of all his rights, but he may not cease to adhere to that which is right.

At this point it is that we may see how it is that the destiny of a man, that is, his highest and ultimate destiny, can never be taken out of his hands. Men may deprive him of every right, but they can bring about no combination of circumstances under which it will be impossible for a man in those circumstances to do right. It may be a fearful alternative, and there may be unspeakable wickedness in presenting it, when a man must be deprived of his rights, even of that to life, or cease to do right, but it is the glory of man's nature that there is in it the capacity of adhering to what is right under all deprivation and all suffering. If it were not for this—the higher estimation of right than of rights—no man could be a martyr. Right belongs to man in his individual capacity, rights from his relation to others.

Of rights as thus originating and thus distinguished from right, some are alienable, and some inalienable; and we find in the distinctions already laid down the ground of this difference. An inalienable right is one which arises in connection with the pursuit of our highest end. With that nothing may interfere; and a right thus based is called inalienable because it cannot be parted with freely without crime, and cannot be rightly taken away unless forfeited by crime.

As has been seen, the moral, no less than the physical nature, has its end; in the use of means for the attainment by that nature of its end, the idea of rights the most sacred would arise; and to whatever is an essential condition for the attainment of that end man has an inalienable right. With that he may not consent to part, and no one may rightfully wrest it from him; but any right which is not thus necessary he may alienate.

After the moral nature, the natural affections and the intellect are next in dignity. That the rights which originate in connection with the exercise of the affections are alienable, appears, since a parent may transfer to another all the rights and responsibilities vested in him as a parent. A child may be wholly given away, its name changed, and the rights of the parents over it vacated according to law. Than this, perhaps a stronger case could not be put under the rights of the affections. Of the intellect it is to be said that its operations are so essential to the full attainment of the ends of the moral nature that it can hardly stand on its own ground; but that a man may employ his intellect for gain at the will of another, and, so far as that is possible, wholly give it up to his control, provided that control does not interfere with the attainment by the moral nature of its end, will, I suppose, be conceded. Why not? The intellect is simply instrumental, and may be employed by the executive power in any way that shall not contravene a moral end. Of the rights that originate from the desires, as that of property, I need not speak, as it is conceded that they are alienable.

All inalienable rights may be included in those of life and liberty. A right to the pursuit of happiness, mentioned in the Declaration of Independence, would be included in that to liberty, since no man can have liberty who is debarred from the pursuit of that. And yet liberty is not wholly inalienable. In some respects, and to some extent, a man may part with his liberty, and it has not always been easy to say how far he may go in this, According to the principles already stated he may part with his liberty in any respect, and up to any point, that shall not interfere with the attainment of his highest end. Beyond this he can make no contract that would not be unlawful, and so not binding; for man has a paramount duty to God respecting himself, which is as fully binding as any other duty. He may never lawfully do anything with himself which shall prevent the great purpose that God had in view in giving him being from being accomplished. Except as an indispensable condition for a higher end, there is nothing sacred about liberty; it is capable of being wholly abused, and if it may be conceived that a higher end may be promoted by giving it up, then may it be given up. According to this those Moravian missionaries who sold themselves into slavery that they might preach the gospel to the slaves, may have been justifiable. They sacrificed liberty for a higher end.

Inalienable rights are those of which a man cannot divest himself by contract; which he may not, under any circumstances, lawfully demit; but he may forfeit them by crime, and be wrongfully deprived of them by others. It is in this last case, in the violation of an inalienable right, that the greatest wrong is committed, and of this we see the reason in what has been said respecting the ground of inalienable rights. To deprive a man of life is everywhere regarded as the highest crime; and next to that, in some circumstances perhaps even greater, is the crime of depriving him of his liberty. When this is so done as to degrade a human being, and to come between him and his highest end, we have a crime that involves in it the essence of all crimes.

Of slavery, so far as it interferes with inalienable rights, our abhorrence cannot be too strong. It interferes with other rights, as those of the desires. It takes property, or the labor that makes property, without an adequate compensation. It violates the rights of the affections. It separates husbands and wives, and parents and children; putting, in the eyes of the law, and often practically, and by the necessities of the system, the natural affections of the slave on the same level with a brute instinct. It interferes with the rights of the intellect. It keeps men in ignorance, and prohibits them from learning to read the word of God. It gives the slave no security for anything. Everything must depend upon the will of the master; and if that will be reasonable, then upon his life. Now, while it is true, as has been said, that no man can be so placed that he cannot adhere to the right, yet such a system, applied to masses of human beings, must degrade them, must come between them and their highest good, and so touch inalienable rights. The highest right of a man is his right to himself, and any right of property that would so contravene this that man shall be treated in any way as a brute, or degraded, and that would come between him and his end as designed by God, is impossible. No man can give it; the man himself cannot; no state can give it, and any attempt to hold such property is *sin per se.*

That there may be a temporary and modified system of involuntary servitude without infringing upon inalienable rights, and with ultimate benefit to those so held; that under a system of perpetual servitude the actual guilt will depend much on the light of the master, and the spirit in which it is administered; and that, under peculiar circumstances, the legal relation of master may be sustained for the good of the slave, not only without guilt, but meritoriously, may be conceded. And it is because this partial alienation of liberty without degradation is possible; and because guilt is so modified by acquiescence in established customs to which men have been used from their infancy, and which they have been taught are right; and because, from obstacles to emancipation through wicked laws and the disabilities they lay upon the freed-man, or from the helplessness of infancy or of old age, the legal relation of master may sometimes be rightly held while yet the system itself is one of utter oppression and wrong, often and generally infringing upon inalienable rights; and because of the immense pecuniary interests at stake, that it is possible for men to hold such discordant views on this subject, and that their views are held in connection with feelings so intense.

Having thus seen what is the origin of rights, and the distinction between those that are alienable and those that are inalienable, we turn to another distinction. There are rights which have it for their object to guard the individual against the encroachments of others. As thus used, the sole correlative of rights is obligation, and it is in this aspect that rights are more generally treated. If I have a right to a piece of property, all others are under obligation to abstain from its use. The object of such rights is so to protect the individual in his freedom, that he may accomplish the ends indicated by his active powers. Such rights respect things, and not persons; or, if they respect persons, it is only as they are so related to us that we may by them accomplish our own ends.

But there are also rights over persons. The object of these is to enable those in whom they are vested to aid others in the accomplishment of their ends. Here the correlative of rights is still obligation. If the parent has a right over the child, the child is under obligation to respect that right. But here the right involves by necessity not only an obligation on the part of others, but also a duty on the part of him in whom the right is vested, and this duty thus necessarily involved in the right, and measured by it, may also properly be called its correlative. The foundation of the right here and in the other case is radically the same, as they both have reference to the attainment of an end; and yet there is an essential difference. In the first case the ground of the right is the necessity of that to which the individual has a right in order to the attainment by himself of his own ends, that is, of those indicated by his various active powers. But in the relations of society human beings are not always capable of attaining these ends without aid from others. In that case others may have rights over them, natural or acquired; but the ground and measure of those rights will be found in the necessity there is for aid in the accomplishment of those ends, and in the power and duty of those who possess the rights to render that aid.

In what has now been said we have a clear distinction between rights over things and those over persons. This distinction was indicated by Blackstone, under the heads "Rights of Things" and "Rights of Persons," but his statement of any ground for it is so indistinct that in a note to Chitty's edition of his work it is said that "the distinction of rights of persons and rights of things in the first two books of the Commentaries seems to have no other difference than the antithesis of the expression." As the most he could make of it, the annotator adds, "The distinction intended by the learned judge in the first two books appears to be in a great degree that of the rights of persons in public stations, and the rights of persons in private stations." This is wholly aside from the real ground of the distinction. As has been said, rights over persons have respect to the accomplishment of ends by those persons, and involve duties; while rights over things respect the accomplishment of ends by ourselves, and do not in the same way involve duties.

This distinction is needed because the rights over persons are numerous and important, and without it we have no way of fixing precisely the ground and limits of those rights. These are the rights of parents, of guardians, of teachers, so far as they have also guidance and control; they are, in general, the rights of those that govern; and have, standing over against them, not only corresponding obligations, but also corresponding rights. Wherever there is a right to govern, there is a corresponding right to be governed rightly. What it is to be governed rightly is implied in what has already been said. A man ought to govern another on the same principle on which he ought to govern each of his separate faculties, and his whole self. He governs those faculties rightly when he causes each to accomplish its end. He governs himself rightly when he accomplishes his own end; and he governs another rightly when his government is wisely directed to enable that other to accomplish his end. This is the law of limitation here. Hence the parent has a right, so far as the destiny of the child is committed to him, to all the control necessary to secure for the child its true end. Whatever power he may use for any other end is not properly that of a parent, since it would not grow out of the parental relation as instituted by God. That relation is one of guardianship of the child with reference to the ends for which he was made, and especially to his highest end; and if the child could certainly know that he could secure his highest end only by disobeying his parent, he would be bound to disobey him. This shows the natural limit to the rights, and so to the authority of the parent. And what is thus true of a parent is equally true of a guardian, a teacher, a magistrate, a government. So God governs. This is the model he sets before us, and he has given no rights to any of his creatures that will justify them in governing upon any other principle.

Very beautiful is the relation thus established between the governing and the governed, and quite in accordance with what has been previously said. We have seen how beautiful is that relation of all things as conditioning and conditioned by which there is a continual subserviency of that which is lower to a higher end, till this universe, as more immediately known to us, is built up from its base to its apex, and culminates in man. In this process the lower force is independent of that which is higher and unmodified by it till we reach organization. In all organization, while the higher is built up by the lower, and constantly sustained by it, yet the higher reacts upon the lower, and becomes in its turn essential to that. The stomach and digestive system are for the brain. They build it up; but the brain reacts upon them, and unless it be healthy they will fail. Where organization begins, the movement within each organism becomes circular, and not merely one of upbuilding from a base. And now, when we pass into the region of intelligence, we find provision not merely for a system of forces acting from below to build up that which is above, but that there shall be forces from above intelligently acting to benefit if not to elevate that which is below. At first, and in mere organizations, the lower builds up the higher, and sustains it, and is wholly for that. Any action from the higher to the lower is simply to sustain the lower in its own place and function as tributary, but never to elevate it out of that sphere. But when we reach the sphere of intelligence the object of the action from above is to elevate the lower. When the summit is reached, then, through this arrangement of rights and of duties, a circle is formed by which the system works from the top, so that that which is spiritual is drawn up from above, since there could have been no force from below adequate to push it up. Certainly the parent, as a parent, is for the sake of the child, and his end in that relation is accomplished when he has brought the child up to his own elevation, or, rather, to what that elevation ought to be. In doing this there may be, there ought to be ties formed that shall be permanent, that, as spiritual, shall be eternal, and so the highest here minister to that which is still higher; but the parental office, and the merely natural affections connected with it, have exhausted themselves when the parent who is what he should be has raised the child to his own elevation. So all analogy teaches. So is it with every animal that has natural affection; and where provision is made for the young independently of the parent, the affection is not given.

Up to the point where giving from above begins to elevate that which is below, if there may be said to be blessedness at all, it had been more blessed to receive than to give. The giving was always by the lower to the higher, and for the sake of the higher. But we now reach a point where the giving is by that which is above, for the sake of that which is below, and God has connected with it, in the end which it accomplishes, in the affections which it gratifies, and in the improvement, and growth, and dignity of the giver, a blessedness that could not come from receiving. It is here, indeed, that we have *the* element of the noblest giving. It is not simply that which addresses itself to the animal nature and satisfies want. It is *that*, when it is needed, always that; but enwrapping and bearing with it a giving of affection and self-sacrifice that would lift up that which is below it; and if this element be wanting, no giving can avail much, and the highest blessedness of it cannot be known.

In speaking of the rights that involve duties, I have referred almost wholly to those of parents; but the principle applies equally to the rights and duties of society and of government. These, scarcely less than the parental relation, are essential for the perfection of the individual. Without them he cannot find his sphere, and scope for the expression of his whole nature. It is, indeed, that constitution by which society is thus necessary, that makes a number of individuals a community, that makes the state an institution of God, and the race a unity. An exclusive capacity to confer such aid, given in the order of nature, confers rights. A necessity that such aid should be conferred is the ground of a claim. Hence the reciprocal rights and duties of the family, of the state, and of humanity.

It is to governments as founded upon this principle that attention is especially needed. Practically, they have too often been instruments of oppression. They have kept down and degraded the governed. It is among the saddest features of the history of our world that the very conception and ground of this beautiful and beneficent function of government should have been so wholly lost sight of, and government so perverted to purposes directly opposite to those for which it was intended. A vast abstraction, or, if you please, a general conception called the state, has been idolized. It has been supposed that the individual was wholly for that; and so, partly through a blind and perverted instinct of patriotism in the people, the very institution which ought to have been the most efficient for their elevation has often been the most potent engine for their oppression and degradation. So it has been; so it is still.

But in the light of our discussion, government has no right *to be*, except as it is necessary to secure the ends of the individual in his social capacity; and it must, therefore, be bound *so to be* as to secure these ends in the best manner. This is the whole principle, and only the full application of it is needed to make governmental and social movements on the earth correspond in their order and beauty to the movements of the heavens. On this principle there could be no conflicting rights as between the individual and the government. The government could require — from the very ground of its rights as already stated, it could have a right to require — nothing that would not be in harmony with the ends of the individual, and whatever the government might need to accomplish its ends that should be thus in harmony, the individual would be bound to concede.

This is the general statement. To obviate practical difficulties, however, it must be observed that when it is said that government is for the individual, it is not meant that it is for any one individual especially, but for all the individuals of whom the society is composed. If, therefore, a case should occur in which the good of the society would require that the alienable rights of the individual should be, not, as is generally said, given up, but alienated for an equitable consideration, the government, as the agent of society, has the right to enforce such alienation. This paramount right government has, and must have, from the end for which it was instituted. Is it for the good of society that it should take the land of a man for a road? It has a paramount right, and takes it; but it gives him an equivalent. It would be thought monstrous to take it otherwise. Is it again for the good of society that it should take the time, more valuable it may be than land, of an innocent but accused man, that he may be tried? It has a paramount right, and takes it, but it makes no compensation. But that society is bound in equity to make it, there can be no doubt.

The right of society is to take, for its own good, the alienable rights of the individual, on condition that those rights shall be surrendered only for a fair equivalent. This the ends of society, and so of government, require. What society says to the individual is, "We will give you as ample means as you now have to accomplish your ends; we interfere therefore with none of your fundamental rights; but we cannot suffer mere will or caprice to stand in the way of the good of the whole." The right to say this I do not suppose society gets from any consent of the individual, or any agreement on his part to surrender certain rights; but because it is of divine origin, and has, therefore, an inherent right to accomplish its ends. This it must do for the sake of the individual, since his perfection can be reached only through society, and hence, according to the doctrine stated, the individual can have no rights not compatible with the ends of society. All alienable rights must be held by him subject to the condition that when they interfere with the good of the whole, they shall so far cease to be rights that they may be alienated by the will of society regularly expressed through its government, and for a fair compensation. According to this view, the rights of the individual and of society would be perfectly harmonized. At least, there could be no conflict in regard to alienable rights. Nor could there be any respecting those that are inalienable, since those are sacred. Those society may not touch. It is impossible that any legitimate end of society should be gained by trenching in any degree upon any inalienable right, and therefore society can have no right to do so. Injustice, tyranny, may do anything. A triumph of wrong there may be, but there can be no conflict of rights.

From the consideration of rights we pass to that of liberty, of which the conception of rights is both the basis and the natural limit. Rights and liberty! These are among the most exciting and stimulating words of the English language, and unless our view of their grounds and limitations be distinct they may become words of delusion and mischief, — cabalistic words for the popular declaimer and demagogue to conjure with. It is a slow process by which the conceptions connected with such words in the popular mind become clear and steady; but nothing is more needed, especially in a government like ours; and whoever contributes to it in any degree is doing the public good service.

It has just been said that rights are the basis and natural limit of liberty. If there were no rights there could be no law. God would have no right to give or to enforce one, and there would be nothing for law to guard. Law is the guardian of rights and the condition of liberty, since without law there would be anarchy, which is the opposite of liberty. It is, I know, usually thought that the idea of liberty is the primary one, and that of law secondary, as coming in to restrain liberty; but if we take law in its widest sense as that which gives stability and regularity, and a rational ground of expectation, we shall see that without the conception of that there could be no ground of choice or of action, and so none for liberty; so that it may well be doubted whether the conception of law does not underlie that of liberty of any kind, as it certainly does that of all desirable and rational liberty. We may, indeed, conceive of what is called absolute liberty, by which is meant a liberty of doing, without question or control, whatever the individual pleases. For a single isolated individual this is conceivable, but not in a community of individuals, each having free will and independent choices. Such a liberty would be an element of utter confusion, like that which would ensue in the physical elements if their affinities were unloosed and wholly capricious, so that there were nothing of regularity in their movements. We may well conclude, then, that the first liberty among created beings was born and cradled and trained amidst the sanctities of law, and that any exercise of it except under the control and guidance of law must be a curse.

Taking liberty, then, as known by us, and desirable for us, we inquire after its different kinds.

And, first, there is natural liberty. This is not absolute liberty. That is not natural. The law of any being is indicated in its nature, and no liberty can be natural that would overstep that natural law. Than this nothing could be more unnatural. But natural liberty is simply that which is commensurate with natural rights. Every man has originally a natural right to use all the means furnished him by God for the attainment of the legitimate end indicated by each of the active principles of his nature; and his natural liberty would be such a freedom from restraint that he could avail himself of all such means for the attainment of those ends. If God has not furnished the means of doing this without encroaching on the rights of others, then his liberty and his rights find their limit together. Let a man have a liberty by which he may attain every end of his being which God has given him the means of attaining; let no man come wrongfully between him and those means, and he has all the liberty that any being ought to have or that can be natural to any. This, then, is natural liberty — a liberty to use all the means that God gives a man for the attainment of the ends indicated through his nature.

A man has natural liberty to use the means above indicated. Has he also a natural right to defend himself in such use? This is commonly said, and that the right of society to defend the individual in the use and enjoyment of these means is from a voluntary transference of such right by the individual to society. But society is natural, and as such has rights and duties; and looking at its end, we shall find it to be its natural right and duty to protect the individual in the use of these means. If, in an unnatural state of isolation, the individual has a right to defend himself in the enjoyment of these means, it may be quite as correct to say that he gets that right by a transference of it from society, as to say that, in ordinary circumstances and in a natural state, society gets the right by a transference of it from the individual. Saying this we avoid all conflict of rights; we avoid the unnatural and violent supposition that man is necessitated to give up any of his natural rights in order to secure the remainder.

We next inquire what civil liberty is. Of this it is thought by some that the notion is so complex that it cannot be defined, but only described, and the circumstances stated in which it is enjoyed. But having seen what natural liberty is, we say that civil liberty is natural liberty under the guardianship and guarantee of an organized society. It is the liberty which a man enjoys when his rights are protected and guarantied by society instead of himself. Hence the only abridgment, if such it may be called, of natural liberty needed that it may become civil liberty will respect the means of attaining the end, and not the end itself. Man has a natural right both to defend and to use and enjoy the property produced by his own labor; but the right of defence vests in society, and by suffering it to remain there he enjoys greater freedom and security in the use of his property. This freedom and security are civil liberty. It consists in a liberty and security in enjoying the end which can be attained only by leaving with society the responsibility, and so the right of protecting ourselves in that enjoyment. But protection is not in itself an end; it is only a means; and therefore we are always to remember that in requiring us to leave with society a portion of our rights civil liberty only requires us thus to leave the right to employ means, but never to abandon the right to enjoy ends.

The perfection of civil liberty will be measured by the degree of freedom and security that can be attained in the enjoyment of every right which can be left to the guardianship of society. Every right cannot be thus left, and the liberty to defend such right must remain with the individual; but perfect civil liberty will be the greatest possible freedom and security under the guardianship of society for every right that naturally belongs to its care. It may be added that, under civil society, such liberty, as essential to the end of the individual as a social being, is a natural right.

In the view of it above taken civil liberty is for the perfection of the individual. It may also be regarded as it stands related to the ends of society as a whole. The object is not only to find the point where the action of the whole shall either be for the good of the individual, or not militate against it; but also where the action of the individual shall either be for the good of the whole, or not militate against that. That these points may be found, and that they would coincide, cannot be doubted by any who know the balancings, and adjustments, and harmonies there are in the works of God, and for which we might expect the most perfect provision in the highest department of those works. This would bring the interests of the individual as an individual and his interests as a member of the community into perfect harmony. In this point of view civil liberty would be conditioned on such a restraint of individual action as should guard the interests of the whole from injury.

Civil liberty, as has been said, is a natural right. Hence,

under a free government, it is accorded to all, whether they are citizens or not. But the right to take a part in the government, to say who shall administer it, and what provisions shall be made for the maintenance of civil liberty, is not a natural right. It belongs to society as a whole, but not to every individual in that society. It is not generally supposed to belong to minors, to women, to foreigners, except on specified conditions, and in the most of our States it is not granted to the free blacks. What the principles are on which this right should be conceded, and what should be their application in particular cases, it is not always easy to say. Here an end is to be secured. Society is bound to secure it in the best way it can, but the means and materials for doing this may be very different at different times and in different nations.

On this point it may be said, first, that a reasonable presumption of hostility to the welfare of the society would be a sufficient ground for excluding any one from having a voice in the government. Hence criminals are excluded; and there may be factions, or races, known to be hostile to the government, who may be justly excluded while that hostility remains.

Secondly. Incompetency to understand and promote the ends of society would be a sufficient ground for exclusion from political rights. It is on this ground that minors are excluded, and foreigners who are presumed to be ignorant of the nature and working of institutions under which they have but recently come. It is true that many minors, and many foreigners not naturalized, are better qualified to exercise political rights, and so for what is sometimes called political liberty, than many who do exercise those rights; but where there is no absolute right society may, and must, fix the best average limit it can. According to this, under institutions like ours, society would have a right to say, as has been proposed, that no man should vote who could not read. It may be expedient in given circumstances that such persons should vote, but they have no right. It may be wrong that they should be permitted to do it. Society cannot be bound to entrust its interests and destinies to ignorance, or chance, or passion.

Once more; if there be such relations established by God that one portion of the community cannot take part in administering the government without injury to the ends of society, then that portion may be excluded. It must be on this ground, if upon any, that women are to be excluded from the right of voting and holding office under our government. They cannot be excluded on the ground that they are not interested in the welfare of the government, or that they are incompetent. But it is never safe to violate any true instinct of humanity. There are some things that depend not so much upon reasoning as upon sentiment and a felt propriety. When a country is invaded and civil liberty is to be defended, it is not so much from any laying down of principles and formal reasoning as from a felt propriety that the women remain at home, while the men go to the battle. In the same way, when civil liberty is to be instituted and sustained, it may be from the same felt propriety that men alone should be concerned in the conflicts of public debate, and at the polls. It may be that in her relations to man, when she is elevated to her true position, God has made provision that her influence shall as effectually reach a free government for good as if she were immediately concerned in it; or if not, there may be obstacles which would render it inexpedient that she should have that power at present; and in either case society would have the right to withhold it. Certainly, if there be such relations established by God that one portion of the community cannot take part in the government without injury to society, then that portion may be excluded. How far this may be the case in any particular instance, each society must judge for itself, as it does upon other and similar questions.

I cannot close this lecture without observing that this subject of rights, regarded as a barrier against encroachment, and as involving duties, demands the especial attention of a free people. Among such a people there will always be a tendency to regard liberty as a right of unrestrained action, and rights as something to be enforced. It is those days when liberty was gained and rights enforced that nations celebrate. But is easier to gain liberty and enforce rights than, having gained them, to practise the self-control that shall respect rights, and the self-denial and faithfulness and patient waiting required in performing the duties that our rights involve. This is the turning point with us. Can we use our freedom and enjoy our rights without encroaching upon the liberty and the rights of others? Will parents, and magistrates, and citizens, fulfil the duties that correspond to their rights? Will they see that individual and unauthorized action is so restrained that all shall have their rights? There is no grander sight than that of a great people, powerful and free, under the guidance of a comprehensive wisdom, always arresting its action at the point where it touches the rights of others, protecting those of the most feeble, and trusting calmly for its aggrandizement to the gradual but resistless power of intelligence, industry, and freedom, under the guidance of justice. And there is no sadder sight than such a people governed by fraud and cunning, torn by faction, disintegrated by selfishness, denying to others what they claim for themselves, with no faith in the natural power of free institutions to perpetuate and extend themselves without force, and thus putting into the hands of others a cup, which, in the circuit and balance of God's retributions, must be returned to their own lips, and which they must be compelled to drain to the very dregs.

LECTURE XII.

A FUTURE LIFE. — ITS RELATION TO MORALITY. — THE PHYSICAL ARGUMENT. — MORAL ARGUMENTS.

WHAT man ought to do will depend on the end for which he was made. If he was made for this world only, then he ought to live for this world. But if he was also made for a life after this, and his conduct in this life would affect his condition in that, then he ought to live with reference to that. We labor for the morrow, because we expect to awake in the morning. It is thus that the doctrine of a future life connects itself with morality; and as we have seen that man is connected with all that is below him, it will be a fitting close of our subject to inquire what indications there are in his nature that he is also connected with that which is beyond and above him.

Than this no inquiry can be of greater interest. Whether there is a God or not; whether this visible structure of the universe is to be eternal or not; whether the generations of men are to be perpetuated, or are to be destroyed by some general convulsion of nature, are questions that little concern the individual man if he is evoked into being like the bubble upon the ocean, to appear but for a moment, and then vanish forever.

The first indication of a future life that I shall mention is drawn from the nature of the mind as simple and indivisible, and so incapable of destruction except by annihilation.

Concerning that which underlies the power of thought three suppositions may be made, and only three. It must belong either to one single, indivisible, ultimate particle of matter; or to a number of such particles united together; or to what we must call an immaterial substance entirely distinct from matter.

Does the power of thought, then, reside in a single, indivisible, ultimate particle of matter? I think not, because these particles are so minute. No microscope can reach them. If a single grain of the salts of iron be put into thirty thousand pints of water, it can be detected by experiment in every drop of that water. A hare, in his flight, leaves particles of insensible perspiration upon the earth at every footfall. These must be inconceivably minute, as they are constantly given off so long as the hound can follow the track. But to suppose that one such ultimate particle has, in addition to the properties of matter, those of thought, feeling, memory, imagination, judgment, that it studies fluxions and metaphysics, indites poems, and governs nations, seems absurd.

But I need not dwell on this, because those materialists who deny a future life do not advocate it, and for the very good reason that it would be a strong argument against them. If the soul be such an ultimate particle, then it can perish only by annihilation, and it seems to be a principle in the government of God not to annihilate anything. What we call destruction is simply a change of form, never an annihilation of substance.

Is, then, the power of thought the property of a number of particles of matter united together?

Here again we must look at the constitution of matter. Concerning this there are two suppositions. One is that of Boscovich, and was adopted by Priestly, a distinguished materialist. The supposition is that what we call matter consists, not of solid particles, but of centres of attraction and repulsion. As other philosophers have said, take away solidity and matter vanishes, so Priestly says expressly, "Take away attraction and repulsion and matter vanishes." This seems to me to deny the existence of matter as a substance, though not as a force, and it cannot be necessary in opposing materialism to show that thought cannot be the property of a number of centres of attraction and repulsion, when, by the supposition, those centres themselves, as material bodies, do not exist.

We take next the common supposition that matter consists of solid extended particles of great minuteness.

Whether such particles are ever so united that there is actual contact between them is not decided; but whether there is or not, we must remember they are separate and independent bodies, and that a body which we call one is not a unit, but a collection of units to which we give a common name. There is no unity till we come to ultimate particles, or to mind.

Now the supposition is that thought, though not the property of any one of these particles separately, is yet the property of a number of them, greater or less, united together.

But this is surely contradicted by the consciousness of every man in regard to the oneness of that being which he calls himself. It is also contradicted by the nature of the mental phenomena, as thought, feeling, consciousness, which are simple, and incapable of division. If this doctrine be true, then the thought, originating not solely in one particle, but in a number, must come, part of it from one, and part from another, and what is thus made up by composition may be again divided. According to this there would, as has been said, be no impropriety in speaking of the half or the eighth of a thought, of the top and bottom of a feeling, of the east and west end of consciousness.

But, again, if this doctrine were true, there could not only be no such thing as simple indivisible thought, but there could be no personal identity. Our bodies undergo constant change; they are no more the same bodies for two days together than the stream which we pass over on two successive days is the same water. The brain participates in these changes. I remember now what happened when I was four years old; but there is not in my system now one particle of matter that was there then. How, then, does this new matter know what happened to the old? How can this consciousness, this sense of identity, be transferred from one particle to another? According to this, we should be undergoing a continual death, for, as the whole brain dies when it ceases to think, so there must be some particles of it, as they are passing off, constantly giving up the ghost, and leaving their transitory honors to their successors. And these others, — how are they exalted! That which was yesterday a portion of a potato or of a calf's brains, may to-day become a part of the soul of a philosopher! That there are any who believe this is the most plausible argument that I know that their souls are thus made.

In reply to this objection I have never seen anything better than the following ironical answer from Martinus Scriblerus: "Sir John Cutler had a pair of black worsted stockings which his maid darned so often with silk that they became at last a pair of silk stockings. Now, supposing those stockings of Sir John's endued with some degree of consciousness at every particular darning, they would have been sensible that they were the same individual pair of stockings both before and after the darning, and this sensation would have continued in them through all the succession of darnings, and yet, after the last of all, there was not, perhaps, one thread left of the first pair of stockings, but they had grown to be silk stockings, as was said before."

But however conclusive the above arguments may seem, I am aware that I have not yet touched the real difficulty as it lies in your minds, if you have been accustomed to read a particular class of writings on this subject. It is, that thought is never manifested except in connection with a brain or nervous system, on which it seems to depend; that as one changes the other changes; when the brain is diseased, thought is disordered, and when that ceases to act thought ceases to be manifest. That it is not to be supposed that any one particle in distinction from the others has the power of thought, but that it is the one simple result of the combined action of the whole, just as music is the result of the combined action of the fiddle-bow and the fiddle, or as secretion is the result of the action of the gland. This, I think, is a fair statement of the doctrine of the materialists, and of the kind of analogies by which it is supported.

In reply to this I observe, first, that we have evidence of the existence of thought without a brain or nervous system, or we have no evidence of the existence and intelligence of God, or of any spiritual being. If there be such beings, doubtless the principle of thought is the same in us as in them.

But allowing that we have no such evidence, I am inclined to think that the statement is absurd, for it supposes the whole to have properties which do not belong to the parts separately. In a piece of silver, however small, we have all the properties we can have in a mass as large as a mountain.

But music is not the property of the fiddle, or of the bow, but the result of the combined action of the two. What, then, is music? What is done in this case? Why, the fiddle and the bow have motion of a particular kind in their particles. This is communicated to the atmosphere, producing vibrations. These vibrations are no more one than the "gales of Araby the blest," and of Lapland. They proceed to the ear, and by means of that make a series of impressions upon the mind which we group under one name and call music. The only one effect produced by the fiddle, or the bow, or both together, is motion, and this is a property or result that belongs to all the parts. There is no *music* till the motion reaches the perceiving mind, which, having an antecedent unity, makes to itself a unity of that which, without it, had been nothing but a succession of different motions. Here certainly is no new property acquired by the aggregation of parts, no unity like that of thought, nor indeed any unity at all except that which is derived from the mind itself. A man might as well speak of the unity of the particles which cause smell because they produce one odor, as of any unity there is in music till it reaches the mind.

But does not the brain secrete thought as the liver does bile? This is a favorite theory with some physiologists. To this there are three objections: 1st. The liver does not secrete bile as mere matter. A dead liver will not do it, and if there were not some one principle of life, different from matter, working through the liver, it would not do it. 2d. The bile that is secreted is made up of separate particles of matter, and has no unity as thought has.

3d. Thought is immaterial, and it seems absurd to suppose that an immaterial result can be secreted by a material organ.

Than the analogies just given I know of none stronger. Particles of matter may be so accumulated and arranged as to produce an effect upon the mind or upon other matter different from that produced before, and may require a new name, but they thus get no new quality or property like the power of thought. Here is a single particle. It has, by the definition of matter, magnitude, figure, mobility, and if any one shall choose to add color I will not now object. Now, you may add other particles to this in any way you please, and unless you change the definition of matter you can have nothing but varieties of color, figure, motion, and magnitude.

But it is said that the mind and brain increase together, are mutually affected, and decay together. This is true to a certain extent, but with such exceptions and limitations as to destroy the force of the argument. "It is certain," says Lord Brougham, "that the strength of the body, its agility, its patience of fatigue, indeed all its qualities, decline from thirty at the latest, and yet the mind is improving rapidly from thirty to fifty, suffers little or no decline before sixty, and therefore is better when the body is enfeebled at the age of fifty-eight or fifty-nine than it was in the acme of the corporeal faculties thirty years before. It is equally certain that while the body is rapidly decaying between sixty or sixty-three and seventy, the mind suffers hardly any loss of strength in the generality of men; that men continue till seventy-five or seventy-six in the possession of all their mental powers, while few can then boast of more than the remains of physical strength, and instances are not wanting of persons, who, between eighty and ninety, or even older, when the body can hardly be said to live, possess every faculty of the mind unimpaired. The ordinary course of life, therefore, presents the mind and the body running courses widely different, and in great part of the time in opposite direction; and this affords strong proof both that the mind is independent of the body, and that its destruction in the period of its entire vigor is contrary to the analogy of nature." Of the above statements Lord Brougham is himself a distinguished example.

No doubt we are intimately connected with certain portions of matter. We are so with our limbs; but cut them off and there is no loss to the mind. Yet these were portions of matter by means of which we had felt and communicated with the external world. Our connection with the brain may be more intimate, but there is no reason to suppose it to be of a different kind. Parts of the brain may be ulcerated, removed by operations or by accident, and the man still remain the same. Indeed, there is no reason to suppose that one piece of matter by means of which we perceive is any part of ourselves more than another. By means of glasses we see objects that we could not without them. The same is true of the eye. The eye is only an optical instrument which we carry in our heads instead of our pockets, and we have no more reason for supposing it a part of ourselves than we have for supposing a telescope a part of ourselves.

As to the decay of old age and the effects of disease and injury upon the brain, they are only what might naturally be expected. To adopt the words of an old English poet, Sir John Davis, —

> " For these defects in sense's organs be,
> Not in the soul, nor in her working might;

She cannot lose her perfect power to see,
Though mists and clouds do choke her window light.

"These imperfections, then, we must impute
Not to the agent, but the instrument;
We must not blame Apollo, but his lute,
If false accords from her false strings be sent:

"As a good harper stricken far in years,
Into whose cunning hands the gout doth fall,
All his old crotchets in his brain he bears,
But on his harp plays ill, or not at all."

The most skilful singer may have a cold, the best musician a cracked fiddle, the best eye can see but imperfectly through furrowed glass. Speaking of this connection and distinction between the agent and the instrument, Cicero says: "Suppose a person to have been educated from his infancy in a cottage where he enjoyed no opportunity of seeing external objects except through a small chink in the window-shutter, would he not consider this chink as essential to his vision, and would it not be difficult to persuade him that his prospect would be enlarged by demolishing the walls of his prison?" You see the application. Old age is the gradual closing up of this chink, but death is the pulling down of the walls of his cottage and letting in the broad daylight upon him.

From a consideration, then, of the nature of the soul, so far as we can judge of it from its attributes, we believe it has an existence independent of the body, and that it is of such a nature that it can perish only by annihilation, which we have no reason to suppose ever occurs in regard to the most inconsiderable of the works of God.

We now pass from the argument from the nature of the soul as a substance, and its connection with the body, and proceed to others derived from its faculties and situation in this life.

The first that I shall mention is the general and well-nigh universal belief of this doctrine. Travellers have said that they could discover no traces of this belief among certain tribes. But those who pass through a tribe ignorant of its language and customs are incompetent judges on such a point, and it has, I believe, been found in every instance, after fuller investigation, that such a belief did exist. If it do not, it is only among those who are raised but one degree above the brutes, and whose faculties consequently have not been developed. Certainly the belief is so universal that it must be supposed to be the work of nature. It arises directly and without reflection from our natural desire of continued existence, and from the expectations excited by the action of the moral nature in hope and remorse.

Can we, then, reason from the constitution of our nature to its destiny?—from the expectations which that nature instinctively excites to our future condition? If not, we can reason from nothing, for nature is not constituted on the principle of good faith. It is said, indeed, that the above principles subserve beneficial purposes in this life, and that they were given for that purpose alone. But if so, nature has mingled them in the constitution too largely. She has so constituted them that man does, in fact, expect a future life. Besides, if they were given for this life only, why is hope strongest in the aged and the good, and why, especially, does remorse increase in the guilty as death approaches? The appetites were given for this life, and they grow weaker with age. What must be thought of the honesty of a system in which it should turn out that the hope of the good man was a lie, and the fear of the bad one a phantom?

A second argument is, that while there is throughout nature an exact adaptation of everything else, especially of every animal in its structure and instincts, to its situation and end, if man is to exist in this life only, we find no such adaptation either in his intellect or in his affections.

While the brutes have no curiosity, instinct supplying the place of experience and of investigation, man wishes to know not only the use of things, but their nature, and that not alone of things with which he is or can be connected in this life. His curiosity fixes upon bodies the most remote as if they were his own proper province which he was one day to investigate and understand. He sees the mountains and valleys of the moon; he follows the track of the comet; he wonders at the rings of Saturn; he explores the nebulæ, and inquires after the "architecture of the heavens." He knows just enough of these bodies to raise his curiosity, but not enough to satisfy it. His intellect is to the distant universe just what the eye of the child is to this world when it first opens upon it. It sees a little, it is adapted to see more; shall it be quenched forever even before it has learned to see? And not only does the intellect seek to know the physical universe, it also inquires after God. It says, "Where is God my Maker?" It is capable of knowing that God as seen in dim reflection from his works. And will God, having revealed himself thus dimly, withdraw? The twilight of this highest of all knowledge having dawned on the soul, shall the sun go back?

Nor is the want of adaptation in the affections less than in the intellect. Even more than curiosity do the yearnings of affection seem like those mute promises of nature which we observe in the animal world, and which are there always fulfilled. Has the chrysalis wings that are folded within? There is an atmosphere prepared without in which it can fly. Does the bee perceive a fragrance on the air? There is a flower on which it can alight. And shall man be as the bee that should perceive the fragrance but not find the flower? Shall bereaved love cherish hope till death only to be disappointed? The only interpretation of affection yearning for something higher than this world can give, and the only solace of that which is bereaved, is to be found in the doctrine of a future life.

A third argument is, that while individuals of every other species attain all the perfection of which their nature admits, there is evidently a foundation laid in the nature of man for an indefinite progression.

A tree rises from its seed, it increases for many years, it is beautiful to the eye, it yields fruit, it furnishes shade. If it were to remain forever it could do nothing worthier or better. It has attained perfection as a tree. So an animal reaches in a short time the limit of its powers. Destitute of reason, of a moral nature, of the power of forming general ideas and following general rules, it goes on in the fulfilment of its destiny guided by instinct and by particulars, and could not, without a different kind of powers, make any essential progress. It is perfect as an animal. The structure, though humble, is complete. It has its capitals and its dome. But no one can say that man, considered as a rational and moral being, reaches here the perfection for which a foundation is laid in the nature of his powers. The philosopher who has traversed the circuit of human knowledge, and has pitched his tent upon its outposts, not only does not approach the limits of knowledge, but, what is important to our present argument, he does not find his powers burdened or embarrassed by the knowledge already acquired. On the contrary, every advance which he makes gives, and from the nature of the powers must give, new light and strength to make further advances, and when old age comes he only feels himself more "like a child gathering pebbles on the shore of the great ocean of truth." So, also, and more so, is it with the good man making progress in goodness. His path is like the shining light. Shall it shine more and more unto the perfect day, or shall it go out in darkness? Here, then, the foundation is laid. Shall the superstructure go up? The ocean is before man, shall he embark upon it? Or shall he, who, as Shakspeare says, is "so noble in reason, so infinite in faculties, in form and moving so express and admirable, in action so like an angel, in apprehension so like a God,"—shall he be left the only fragmentary being, as if God had completed everything else and had failed in his grandest undertaking; as if he had indeed made him not only the "glory," but the jest and riddle of the world?

The force of this argument from the nature of the human powers as progressive, is greatly heightened when it is considered in connection with a fourth which I now adduce, and which is from analogy.

The effect of this argument upon our minds will depend much upon the care with which we have studied the works of God, and our consequent conviction of the connection, and uniformity, and consistency of those works. It was once supposed that different parts of the earth were governed by different powers and laws. The heavens had their Jupiter, and the ocean its Neptune. Ignorant nations think so still. But we now know that it is all one system of mutually dependent elements, and subject to one code of physical laws. And not only so, it is now settled that the physical universe is one great system in which every part is related to every other part. Every particle of matter, or, as Paley says, "the chicken on its roost," is related to the sun and to other systems; and while this is so, we say that it is contrary to all analogy that this great intellectual and moral system of man should have no relations beyond itself. The inference undoubtedly is that as matter is here subordinated to mind, it is so elsewhere, and that there is a vast intellectual and moral system, the parts of which have relations that are to be unfolded in future time. I believe that we shall one day know the history of other worlds and other orders of beings, and that they will know ours. Certain it is, however, that we are in the midst of a *system;* it is one of gradation and mutual dependence from the infinitely minute up to man, each that is below being united to that which is above, till we come to man, who is the topmost of the series. Now, does the series stop with him? Is it probable, when we see, as we do see, the hooks and grappling-irons fastened into the centre of his being, by which he is to lay hold on somewhat above him, that there will be nothing found on which he may fix? Our superior knowledge of nature in its connections gives us a great advantage over the ancients in this analogical argument. It enables us to see more completely what is wanting that man may be wrought in and form, without discrepancy, a part in the one great system; and I would sooner believe in such monsters as centaurs and satyrs and hippogriffs, than in such a monster as man would be if cut off from anything higher than himself and beyond the present life.

> "Unless above himself he can
> Erect himself, how mean a thing is man."

But the argument which has probably been most effective with men in general is that indicated in the soliloquy of Cato:—

> "If there's a power above us,—
> And that there is, all nature cries aloud
> Through all her works,—He must delight in virtue;
> And that which he delights in must be happy;—
> But when? or where? This world was made for Cæsar."

"When," says Jeremy Taylor, "virtue made men poor, and the free speaking of brave truths made men lose their lives, or at least all the means and conditions of enjoying them, it was but time to look about for another state of things where justice should rule and virtue find her own portion."

No thoughtful man can contemplate the unredressed wrongs of this world without perplexity. He cannot but ask if there be not a supreme power somewhere who will regard the appeal of the martyr which he writes in his own blood,—if there be not a supreme power somewhere who will disown the atrocities perpetrated in his name on the field of battle and in the dungeons of the inquisition. For the difficulties thus presented there is no solution but in a future state.

What has just been said goes on the supposition that the distribution of good and evil in this world is promiscuous; but if it should appear that it is not wholly so, but that there is an undertone in the natural government of God that chimes in with the voice of conscience, the argument would be much strengthened. Are there discoverable amidst this apparent confusion the beginnings of a righteous administration, which carry with them a promise of their own completion?

This is a subject of wide compass, and for its full illustration I must refer you to a chapter upon it in Butler's Analogy. Suffice it to say, that from the serenity of virtue on the one hand, and the uneasiness of vice on the other; from the different treatment which virtue and vice, as such, necessarily receive in civil society, the constitution of which is natural; from the forebodings of conscience; from the natural tendencies of virtue and vice, — the one tending to order and strength, the other, though it may have at times an accidental ascendency, to disorder and confusion, — from all these He who is supreme in nature has sufficiently indicated to which side he belongs. His object seems to be to manifest himself just so far as to give room for moral election, — to give such indications of his will as may suffice for the sincere, the humble, and the diligent, but not such as shall be obtrusive, and withhold the reckless, through fear, from pursuing their own course.

But whatever the object may be, certain it is that the moral feelings of man are not the only ground of argument on this subject. There is a righteous administration already begun here, and on the scroll of Providence, as it is unrolled in its grand and solemn movements, there are written characters, which vice, if it were not infatuated, would read and tremble. If, therefore, there be no future state in which these silent prophecies may be accomplished, then is there falsehood inscribed not alone on the intellectual and rational powers, not alone on the mere natural government of God, but also upon his moral government so far as it can be discovered, and in the very sanctuary of the moral nature of man.

If, after these arguments, there should still remain some vague impression that in the shock of so great a change as that of death the principle of thought should not survive, there are analogies of nature which may bring us some relief. If all the philosophers on earth had been shown an egg for the first time, and been asked what it would become, they could as little have thought it possible that it should be such a creature as a swan or a peacock, as the greatest skeptic now thinks it possible for man to survive. Or, to take a case sometimes thought to be more in point, what can be a greater change than the chrysalis undergoes in its manner of life, when it passes from its dormant condition to that of a beautiful butterfly, seeming, as Bryant says, "a living blossom of the air"? So striking, indeed, is this analogy that the Greeks gave the soul the same name as the butterfly, from the expectation that it would undergo a similar change.

The strongest case, however, is that put by Butler. It respects the change in man from the mode of his existence before birth to that which he at present enjoys. He is still the same being, but his mode of existence was so different that had he been endowed with the powers of reason he would have been much less able to form any conception of his present mode of being than he now can of a future state. He might have perceived some indications in his structure, as in the eyes and the lungs, of a preparation for a state then future, as we now do for one still future, but the necessary change would have been quite as mysterious as that which must pass upon us at death.

It is to be remarked, also, in thinking of this change, in

what part of our nature it occurs. We have two modes of being, that of sensation and that of reflection, which seem in a great degree independent of each other. Reflection, having once commenced, is independent of sensation, and is most active and intense when sensation is weakest. If we wish to reflect we shut out sensation. But it is upon the sensitive life that this shock of death seems to spend itself. The power of reflection often continues in full vigor up to the last moment. Since, then, the power of reflection is so independent of the sensitive life, and of the organs of sensation, it seems rational to conclude that it may hereafter maintain a separate existence.

Such are some of the arguments drawn from nature which I would urge in favor of the probability of a future life. To me they seem to have no little weight. But if they were less forcible than they are, so that their opponents could bring against them those of equal or greater force, I could never understand, unless something different from mere argument is concerned, the triumph which some men appear to feel when they suppose themselves to have quenched the hope of man, and to have levelled themselves with the clod. Surely, if a man were to think himself obliged, as the result of a candid investigation, to believe that to be true which "nature never told," we should expect, instead of exulting, that he would

> "Read, nor loudly nor elate,
> The doom that bars him from a better fate,
> But, sad as angels for the good man's sin,
> Weep to record, and blush to give it in."

These few arguments from nature for a future life I offer, not as affording absolute proof, but a presumption so strong that a prudent man might act upon it even if he had no other light; a presumption stronger than that upon which we often act, and upon which it would be madness not to act in the ordinary concerns of life. I wish, also, to have you see that skeptics may be met on their own ground, and that no impression may be left upon your minds which shall prevent you from receiving in its full force the evidence for that revelation by which alone, in all its clearness, "life and immortality are brought to light."

SUMMARY.

Having completed the several lectures, it remains to give a summary of the course of thought passed over. That course has been one, and in itself entirely simple.

The three questions proposed concerning duty — 1st. What ought to be done? 2d. Why ought it to be done? 3d. How ought it to be done? — we attempted to answer by a consideration of ends. We saw that all rational arrangement, construction, and action, must have reference to an end, and can be comprehended only in the light of that end; and that all rules and laws have their significance and value in the same way.

We assumed that from a study of the structure of man, physical and mental, some knowledge may be gained, not only of his separate organs and faculties, and of their use, but also of the end of man himself. If man cannot know his own end there can be no philosophy of man — no comprehensive or satisfactory knowledge of him. Whether he could know this as he now is, without revelation, may be doubted. There is no philosophy in a ruin; and where the Bible has not been it does not appear that men have retained a knowledge of their end. But however this may be, a knowledge of the end must greatly aid us in tracing the arrangements and correlations for the attainment of that end, and so of comprehending the whole system as one of means and ends.

Ends were distinguished as subordinate, ultimate, and supreme.

As the conception of an end involves that of some good, we considered the nature and sources of good. This we found to result from activity, and that the highest good would be from the activity of the highest powers in a right relation to their highest object. We discriminated the different kinds of good as it comes from the susceptibilities and the powers, finding from one what is distinctively pleasure, from the other happiness and blessedness.

We then sought to classify the powers, and consequently the good derived from their action, as higher and lower. In doing this we found a common law of gradation, and so of activity for forces and faculties — for those forces by which the universe is governed, and for those faculties by which man ought to be governed..

Commencing with the lowest and most general force known to us, we passed up till we came to vegetable or organic life, where a great transition is made, and which subordinates to itself all lower forces. We then came to that sensitiveness and intelligence in the service of which life works; and then to those rational and moral powers in which is personality, and by which we are made in the image of God. At every step from the lowest sensitiveness, while we found, as in that, an end in itself, we also found a beautiful subordination to that which is higher, and in that subordination we found the law of limitation for the activity of every lower power and faculty. We saw how perfectly God regards this law in that part of the chain where our wills do not intervene, and how perfect is the model he sets before us for the regulation of our own lives. We saw that when we reached the highest form of activity and of good the law of limitation ceased, and became that of the highest capacity of the faculties in a form of activity, and so of blessedness, like that of God himself. Our conception of him is that he is perfectly blessed in a holy activity. Being made in the image of God, our whole duty and end, as might have been supposed, is to be like him; and if we are like him in his activity we must be in his blessedness.

In thus passing upward from a broader basis, retaining all that is below, and adding something for every new and narrower platform, till we reach man at the summit of the pyramid, we find for the universe so far as we know it, the principle of unity. This is in the fact that each lower force is always the condition of the higher. This would give us a universe; but it is the fact that each lower force is precisely such in degree as to be the most favorable condition for that which is higher that gives us an orderly universe. This fact and relation we find everywhere in nature, — in all the systems of which the body is composed, from the digestive upwards, and in all the powers and faculties of the mind; and everywhere we find the proportion of force accurately observed till we come to the intervention of finite will. We thus find provision for every inferior form of good. We omit nothing; we undervalue nothing. We find provision for the harmonious operation and symmetrical growth of every propensity, appetite, and power, whether of body or of mind, and especially full provision for those powers by which man is connected with what is infinite and eternal.

Having thus obtained a knowledge of good in its sources and gradations, we proceeded to a classification of those activities and faculties in which good originates.

And here we considered the forms of mental activity, first as spontaneous, and second as voluntary. In the first we found a spontaneous or automatic life which is conditional for a voluntary life, into which the voluntary or personal life is put, as into a garden, to dress and to keep it, and which, without the personal life, would go on always as the mind does in dreams, and be a thinking thing. Perfection here would be in the coincidence of the two without effort.

We then proceeded to classify the faculties as they are related to ends.

Here the first class is of those which are instrumental for the attainment of ends beyond themselves. Under this are, first, those which indicate ends; and, second, those in the light of which we pursue ends.

The second class are those powers in whose activity we find ends beyond which there are no others, and which are our moral nature.

Under the first class we considered separately, and at some length, the Instincts, the Appetites, the Desires, and the Natural Affections. We considered the Intellect, also, as far as that is subject to the will. All these we regarded as having no moral quality in themselves,—as neither good nor evil, except as they are controlled. To any particulars of these discussions which occupied us during four lectures we need not now recur.

We next passed upwards to those powers that are directive, that *are* our moral nature, and in whose activity are ends beyond which there are no others. These we found to consist of the moral reason, having inseparably connected with it moral affections and conscience; and of free will. In the union, or rather synthesis of these, we found a *person*, and so reached the highest known and possible form of being. Not that the person is composed of these as elements, but that this person *is* as a simple form of being, and that these are forms of its manifestation without which personality could not be conceived of. Here we find a being moral and responsible.

In the activity of such a being, naturally knowing his own end, and necessarily affirming obligation to choose it, we have the intuitional side of a true moral system; and in the activity of the discursive and practical powers in coincidence with this we have its inductive side. We thus harmonize intuitional and teleological systems. In this connection, also, we have the characteristic of complete virtue or holiness as manifesting itself in two directions; we have the point of moral responsibility, and the genesis of our chief moral ideas. Here, too, we considered the moral nature in its double function, as both originating moral acts, and judging of them; and here we sought for the proper sphere of conscience, and pointed out the ambiguity of the term.

Of a person thus endowed with reason, moral affections, conscience, and free will, the highest form of activity is rational love; and hence, according to the philosophical formula for the highest good, we found it here. At this point, therefore, we identified the teachings of the human constitution, as drawn from a consideration of ends, with the summary of the revealed law of God as given by our Saviour.

We next investigated the relation between holiness or virtue, and happiness. In doing this we distinguished between moral good, as the natural and necessary result of moral goodness, and natural good; and also considered the good there is from the approbation of goodness. Moral good and that from approbation were shown to be infallibly connected with moral goodness. Natural good is not necessarily thus connected, but there is a tendency towards it. There is between them no contrariety or opposition, or "antinomy," and they ought to be connected by will in the way of reward. That they are not thus connected in the present state, is an evidence of disorder, and an indication of a state yet future.

In connection with this we affirmed the duty of each one to secure his own good through moral goodness, and found that this was not only compatible with the good of the whole, but necessary to it, — thus bringing into harmony a rational self-love and benevolence.

Regarding not only the quantity, but also the quality of enjoyment, we saw that the good and end for man was not to be found either in holiness by itself, or in happiness by itself, but in *holy happiness*, or *blessedness*. That these are thus necessarily united, no doubt God intended we should know; also that we should seek them as thus united; and our idea of perfection is the highest possible union of these, together with all natural good following in their train.

In determining, next, more specifically, the sphere of moral science, we took our point of observation at the performance of an outward act, and going backwards to its source, we found an immediate recognition of the moral quality of the act as good or evil; while, in going forwards and outwards to its consequences, we found the ideas of utility, and, in one sense, of right and wrong. In the one case we were wholly concerned with the person and the motive; in the other, with the outward act and its results. Separated from its origin in a person, and its motive, an act can have no moral quality; but it may be outwardly conformed to law, and have consequences beneficial or injurious, and be, in ordinary language, right or wrong; and an attempt was made to show the confusion that has arisen at this point, and the need of greater precision both of ideas and of terms.

We also considered the province of conscience, its infallibility, the two spheres in which it acts, and its relation to other active principles; and we inquired whether, in order to be virtuous, an act must be done from a sense of duty.

Leaving personality and motives, we next went outward to the consideration of those fixed relations established by God, and which indicate his will. Here we saw that virtue and rectitude are so far coincident that where virtue exists there can fail to be rectitude only from mistake; and also the difference between those calculable consequences from acting in violation of fixed relations or in accordance with them, and those incalculable and illimitable consequences that may flow from guilt or its reverse. We sought the character of a true expediency, and the difference between prudence and virtue. We even ventured to speak of the nature of God, and so far to call in question the common view as to suggest whether it be not his nature to be wholly supernatural; and whether there can be anything more ultimate for the conscience than his character as the standard of moral excellence, and his will as the expression of that character.

At the opening of our discussions it was said that besides pursuing an end as rationally comprehending it, we may also do so from Instinct and from Faith; and we next showed that between the action of these and of reason there might so be a coincidence that a man may be rational in acting both from instinct and from faith. Reason and faith being thus reconciled; reason being at the basis of moral philosophy, and faith being the distinctive principle of religion, just as it is in the relation between parent and child, it was easy to see what must be the points of coincidence and mutual support between moral philosophy and religion, whether natural or revealed — whether a system of pure revealed law, or of forgiveness and restoration after law had been broken.

We next had before us the subject of rights as connected with our previous speculations. We showed their origin in the will of God — uttered through the several active principles of our nature — that man should attain his end. We ascertained their gradations as growing out of previous classifications. We drew the distinction between alienable and inalienable rights, and also between those over persons and over things. We showed the foundation and limits of the rights of parents and of governments. We spoke of liberty in its various kinds as related to rights; also of the rights of different classes of the community; and closed by a reference to the duty of all in a government like ours to secure the rights of all.

In the closing lecture we have passed from the relations of time, and considered the great question of a future life, thus giving to morality weightier sanctions, and a loftier perspective. The details of the argument we need not reproduce.

We have thus, my friends, in accordance with that ancient precept, "know thyself," which is said to have descended from heaven, examined the human constitution in its relation to ends. In doing this it has been my wish to avoid technical terms, and to appeal directly to the consciousness of my hearers. That appeal has been met by an attention that has been all I could desire. Upon such a course probably no independent thinker could enter without discovering new relations both between the faculties themselves, and between them and the ends for which they were intended. How far such relations have now been presented, or the point been reached towards which the great lines of thought converge, you will judge. That these views will be accepted by all, I do not expect. That they will not be without their value in advancing the science, I cannot but hope. As was said in the first lecture, that advance must be slow; but we are not to be discouraged. The moral sphere is more intimate to us than any other; it is the highest of all; it is there that we find our true selves; and it cannot be that we should be capable of tracing the harmony of suns and of planets, and be forever incapable of apprehending those higher harmonies which we have now attempted to trace, between man and nature, between man and himself, between man and his fellows, and between man and God.

THE END.

Valuable Works,

PUBLISHED BY

GOULD AND LINCOLN,

59 WASHINGTON STREET, BOSTON.

CHRISTIAN'S DAILY TREASURY: a Religious Exercise for every day in the year. By Rev. H. Temple. 12mo, cloth. $1.00.

WREATH AROUND THE CROSS; or, Scripture Truths Illustrated. By Rev. A. Morton Brown, D. D. 16mo, cloth. 60 cents.

SCHOOL OF CHRIST; or, Christianity Viewed in its Leading Aspects. By Rev A. R. L. Foote. 16mo, cloth. 50 cents.

THE CHRISTIAN LIFE, Social and Individual. By Peter Bayne, M. A. 12mo, cloth. $1.25.

THE PURITANS; or, The Church, Court, and Parliament of England. By Rev. Samuel Hopkins. In 3 vols., octavo. Vol. I., cloth, *ready.* $2.50.

MODERN ATHEISM; under its various forms. By James Buchanan, D.D. 12mo, cloth. $1.25.

THE MISSION OF THE COMFORTER; with copious Notes. By Julius Charles Hare. American edition; Notes translated. 12mo, cloth. $1.25.

GOD REVEALED IN NATURE AND IN CHRIST. By Rev. James B. Walker. 12mo, cloth $1.00.

PHILOSOPHY OF THE PLAN OF SALVATION. New, improved, and enlarged edition. 12mo, cloth. 75 cents.

YAHVEH CHRIST; or, The Memorial Name. By Alex'r MacWhorter. Introductory Letter by Nath'l W. Taylor, D.D. 12mo, cloth. 60 cents.

SALVATION BY CHRIST: Discourses on some of the most important Doctrines of the Gospel. By Francis Wayland, D.D. 12mo, cloth. $1.00.

THE SUFFERING SAVIOUR; or, Meditations on the Last Days of Christ. By Frederick W. Krummacher, D. D. 12mo, cloth. $1.25.

THE GREAT DAY OF ATONEMENT; or, Meditations and Prayers on the Sufferings and Death of our Lord. 75 cents.

EXTENT OF THE ATONEMENT IN ITS RELATION TO GOD AND THE UNIVERSE. By Thomas W. Jenkyn, D.D. 12mo, cloth. $1.00.

THE IMITATION OF CHRIST. By Thomas à Kempis. With a Life of à Kempis, by Dr. C. Ullmann. 12mo, cloth. 85 cents.

THE HARVEST AND THE REAPERS. Home Work for all, and how to do it. By Rev. Harvey Newcomb. 16mo, cloth. 68 cents.

(*RELIGIOUS.*)

LIMITS OF RELIGIOUS THOUGHT EXAMINED. By Henry L. Mansel, B. D. Notes translated for American ed. 12mo, cl. $.100.

THE CRUCIBLE; or, Tests of a Regenerate State. By Rev. J. A. Goodhue. Introduction by Dr. Kirk. 12mo, cloth. $1.00.

LEADERS OF THE REFORMATION. Luther — Calvin — Latimer — Knox. By John Tulloch, D. D. 12mo, cloth. $1.00.

BARON STOW. *Christian Brotherhood.* 16mo, cloth. 50 cents.

——— *First Things;* or, the Development of Church Life. 16mo, cloth. 60 cents.

JOHN ANGELL JAMES. *Church Member's Guide.* Cloth. 33 cts.

——— *Church in Earnest.* 18mo, cloth. 40 cts.

——— *Christian Progress.* Sequel to the Anxious Inquirer. 18mo, cloth. 31 cents.

THE GREAT CONCERN. By N. Adams, D. D. 12mo, cloth. 85 cents.

JOHN HARRIS'S WORKS. *The Great Teacher.* With an Introductory Essay by H. Humphrey, D. D. 12mo, cloth. 85 cents.

——— *The Great Commission.* With an Introductory Essay by William R. Williams, D. D. 12mo, cloth. $1.00.

——— *The Pre-Adamite Earth.* Contributions to Theological Science. 12mo, cloth. $1.00.

——— *Man Primeval:* Constitution and Primitive Condition of the Human Being. Portrait of Author. 12mo, cloth. $1.25.

——— *Patriarchy;* or, The Family, its Constitution and Probation. 12mo, cloth. $1.25.

——— *Sermons, Charges, Addresses, &c.* Two volumes, octavo, cloth. $1.00 each.

WILLIAM R. WILLIAMS. *Religious Progress.* 12mo, cloth. 85 cts.

——— *Lectures on the Lord's Prayer.* 12mo, cloth. 85 cents.

THE BETTER LAND. By Rev. A. C. Thompson. 12mo, cloth. 85 cents

EVENING OF LIFE; or, Light and Comfort amid the Shadows of Declining Years. By Jeremiah Chaplin, D. D. 12mo, cloth. $1.00.

HEAVEN. By James William Kimball. 12mo, cloth. $1.00.

THE SAINT'S EVERLASTING REST. Baxter. 16mo, cl. 50 cts.

Gould and Lincoln's Publications.

(LITERARY.)

THE PURITANS; **or, the Court, Church, and Parliament of England. By SAMUEL HOPKINS. 3 vols., 8vo, cloth. $2.00 per volume.**

HISTORICAL EVIDENCES OF THE TRUTH OF THE SCRIPTURE RECORDS, STATED ANEW, **with Special Reference to the Doubts and Discoveries of Modern Times. Bampton Lecture for 1859. By GEORGE RAWLINSON. 12mo, cloth. $1.00.**

CHRIST IN HISTORY. **By ROBERT TURNBULL, D. D. A New and Enlarged Edition. 12mo, cloth. $1.25.**

THE CHRISTIAN LIFE; **Social and Individual. By PETER BAYNE. 12mo, cloth. $1.25.**

ESSAYS IN BIOGRAPHY AND CRITICISM. **By PETER BAYNE. Arranged in two series, or parts. 2 vols., 12mo, cloth. $1.25 each.**

THE GREYSON LETTERS. **By HENRY ROGERS, Author of the "Eclipse of Faith." 12mo, cloth. $1.25.**

CHAMBERS' WORKS. CYCLOPÆDIA OF ENGLISH LITERATURE. **Selections from English Authors, from the earliest to the present time. 2 vols., 8vo, cloth. $5.00.**

———— ***MISCELLANY OF USEFUL AND ENTERTAINING KNOWLEDGE.*** **10 vols., 16mo, cloth. $7.50.**

———— ***HOME BOOK;*** **or, Pocket Miscellany. 6 vols., 16mo, cloth. $3.00**

THE PREACHER AND THE KING; **or, Bourdaloue in the Court of Louis XIV. By L. F. BUNGENER. 12mo, cloth. $1.25.**

THE PRIEST AND THE HUGUENOT; **or, Persecution in the age of Louis XV. By L. F. BUNGENER. 2 vols, 12mo, cloth. $2.25.**

MISCELLANIES. **By WILLIAM R. WILLIAMS, D. D. 12mo, cloth. $1.25.**

ANCIENT LITERATURE AND ART. **Essays and Letters from Eminent Philologists. By Profs. SEARS, EDWARDS, and FELTON. 12mo, cloth. $1.25.**

MODERN FRENCH LITERATURE. **By L. RAYMOND DE VERICOUR. Revised, with Notes by W. S. CHASE. 12mo, cloth. $1.25.**

BRITISH NOVELISTS AND THEIR STYLES. **By DAVID MASSON, M. A., Author of Life of Milton. 16mo, cloth. 75 cents.**

REPUBLICAN CHRISTIANITY; **or, True Liberty, exhibited in the Life, Precepts, and early Disciples of the Redeemer. By E. L. MAGOON. 12mo, cloth. $1.25.**

THE HALLIG; **or, the Sheepfold in the Waters. Translated from the German of BIERNATSKI, by Mrs. GEORGE P. MARSH. 12mo, cloth. $1.00.**

MANSEL'S MISCELLANIES; **including "Prolegomina Logica," "Metaphysics," "Limits of Demonstrative Evidence," "Philosophy of Kant," etc. 12mo. *In press.***

Gould and Lincoln's Publications.

(RELIGIOUS.)

GOTTHOLD'S EMBLEMS; or, Invisible Things Understood by Things that are Made. By CHRISTIAN SCRIVER. Tr. from the 28th German Ed. by Rev. ROBERT MENZIES. 8vo, cloth, $1.00 Fine Edition, Tinted Paper, royal 8vo, cloth, $1.50.

THE STILL HOUR; or, Communion with God. By Prof. AUSTIN PHELPS, D. D., of Andover Theological Seminary. 16mo, cloth. 38 cents.

LESSONS AT THE CROSS; or, Spiritual Truths Familiarly Exhibited in their Relations to Christ. By SAMUEL HOPKINS, author of "The Puritans," etc. Introduction by GEORGE W. BLAGDEN, D. D. 16mo, cloth. 75 cents.

NEW ENGLAND THEOCRACY. From the German of Uhden's History of the Congregationalists of New England. Introduction by NEANDER. By Mrs. H. C. CONANT. 12mo, cloth. $1.00.

EVENINGS WITH THE DOCTRINES. By Rev. NEHEMIAH ADAMS, D. D. 12mo, cloth.

THE STATE OF THE IMPENITENT DEAD. By ALVAH HOVEY, D. D., Prof. of Christian Theology in Newton Theol. Inst. 16mo, cloth. 50 cents.

FOOTSTEPS OF OUR FOREFATHERS; what they Suffered and what they Sought. Describing Localities, Personages, and Events, in the Struggles for Religious Liberty. By JAMES G. MIALL. Illustrations. 12mo, cloth. $1.00.

MEMORIALS OF EARLY CHRISTIANITY. Presenting, in a graphic form, Memorable Events of Early Ecclesiastical History, etc. By Rev. J. G. MIALL. With Illustrations. 12mo, cloth. $1.00.

THE MISSIONARY ENTERPRISE. The most important Discourses in the language on Christian Missions, by distinguished American Authors. Edited by BARON STOW, D. D. 12mo, cloth. 85 cents.

THE RELIGIONS OF THE WORLD, and their Relations to Christianity. By FREDERICK DENISON MAURICE, Prof. of Divinity in King's Coll., London. 16mo, cloth. 60 cents.

THE CHRISTIAN WORLD UNMASKED. By JOHN BERRIDGE, A. M., Vicar of Everton, Bedfordshire. With a Life of the Author, by Rev. THOMAS GUTHRIE, D. D. 16mo, cloth. 50 cents.

THE EXCELLENT WOMAN, as described in the Book of Proverbs. With an Introduction by W. B. SPRAGUE, D. D. Twenty-four splendid Illustrations. 12mo, cloth. $1.00.

MOTHERS OF THE WISE AND GOOD. By JABEZ BURNS, D. D. 16mo, cloth. 75 cents.

THE SIGNET-RING, and its Heavenly Motto. From the German. Illustrated. 16mo, cloth, gilt. 31 cents.

THE MARRIAGE-RING; or, How to Make Home Happy. From the writings of JOHN ANGELL JAMES. Beautifully Illustrated edition. 16mo, cloth, gilt. 75 cents.

Gould and Lincoln's Publications.

(SABBATH SCHOOL.)

POPULAR CYCLOPÆDIA OF BIBLICAL LITERATURE. Condensed, by JOHN KITTO, D. D. Numerous Illustrations. 8vo. $3.00.

THE HISTORY OF PALESTINE; with Chapters on its Geography and Natural History, its Customs and Institutions. By JOHN KITTO, D. D. With Illustrations. 12mo. $1.25.

ANALYTICAL CONCORDANCE TO THE HOLY SCRIPTURES; or, The Bible under Distinct and Classified Topics. By JOHN EADIE, D. D. 8vo. $3.00.

CRUDEN'S CONDENSED CONCORDANCE. By ALEX. CRUDEN. 8vo. Half boards, $1.25. Sheep, $1.50.

COMMENTARY ON THE ORIGINAL TEXT OF THE ACTS OF THE APOSTLES. By H. B. HACKETT, D. D. 8vo. $2.25.

ILLUSTRATIONS OF SCRIPTURE. Suggested by a tour through the Holy Land. With Illustrations. New, Enlarged Edition. By H. B. HACKETT, D. D. 12mo, cloth. $1.00.

PROF. H. J. RIPLEY'S NOTES.

——— *ON THE GOSPELS.* For Teachers in Sabbath Schools, and as an Aid to Family Instruction. With Map of Canaan. Cloth, embossed. $1.25.

——— *ON THE ACTS OF THE APOSTLES.* With Map of the Travels of the Apostle PAUL. 12mo, cloth, embossed. 75 cents.

——— *ON THE EPISTLE OF PAUL TO THE ROMANS.* 12mo, cloth, embossed. 67 cents.

COMMENTARY ON THE EPISTLE TO THE EPHESIANS. Explanatory, Doctrinal, and Practical. By R. E. PATTISON, D. D. 12mo. 85 cents.

MALCOM'S NEW BIBLE DICTIONARY of Names, Objects, and Terms, found in the Holy Scriptures. By HOWARD MALCOM, D. D. 16mo, cloth. 60 cents.

HARMONY QUESTIONS ON THE FOUR GOSPELS, for the use of Sabbath Schools. By Rev. S. B. SWAIM, D. D. Vol. I. 18mo, cloth backs. 13 cents.

SABBATH-SCHOOL CLASS-BOOK. By E. LINCOLN. 13 cents.

LINCOLN'S SCRIPTURE QUESTIONS; with Answers. 8 cents.

THE SABBATH-SCHOOL HARMONY; with appropriate Hymns and Music for Sabbath Schools. By N. D. GOULD. 13 cents.

EVIDENCES OF CHRISTIANITY, as exhibited in the writings of its apologists, down to Augustine. By Prof. W. J. BOLTON, Cambridge, England. 12mo, cloth. 80 cents.

Gould and Lincoln's Publications.

(LITERARY.)

CYCLOPÆDIA OF ANECDOTES OF LITERATURE AND THE FINE ARTS. Containing a copious and choice Selection of Anecdotes of the various forms of Literature, of the Arts, of Architecture, Engravings, Music, Poetry, Painting, and Sculpture, and of the most celebrated Literary Characters and Artists of different Countries and Ages, etc. By KAZLITT ARVINE, A. M. Numerous Illustrations. Octavo, cl. $3.00.

This is unquestionably the choicest collection of *Anecdotes* ever published. It contains *three thousand and forty Anecdotes:* and such is the wonderful variety, that it will be found an almost inexhaustible fund of interest for every class of readers.

KNOWLEDGE IS POWER. A View of the Productive Forces and the Results of Labor, Capital, and Skill. By CHARLES KNIGHT. With numerous Illustrations. Revised by DAVID A. WELLS. 12mo, cloth. $1.25.

LANDING AT CAPE ANNE; or, The Charter of the First Permanent Colony on the Territory of the Massachusetts Company. By J. WINGATE THORNTON. 8vo, cloth. $1.50.

☞ "A rare contribution to the early history of New England."— *Mercantile Journal.*

THE CRUISE OF THE NORTH STAR. Excursion to England, Russia, Denmark, France, Spain, Italy, Malta, Turkey, Madeira, etc. By Rev. JOHN O. CHOULES, D. D. With Illustrations, etc. 12mo, cloth, gilt. $1.50.

PILGRIMAGE TO EGYPT. A Diary of Explorations on the Nile, the Manners, Customs, and Institutions of the People, the condition of the Antiquities and Ruins. By Hon. J. V. C. SMITH. Numerous Engravings. 12mo, cloth. $1.25.

VISITS TO EUROPEAN CELEBRITIES. Graphic and life-like Personal Sketches of the most distinguished men and women of Europe. By the Rev. WILLIAM B. SPRAGUE, D. D. 12mo, cloth. $1.00.

THOUGHTS ON THE PRESENT COLLEGIATE SYSTEM in the United States. By FRANCIS WAYLAND, D. D. 16mo, cloth. 50 cents.

SACRED RHETORIC; or, Composition and Delivery of Sermons. By H. J. RIPLEY, D. D. With Dr. WARE'S Hints on Extemporaneous Preaching. 12mo, cloth. 75 cents.

MANSEL'S MISCELLANIES; including "Prolegomina Logica," "Metaphysics," "Limits of Demonstrative Evidence," "Philosophy of Kant," etc. 12mo, cloth. *In preparation.*

MACAULAY ON SCOTLAND. A Critique, from HUGH MILLER'S "Edinburgh Witness." 16mo, flexible cloth. 25 cents.

NOTES ON THE UNITED STATES OF AMERICA. By T. H. GRAND PIERRE, D. D., Pastor of the Reformed Church, Paris. 16mo, cloth. 50 cts.

HISTORY OF CHURCH MUSIC IN AMERICA. Peculiarities; its legitimate use and its abuse; with notices of Composers, Teachers, Schools, Choirs, Societies, Conventions, Books, etc. By N. D. GOULD. 12mo, cloth. 75 cents.

THE CAPTIVE IN PATAGONIA; or, Life among the Giants. A Personal Narrative. By B. FRANKLIN BOURNE. With Illustrations. 12mo, cloth. 85 cents.

Gould and Lincoln's Publications.

(SCIENTIFIC.)

ANNUAL OF SCIENTIFIC DISCOVERY. 11 vols., from 1850—1860. By D. A. WELLS, A. M. With Portraits of distinguished men. 12mo. $1.25 each.

THE PLURALITY OF WORLDS; a new edition, with the author's reviews of his reviewers. 12mo. $1.00.

COMPARATIVE ANATOMY OF THE ANIMAL KINGDOM. By Profs. SIEBOLD and STANNIUS. Translated by W. I. BURNETT, M. D. 8vo. $3.00

HUGH MILLER'S WORKS. *TESTIMONY OF THE ROCKS.* With Illustrations. 12mo, cloth. $1.25.

——— *FOOTPRINTS OF THE CREATOR.* With Illustrations. Memoir by LOUIS AGASSIZ. 12mo, cloth. $1.00.

——— *THE OLD RED SANDSTONE.* With Illustrations, etc. 12mo, cloth. $1.25.

——— *MY SCHOOLS AND SCHOOLMASTERS.* An Autobiography. Full-length Portrait of Author. 12mo, cloth. $1.25.

——— *FIRST IMPRESSIONS OF ENGLAND AND ITS PEOPLE.* With fine Portrait. 12mo, cloth. $1.00.

——— *CRUISE OF THE BETSEY.* A Ramble among the Fossiliferous Deposits of the Hebrides. 12mo, cloth. $1.25.

——— *POPULAR GEOLOGY.* 12mo, cloth. $1.25.

HUGH MILLER'S WORKS, 7 vols., embossed cloth, with box, $8.25.

UNITED STATES EXPLORING EXPEDITION, under CHARLES WILKES. Vol. XII., Mollusca and Shells. By A. A. GOULD, M. D. 4to. $10.00.

LAKE SUPERIOR. Its Physical Character, Vegetation, and Animals. By L. AGASSIZ. 8vo. $3.50.

THE NATURAL HISTORY OF THE HUMAN SPECIES. By C. HAMILTON SMITH. With Elegant Illustrations. With Introduction, containing an abstract of the views of eminent writers on the subject, by S. KNEELAND, M. D. 12mo. $1.25.

THE CAMEL. His organization, habits, and uses, with reference to his introduction into the United States. By GEORGE P. MARSH. 12mo. 63 cents.

INFLUENCE OF THE HISTORY OF SCIENCE UPON INTELLECTUAL EDUCATION. By W. WHEWELL, D. D. 12mo. 25 cents.

SPIRITUALISM TESTED; or, the Facts of its History Classified, and their causes in Nature verified from Ancient and Modern Testimonies. By GEO. W. SAMSON, D. D. 16mo, cloth. 38 cents.

Gould and Lincoln's Publications.

(EDUCATIONAL.)

LECTURES ON METAPHYSICS. By Sir William Hamilton. With Notes from original materials. 8vo, cloth. $3.00.

LECTURES ON LOGIC. By Sir William Hamilton. With an Appendix, containing the author's latest development of his new Logical theory. 8vo, cloth.

ELEMENTS OF MORAL SCIENCE. By Francis Wayland, D. D., late President of Brown University. 12mo, cloth. $1.25.

THE SAME, Abridged for Schools and Academies, half morocco. 50 cents.

ELEMENTS OF POLITICAL ECONOMY. By Francis Wayland, D. D. 12mo, cloth. $1.25.

THE SAME, Abridged for Schools and Academies, half morocco. 50 cents.

MENTAL PHILOSOPHY; including the Intellect, the Sensibilities, and the Will. By Joseph Haven, D. D. 12mo, cloth. $1.50.

MORAL PHILOSOPHY; including Theoretical and Practical Ethics. By Joseph Haven, D. D. 12mo, cloth. $1.25.

THE EARTH AND MAN; Lectures on Comparative Physical Geography in its relation to the History of Mankind. By Arnold Guyot. 12mo, cloth. $1.25.

THE ELEMENTS OF GEOLOGY; adapted to Schools and Colleges. With numerous Illustrations. By J. R. Loomis, President of Lewisburg University. 12mo, cloth. 75 cents.

PRINCIPLES OF ZOÖLOGY; for the use of Schools and Colleges. With numerous Illustrations. By Louis Agassiz and Augustus A. Gould, M. D. 12mo, cloth. $1.00.

PALEY'S NATURAL THEOLOGY. Illustrated by forty Plates. Edited by John Ware, M. D. 12mo, cloth. $1.25.

GUYOT'S MURAL MAPS; A series of elegant colored maps, exhibiting the Physical Phenomena of the Globe.

MAP OF THE WORLD, mounted. $10.00

MAP OF NORTH AMERICA, mounted. $9.00.

MAP OF SOUTH AMERICA, mounted. $9.00.

MAP OF GEOGRAPHICAL ELEMENTS, mounted. $9.00.

GEOLOGICAL MAP OF THE UNITED STATES AND BRITISH PROVINCES; with Geological Sections and Fossil Plates. By Jules Marcou. 2 vols., 8vo, cloth. $3.00.

www.ingramcontent.com/pod-product-compliance
Lightning Source LLC
LaVergne TN
LVHW020238110826
845151LV00003B/962

* 9 7 8 1 4 2 5 5 2 9 5 9 8 *